THE LIVING MONUMENT

THE
LIVING
MONUMENT

SHAKESPEARE AND
THE THEATRE OF
HIS TIME

M. C. BRADBROOK

CAMBRIDGE UNIVERSITY PRESS

CAMBRIDGE

LONDON · NEW YORK · MELBOURNE

Published by the Syndics of the Cambridge University Press
The Pitt Building, Trumpington Street, Cambridge CB2 IRP
Bentley House, 200 Euston Road, London NW1 2DB
32 East 57th Street, New York, NY 10022, USA
296 Beaconsfield Parade, Middle Park, Melbourne 3206, Australia

First published 1976

Printed in Great Britain
by W & J Mackay Limited, Chatham

Library of Congress Cataloguing in Publication Data
Bradbrook, Muriel Clara.
The Living Monument.
Includes bibliographical references and index.
1. Shakespeare, William, 1564–1616–Stage history–To 1625. 2.
London–Theatres. 3. English drama–Early modern and Eliza-
bethan, 1500–1600–History and criticism. I. Title.
PR3095.B66   822.3'3   76–7142
ISBN 0 521 21255 3

CONTENTS

PLATES

Between pages 64 and 65

PREFACE

The year 1976 is the four hundredth anniversary of the founding of James Burbage's Theatre, the first in England; today, London remains the theatrical capital of Britain – some would say, of the world.

No physical likeness of Burbage's Theatre survives, although external views exist of its near neighbour, the Curtain (see Plate 1), of the Rose on Bankside which followed, and of the Swan, whose interior, too, was sketched by Johannes de Witt, a foreign visitor. Theatres are for people, so that extensive attempts by scholars to establish the nature of fabric and structure are significant only as these provided an environment where interaction between playwrights, actors and audience eventually produced the work of the greater poet-dramatists.

There have been many significant changes over the past four hundred years, but within the last *thirty* years, the new drama departments in our universities have transformed theatrical history by a keener sense of the living art, which in turn has affected the building of modern theatres; these now provide stages nearer to the Elizabethan model than anything known since the mid-seventeenth century. Leading Shakespearean directors have taken full advantage of the latest scholarship, with the result that all of Shakespeare's plays and many of those of his contemporaries are now being produced. In addition, the history of theatre has been linked with the general history of art, and with social history; the results have been seen in many exhibitions of Tudor and Stuart art, of the work of Inigo Jones, and in the developing projects for a theatre museum.

The present study is first of all concerned with the sociology of the theatre, the subject of Part 1. In the evolution of the new drama, the Theatre of Burbage offered a focus for the manifold pageantry, ceremonies and activities delineated in Chapter 2. These were

vii

given poetic shape in Shakespeare's English history plays, the most characteristic product of the Theatre. The masque at court, which also had traditional roots, evolved more slowly; but structurally, in terms of stage and auditorium, it proved to be the direct ancestor of yesterday's theatre, with its proscenium arch and curtain that 'flew up suddenly' to show the painted scene. The interaction of various forms of theatre is the subject of Chapter 6, whilst the changing image of London itself is the subject of Chapter 5.

In Part II, the effects of this interaction are traced in the works of the Jacobean Shakespeare. By this time, popular drama had evolved its own conventions, whereas in Elizabethan times the shaping force of non-dramatic poetry and of rhetorical forms was still stronger than the emergent dramatic tradition, as it emerged in the workshop conditions of the nineties. I have dealt with these aspects of sixteenth-century drama in *Shakespeare and Elizabethan Poetry* and *Shakespeare the Craftsman*, so that Part II of the present study is confined to the fully-developed art of the Jacobean Shakespeare in the theatrical context which had evolved, and which was largely of his own making. The treatment of his Jacobean plays is limited to the social context indicated in Part I; whilst necessarily omitting many important aspects, it shows Shakespeare first reacting against but finally absorbing and transmuting elements of the Jonsonian court masque. 'Shakespeare as collaborator' treats of one early and one late play.

To round off the story, in Part III a final chapter on post-Shakespearean developments brings out what might be called his posthumous relations with Jonson and the young Milton, in the form which predominated in Caroline times, the court masque.

Without attempting the hopeless task of presenting all the evidence, I have tried to give enough selective detail to illustrate and support my general thesis. I hope that the result may be justified as work in progress, in a field where development is constantly bringing about changes of emphasis (a recent example is the growth of information about inn-yard stages).

The field of social relations in dramatic art is perhaps the least explored, and whilst I attempted in *The Rise of the Common*

Preface

Player to treat of the actors and their audience, I hope here to suggest lines of development in the more complex and difficult area of social relations as reflected in dramatic art. Chapters 1 and 2, however, are directly developed from that work.

At first sight it may seem incongruous that in a volume which opens with the Shoreditch Theatre, four chapters should be devoted to Shakespeare's final plays. My justification would be that in these plays, we see reflected in the mirror of dramatic poetry, what Shakespeare had absorbed as pure theatre in his youth. The reflection alone can show truly what, at that time, could not be put into words at all. Of course the plays contain much more; the accumulated experience of a life spent in the theatre. Yet, I would consider it took even Shakespeare the length of his working life to learn to project what he had found. In poetry, and in poetry alone, that moment was fully caught and transmitted, as no records could transmit it, and as no lesser poet could have done. This is the Theatre's living monument. Similarly, we cannot tell what the interior of Burbage's Theatre would look like. But the Globe Theatre was built from its timbers, and we do have more details of 'that virtuous fabric'.

Cambridge
October 1975   M. C. BRADBROOK

ACKNOWLEDGEMENTS

I am indebted to the following for permission to use material which has appeared elsewhere: to Professor Joseph G. Price and the Pennsylvania State University Press for permission to use for Chapter 2 material published in the volume entitled *The Triple Bond* (1975); to the editor of the *Review of National Literatures* III, 2, and St John's University New York for material used in Chapter 3; to the editor of *Studies in the Literary Imagination* VI, 1, and the Georgia State University Press for material used in Chapter 4; to Mme Jones-Davies and the Librairie Marcel Didier for material used in Chapter 9; to the editor of *English Literary Renaissance* I, 3, and the University of Massachusetts for material used in Chapter 12 and to the editors of *Shakespeare 1971* and the Toronto Press for material used in Chapter 13; to Professor Reavley Gair for permission to reproduce his reconstruction of the second theatre at St Paul's; and to Routledge and Kegan Paul for permission to reproduce the map on pp. xii–xiii from their 1963 publication of Glynne Wickham's *Early English Stages*, Volume II.

I wish also to acknowledge the invaluable assistance and co-operation of Mrs P. C. Rignold at all stages in the preparation of this work, and the invaluable contribution made by the staff of Cambridge University Press.

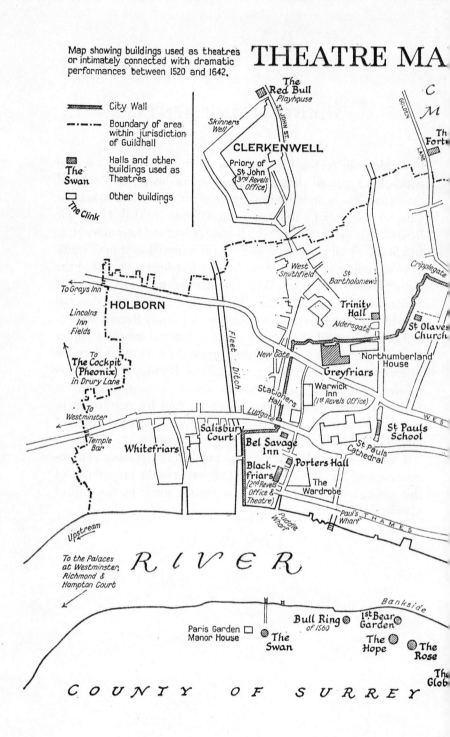

Map showing buildings used as theatres or intimately connected with dramatic performances between 1520 and 1642.

THEATRE MA

Legend:
- City Wall
- Boundary of area within jurisdiction of Guildhall
- The Swan — Halls and other buildings used as Theatres
- Other buildings
- The Clink

The Red Bull Playhouse

Skinners Well

ST JOHN ST.

CLERKENWELL

Priory of St John (3rd Revels Office)

GOLDEN LANE

C M

Th Fort

West Smithfield

St Bartholomews

Cripplegate

To Grays Inn

HOLBORN

Lincolns Inn Fields

To The Cockpit (Pheonix) in Drury Lane

To Westminster

Temple Bar

Fleet Ditch

New Gate

Trinity Hall

Aldersgate

St Olaves Church

Northumberland House

Greyfriars

Warwick Inn (1st Revels Office)

Stationers Hall

Ludgate

St Pauls School

WES

Whitefriars

Salisbury Court

Bel Savage Inn

Black-friars (2nd Revels Office & Theatre)

Porters Hall

The Wardrobe

St Pauls Cathedral

Puddle Wharf

Paul's Wharf

THAMES

Upstream

To the Palaces at Westminster, Richmond & Hampton Court

R I V E R

Bankside

Paris Garden Manor House

The Swan

Bull Ring of 1560

1st Bear Garden

The Hope

The Rose

The Glob

C O U N T Y   O F   S U R R E Y

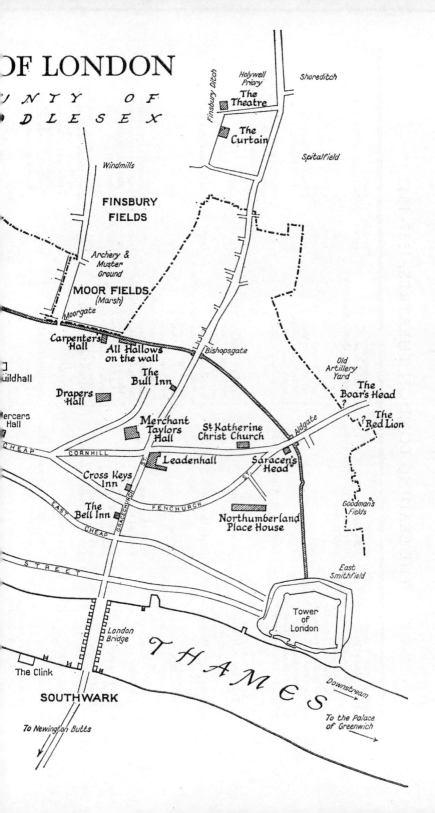

THE LEADING LONDON THEATRES, 1557–1642

	Builder	Acting companies	Opened	Closed
A. INN-YARD THEATRES				
1. The Boar's Head, Whitechapel	John Brayne Rebuilt 1594: Robert Browne	Leicester's Men Worcester's/Queen Anne's Men	c.1557	Not heard of after 1608
2 The Red Lion, Stepney	John Brayne		1567	City
3 The Bell Inn, Gracechurch Str.		Queen's Men	1576	Inns
4 The Bull Inn, Gracechurch Str.		Queen's Men	c.1575	
5 The Cross Keys Inn, Gracechurch Str.		Lord Strange's Men Lord Hunsdon's Men	c.1579	Closed 1597 by order of the Lord Mayor
6 The Bel Savage, Ludgate		Queen's Men	c.1575	Standing at the Restoration in 1660. In use throughout the Commonwealth for Shows, etc.
7 The Red Bull, Clerkenwell	Rebuilt 1604: Aaron Holland	Queen Anne's Men	by 1594	
B. ARENA THEATRES				
1 The Theatre, Holywell	James Burbage	Leicester's/Queen's Men Lord Strange' Mens Lord Hunsdon's Men	1576	1598
2 The Curtain, Holywell	Henry Laneham	Worcester's/Queen Anne's Men Prince Charles's Men	1577	Not heard of after 1627
3 Newington Butts, ?possibly small roofed house	Jerome Savage	Lord Strange's Men Lord Oxford's Men Lord Admiral's and others	1577	1597
4 The Rose, Bankside	Philip Henslowe	Lord Admiral's Men	1587	No record of plays after 1605
5 The Swan	Francis Langley	Lord Pembroke's (caused closure by playing *Isle of Dogs*)	c.1594	Closed 1597 Standing 1621
6 The Fortune I	Philip Henslowe and Edward Alleyn	Lord Admiral's/Prince Henry's/Palsgrave's Men	1600	Burnt 1621
7 The Fortune II	Edward Alleyn	Palsgrave's Men	1625	1649 dismantled. 1662 demolished
8 The Globe I	The Burbages and associates	Lord Hunsdon's/King's Men	1599	Burnt 1613 (built from timbers of The Theatre)
9 The Globe II	The Burbages	King's Men	1614	1642 (expiry of lease) 1644 demolished
10 The Hope	Philip Henslowe, Edward Alleyn and Jacob Meade	Lady Elizabeth's Men	1614	1656 (built over Bear Garden; theatre and bear-ring)
C. PRIVATE THEATRES ★				
1 St Paul's I (exact vicinity	Sebastian Westcott	Paul's Choir	c.1560	1590

xiv

					other theatres)
3	Blackfriars I (The Old Buttery)	Edward Kirkham, William Hunnis, Richard Farrant	Children of the Chapel Royal, combined with Oxford's Boys	c.1576	1584
4	Blackfriars II (The Upper Frater)	John Lyly, James Burbage, Leased to Giles, Henry Evans, Edward Kirkham and others	Children of the Chapel R. Children of the Queen's Revels; Children of the Revels; Children of the 2nd Queen's Revels	1596	1655 demolished
5	Whitefriars	Philip Rosseter	Children of the Revels	1608	?disused after 1613
6	Cockpit, Drury Lane or Phoenix	Christopher Beeston, William Beeston, William Davenant	Queen Anne's Men, Prince Charles's Men, Lady Elizabeth's Men, Queen Henrietta's Men, Beeston's Boys	1616	Demolished in riot. Rebuilt 1617; standing in 1660–reopened then
7	Salisbury Court (a barn near Whitefriars site)	Richard Gunnell, William Blagrave, Henry Herbert	Children of the Revels, Prince Charles's (II) Men, Queen Henrietta's Men	1629	Dismantled 1649. Reopened 1600 as Dorset Garden

D. ROYAL THEATRES

Queen Elizabeth used the Great Hall at Hampton Court, Greenwich, Nonsuch and her other 'standing houses'. At Whitehall she had utilized wooden structures – 'banqueting houses' – of a temporary kind, until 1581.

1	First Elizabethan Banqueting House	'a long square'; timber; on site of later houses		1581	Demolished 1607
2	First Jacobean Banqueting House	Adjoining tiltyard S.W. of Great Hall 120' × 53' Built by Inigo Jones	Opened with Masque of Beauty		Burnt January 1619
3	Second Jacobean Banqueting House	Built by Inigo Jones on same site		1621	Disused for masques after Rubens ceiling was put in, 1637
4	Cockpit-in-Court	Built by Henry VIII. Used for plays from c.1608. Rebuilt as theatre 1629. Reconditioned 1660		c.1608	Demolished c.1674
5	The Masquing House (known as 'The Queen's Dancing Barn')	Timber built in 1637 to replace the Banqueting House for large assemblies. Designed by Inigo Jones. Between Hall and Banqueting House			Demolished 1645

The Second Jacobean Banqueting House is the only theatrical building to survive, apart from the Halls of the Inns of Court. It was also used for Audiences, and other State functions.

★ Private theatres are roofed buildings in which, at first, resident players, incorporated for some other purpose, gave performances. After 1600, the description usually meant roofed and more expensive, smaller theatres, used only by players.

xv

Part I

THE SOCIOLOGY OF THE THEATRE

1

THE THEATRE AND ITS POET

In the year 1576, the seventeenth year of the reign of Elizabeth I, James Burbage, leader of the Earl of Leicester's Men and by trade a joiner, opened outside the north-east gate of London the first modern public theatre in England, perhaps in Europe. It stood in the parish of St Leonard's, Shoreditch, not very far north of the present Liverpool Street Station. Its honorific classical name *Theatre*, did not prevent the City Fathers from recognizing it as built on an established model – 'the gorgeous playing place erected in the fields' resembled those familiar game places to be found all over England – the circular or polygonal ring, within which scaffolds were erected.[1] In this case galleries for the spectators surrounded the open 'ground', and within there stood also a permanent, or perhaps at first a semi-permanent stage, backed by a 'tiring house' (basically, where the actors attired themselves). The strolling players had found a home, or rather had opened a shop, although the theatre was not restricted to acting nor was acting confined to the theatre. Tumblers, performing animals, swordsmen took the boards, whilst the players were ready to appear on call at a private mansion, a gildhall, or one of the Inns of Court.

Following a favourite custom of strolling players in performing at country inns, players were regularly found in inn-yards both within and outside the city walls; Burbage's brother-in-law, who shared his enterprise, had converted an inn in Stepney and was to convert another in Whitechapel. South of the Thames, the old gamehouses for bull- and bear-baiting were joined in 1587 by a new playhouse, the Rose, built by Philip Henslowe in the garden of an inn; nearby, in 1599, the timbers of the old Theatre were re-erected inside a new ring, to form the Globe Theatre. This became the joint property of the leading members of Burbages'

3

troupe, now known as the Lord Chamberlain's Men; they had moved quarters after a dispute with their landlord, but had dismantled and ferried across the river the timbers of their old Theatre, of which the first Globe was thus the direct descendant.

For some years the Lord Chamberlain's Men had had as their leading playwright and a full member of the company, William Shakespeare – in 1599 aged thirty-five. Shakespeare's settled working life began in the Shoreditch Theatre, and the inn associated with it, the Cross Keys in Gracechurch Street. His name stood first in the lease of the Globe, made out to 'Will(elmo) Shakespeare et aliorum'. The most important kind of play which he had evolved, the English chronicle history, belonged to his days at the Theatre, and remains its living monument; at the end of his life he returned to material recollected from his earlier acting days and refashioned it in his final romances. If anyone has a claim to be regarded as the poet of the Theatre, it is Shakespeare; no other writer had so prolonged an association with that particular 'virtuous fabric'.

By the end of the sixteenth century, a whole family of London theatres, descended from James Burbage's original venture, had appeared. There were other centres of playing; the dwellings of two groups of choristers – St Paul's and the Children of the Chapel Royal – the Revels Office, a court institution, established at one time in the old Blackfriars building and later in the Priory of St John's, Clerkenwell, each of which in consequence became a theatre district. The two men's companies which emerged as the leading troupes were by then based south and north of the river – Burbage's and Shakespeare's company at the Globe, Henslowe's and Edward Alleyn's (The Lord Admiral's Men) at the Fortune near Cripplegate – though Henslowe also controlled the Rose. Two competitors seems to be the natural pattern. A third company, Worcester's, well established at one of the inn-yards outside the city, began to cater for more popular and spectacular needs; just as in the eighteenth century, Covent Garden and Drury Lane, the two licensed houses, were to be supplemented by the 'little Theatre in the Haymarket' (as it was known at that time).

By 1600, Shakespeare was the most seasoned playwright re-

maining in regular production and was therefore the chief means
by which the work of the older theatres passed into the theatrical
repertoire of the seventeenth century; however, Ben Jonson was
his junior by only eight years. The battles of wit between Shakespeare and Jonson, recorded by Fuller, probably took place at the
tavern suppers which actors gave each other or which were given
them by friends – as it might be today at the Ivy or the Dirty Duck.
The social life of the theatre extended beyond its walls, perhaps in
some of those inns within the city walls which in 1597 had been
closed to players. The City Fathers, whose objections were both
moral and prudential (they were afraid of the kind of scenes that
are now common at football matches) had succeeded in this, only
to have playing break out in alternative forms – the Children of
St Paul's and the Children of the Chapel Royal, in their 'private'
theatres, within the city but outside its jurisdiction, reappeared in
1599–1600 – so whilst the date 1597 is rightly considered a very
important one, London theatres were only strengthened by such
an act of pruning. The stronger branches flourished, the weaker
ones fell away. A 'private theatre' – the term did not come into use
till 1604 – implied that in the hall of their own dwelling, some
incorporated privileged group, in this case choristers, were giving
performances for money. A truly private performance for a great
house can be found in *Summer's Last Will and Testament* (see below,
pp. 20–1) – however, if too polemical a tone were introduced into
the choristers' plays, they could be suppressed by clerical superiors.
In the public theatres they had built, men still claimed the status of
retainers to their lord; but they received neither wages nor main-
tainance and for a range of charges, starting at a penny, they
purveyed for the public demand. Defying the literary canons of
art imposed by the learned poets of the Sidney circle, as the
common players grew to resemble craft gilds rather than household servants, so their poets in the course of the 1590s developed
craft skills, based on experience (see below, Chapter 3, p. 41).

In the 'workshop' conditions of the sixteenth century, the playwrights had evolved certain types or genres of drama, Polonius'
pseudo-classical list – comedy, tragedy, history, pastoral – supplemented with various other 'kinds'.[2] Whilst Shakespeare remained

faithful to his company and its public stage, he did not conform to all the fashions; he did not set a revenge tragedy in Italy, but put most of his comedies there, which elevated them above city comedy; he did not attempt – or was not asked – to write a masque. Ben Jonson was not so wholly committed to the stage; he liked to think of himself as a poet and poetic legislator and for ten years, as the chief writer of Jacobean court masques, he was to retire from playwriting. Nevertheless, their work shows the influence which each poet exerted on the other; and when, finally, Jonson did return to the Caroline stage, he was to turn to a more Shakespearean way of writing.

In the course of the present century, the physical structure of some of the old playhouses has been reconstructed in detail from the remaining evidence. Court and city records and other documents ranging from parish records to the Commission for Sewers have yielded data; a building contract, Henslowe's papers in general, and the views of London by contemporary artists, some of which show the exterior of the playhouses, have been worked over by professional architects and men of the theatre, who can bring so much more than the academic student to their interpretation. There are still many gaps; we know that we cannot reconstruct any one theatre as it was, but we can claim to be able to rebuild something that an Elizabethan would find recognizable as a fairly normal playhouse. New evidence brings new forms into prominence; in the last seven years work on the inn-yards has revived interest in this type of theatre. Of course several important buildings which were in use as 'private' theatres are still standing today – the halls of the Inns of Court, Inigo Jones's banqueting hall at Whitehall, the hall of Hampton Court Palace still remain; the streets of London and the River Thames still follow the old lines along which moved the pageants and processions that constituted the civic and royal street theatre. The influence of this last upon the professional stage has recently been studied by art historians; through the modern productions which stress visual form (often at the expense of Shakespeare's text), it has been recreated for modern playgoers.

However, the need now is for what might be termed a sociology of the theatre as distinct from its archaeology. By 'sociology of the theatre' I mean the actor – audience relationships (discussed in Chapter 2) and their effect on plays and playwrights. The subject is at once more elusive and more conjectural than that of theatre structure,[3] but as the end of theatre study is to throw light on the drama and on the age as a whole, such attempts are essential if the enquiry is not to degenerate into antiquarianism.

The evidence of the social historian is very valuable here, since, as the most social of the arts, drama was an integrative force in the reigns of Elizabeth and James, when the first saw an important religious–political adjustment which has largely endured to the present day, the second a political debate which has been revived in our time, on the union of government between England, Scotland and Ireland. In spite of censorship, national concerns could be generally reflected; and at their happiest the playwrights became something like the Crown's public-relations men. As in Elizabeth's reign, sonneteers could put discussions of religion or education into that capacious hold-all, the Petrarchan sonnet sequence ('She may be some College', observed one sonneteer of his mistress); as the ability to produce a poem adaptable in many contexts was a merit, so the theatre could absorb, reflect and attempt to reconcile very different social levels, which were being even more rapidly stratified by social change.[4]

Shakespeare and his company catered for the widest range and, like St Paul, strove to be all things to all men. Ben Jonson, and the managers of the choristers, seeking the approval of the discriminating, either castigated or bantered those who did not belong to the in-group. Whilst the division between popular and 'private' theatres postulated by Alfred Harbage in *Shakespeare and the Rival Traditions* (1952) is now generally agreed to be over-simplified, there were other players, even the most popular, who acknowledged the problem of their diversified audience. Heywood draws a parallel with wine-tasting:

> Thus, gentlemen, you see how in one hour,
> The wine was new, old, flat, sharp, sweet and sour.

The sociology of the Theatre

Unto this wine we do allude our play,
Which some will judge too trivial, some too grave.
(Epilogue to *A Woman Killed with Kindness*, 1603)

By the accession of James, the theatres had learned from one another, and learnt also to steal one another's thunder. The interplay becomes much more sophisticated than it had been in 1597, when Alleyn's troupe put on *Sir John Oldcastle* to rival *King Henry IV*, a simple case of rechristening Falstaff as Sir John of Wrotham and turning him into a fat friar. This complex interplay is the subject of Chapter 6.

Whatever the relationship between Shakespeare's *Hamlet* and the choristers' play, *Antonio's Revenge*, it cannot be doubted that there is a connexion and that Shakespeare, no less than Jonson, influenced his younger contemporaries. A less familiar example of a 'theatre war' – which may have been quite amicable, even a matter of collusion – is John Marston's *Sophonisba* (1605–6) and its debts to the success of the previous season, Shakespeare's *Othello*. Not only does the villain open with a speech on Reputation; before the end of the act the Moor is called away to join battle on his wedding night and Marston actually improves the occasion by having the messenger enter the bridal chamber as the bridegroom, in preparation for getting into bed, is ceremoniously withdrawing the white ribbon from the bride's waist. The boys of the Chapel went in for peppery excitement, and this is sustained by a number of summary executions on stage, by the hero entering from battle 'his arm transfixed with a dart', and by a witch replacing Sophonisba in the bed of Syphax the villain; a stoical suicide from the much-tried heroine (still a virgin bride) completes the dish.[5] This play, given at Blackfriars, would seem from its preface to be aimed against Ben Jonson's classic way of writing history, as the author proudly boasts that he does not cite authorities or translate Latin orations; he is writing as a poet, not a historian.

In the course of the next few years, Shakespeare turned back to Roman tragedy, depicting a warrior who, like Marston's hero, sides with the enemies of his country, and an African queen whose death gives the complete answer to her Roman conqueror. But the full heavy-weight resources of the men's company were put into the plays, both in the fighting scenes, and particularly in showing two mature women, Volumnia and Cleopatra, whose force and prominence demand, in my view, that they be played by men. (The choristers, of course, were not all juvenile; Nat Field was thirteen in 1600 and by the time he played in *Sophonisba* or *Epicoene* he must have been in or approaching his twenties.)

In the meantime, from 1604, the Stuart masque had created a new dramatic form which found its own type of stage setting. Shakespeare, who began by reacting against it, finally succeeded by absorbing, not imitating, some features in creating a stage equivalent, which he combined with even stronger memories of the plays of his youth.[6] The effect was irresistible, and his romances appealed to high and low. Milton was paradoxically to term him 'Fancy's child' – that is, a practitioner of art in its unrealistic forms – and yet to speak of his verse as 'native woodnotes wild'. As Shakespeare had made one of his characters observe, the art itself is nature.

If the history of pre-Restoration drama is seen as a play consisting of prologue and five acts, the divisions might be set out in this way:

Prologue: the period before the opening of Burbage's Theatre. Plays given in the halls of great houses, often of a daring kind, were written by young academics, clerics or lawyers; there were open-air pageants and shows in summer in which town gilds took part. Occasionally the splendour of a Royal Entry would call on all city resources.

Act I (1575–88): from the opening of the Theatre to the arrival of the University Wits, Marlowe and his fellow poets – a period of popular entertainment at the Theatre, and of the first choristers' theatres.

Act II (1588–99): from the arrival of these poets and the new shaping they gave to entertainment, to the gradual build-up of a distinctive theatrical literary tradition. At first the playwrights were still drawing largely on the poetical and rhetorical style of the non-dramatic poets[7] – the shaping impulses came into the theatre from romances, from Spenser, from *The Mirror for Magistrates*. But by the end of this decade when Shakespeare alone remained as an active playwright – supported perhaps by the grave but untheatrical Chapman and challenged by the sprightly John Marston, who began writing in his teens – the whole theatrical enterprise was so well established that the Privy Council had taken steps which for once seem to have had an effect on the turbulent world of the playing places, to allocate given theatres to given troupes, to limit the number and formally to recognize those who were designated as being engaged in a lawful occupation.[8]

Act III (1600–13): from the building of the Globe to Shakespeare's retirement, ending with the great wedding festivities at court for the marriage of the King's eldest daughter, Princess Elizabeth. During this period the boys' theatres re-emerged as rivals to the men's troupes, but the vogue did not continue. This was the Golden Age, the period of Shakespeare's greatest tragedies and his final plays, of Ben Jonson's best plays, of the brilliant work of Marston, Tourneur, Webster, Chapman. It was a period in which the drama had become fully self-sufficient as a form of poetry and so far outstripped any other form of that time as to draw into itself all the interests of an age where new conflicts were developing between different systems of religious and political thought. 'The Century of Revolution', as Professor Hill has termed it in his book with that title, had begun. The Lord Chamberlain's Men had become the King's Men in 1603, and their alignment in the future struggle was decided.

The later period is not now strictly in question, but *Act IV*, the second part of the reign of James (1613–25), saw Jonson dominating the London scene (although from a distance). In a period of witty comedy, of growing sophistication, with Fletcher and Middleton representing, as it were, the gentry and the city interest, some new theatres appeared – notably the Cockpit in Drury Lane, the first theatre on that historical site. It was opened in 1616 by Christopher Beeston, who had been trained by Burbage and who was to become the most successful entrepreneur of the time.[9] A great outbreak of plague, coinciding with the death of the King, led to a prolonged closing of all theatres and ended an era. The King's Men survived when almost everyone else went under, to dominate the reign of Charles I, the long *Act V* (1625–42). The theatre became a much more limited and less popular form of entertainment at the top end of the scale, and a spectacular, rather than literary form at the other: all writers were conscious of the history that lay behind them, and the influence of Shakespeare on the later Jonson, the best of Ford, and on Shirley is clear.

The most crucial development came in the middle of *Act III*. The boys' theatre had always been exclusively an indoor theatre, and when they revived in London, the children of St Paul's and the children of the Chapel Royal at Blackfriars performed to relatively small audiences.[10] In 1608, the Blackfriars, which belonged to Burbage (who had acquired it when the city inns were closed to his troupe, but had not been allowed to play there), became the second theatre of the King's Men.[11] The effect of having two quite different houses, at which nevertheless the same repertory was produced, was gradually to change the balance of interest among playwrights towards writing for an indoor stage.[12] The modern theatre descends from the Blackfriars and not from the Globe. Yet again there was continuity, a long overlap of nearly a quarter of a century as the King's Men alternated between the two houses, and even their 'machines' must have been transported. For example, in his examination of the Second Globe Theatre (built when the first was burnt down in 1613, but upon the old foundations), Walter Hodges has deduced that the roof over the stage was not supported by pillars but only by the external walls in a great arch. It looks exactly like the cross-section of a roof from some great hall. That, I think, is what it was built to be. For the Blackfriars Theatre had such a roof, and the King's Men, when they moved from their winter quarters below St Paul's to their summer quarters on the Bankside, would transport across the river their machines for ascent and descent – such as Jupiter's eagle in *Cymbeline* – and would re-erect them on a site where they needed just such a replica. Even more recently, Glynne Wickham has suggested that the stage roof of Burbage's Theatre was unsupported.

By similar reasoning, the bear in *The Winter's Tale* cannot have been a live bear. (Ariel as a harpy 'clapped his wings' and was attended by strange 'shapes'.)[13]

The details of the theatrical setting may thus be deduced in part from the plays themselves, and it is for their effect on the plays that the playhouses concern the student of drama. The Theatre of James Burbage lasted for nearly a quarter of a century, but its form continued, and through the plays, which were shaped partly by its conditions, its influence can be felt today. The literary form which emerged from Burbage's first Theatre reached maturity as the Theatre itself disappeared. The achievement should be judged by the best and highest issue from this fertile centre, the 'Wooden O' of timbered galleries, thatched lath-and-plaster walls, painted stage, those final plays of Shakespeare that Jonson saw as old-fashioned stuff from Shoreditch.

The struggle for supremacy of the various types of Jacobean stage, which can to some extent be envisaged as a conflict between Shakespeare and Jonson, was a fruitful one. After Shakespeare's death, and after Jonson's replacement at court, the physical features of later stages were further developed by Inigo Jones. To the Jacobean proscenium arch and scenic flats worked on sliding shutters, he added a curtain that could be 'flown', before reaching that final 'curtain act' which events imposed on the whole Caroline theatre.

2

THE TRIPLE BOND:
ACTORS, AUDIENCE, PLAYWRIGHTS

The variety of buildings that served as Elizabethan playhouses, the social constitution, size, and customary manners of the audience made up one part of that 'two hours' traffic of the stage', to which Shakespeare, more than anyone else, gave unity. The audience was part of the performance.

'Poetry is a deed' as Tarlton and the Epilogue to *Cambises* (1561) proclaim.[1] The oral art and the scenic display by which actors and audience participated in an *event*, in the city streets, the game place, or the hall were supported by music and other 'activities' and in the earlier sixteenth century had been directed toward a common function or shared task – worship and religious observance, welcomes, triumphs, civic installation; seasonal rites of spring, harvest, winter solstice; weddings and natal feasts; vassals' tributes to a lord or lady – or, contrariwise, flouting, social mockery, and scorn, directed toward a common enemy.

Any relationship, social or personal, depends on both parties maintaining roles that are mutually acceptable and recognized; the alteration of any one role will change or disrupt the relationship, and thereby change also the nature of the events in which it is embodied. Sharing a task is a sure way to stabilize personal relations – whether bringing up children or cooking a meal, whether customary or contractual. During the sixteenth century, as I shall show below, the relation of actors to audience moved from the customary to the contractual. The actors' rôle became increasingly interpretative, that of the audience differentiated, while in certain kinds of play the author acquired independent status.

At the beginning of Elizabeth's reign, the gildhall of a London church might serve as a stage for players one week and for a wedding feast the next.[2] In 1565 two inns began staging fencers' prizes – as we know from records of the Masters of Fence – which implies some kind of auditorium;[3] the Bull and the Bel Savage later became well known as players' inns. Another, the Bell, kept a stock of theatrical properties for hire.[4] An atmosphere of holiday and revelry was proper to inns. Along with the appearance of the great Theatre of Shoreditch in 1576, an actor belonging to the Earl of Warwick's Men erected a small playing place in the garden of his house at Newington Butts, which, enjoying pleasant and reputable surroundings, survived to be used by Oxford's Men and, in 1592, Lord Strange's Men (who reopened there after a plague season with two of Shakespeare's plays).[5] This little suburban playhouse, which was left standing till 1597, may represent the casual playing, which dwindled and almost vanished by the end of the century. O. L. Brownstein has established that the Bel Savage, Ludgate, adjoining the Fleet prison, served a gentlemanly but partially captive audience!

Within the City of London, the Inns of Court maintained varied traditions of revelry at Christmas, which might have significant political implications; the production of *Gorboduc* in 1569 was part of Robert Dudley's campaign for favour.[6] They also offered training in public speaking, which began with the study of drama at the grammar schools. Thomas Kyd attended the Merchant Taylors' School; he may have performed on that occasion in 1574 when the Livery protested that they were kept out of the best places to see the school play because an admission charge had brought too many of the general public.

The singing children of St Paul's may have presented their plays to so select an audience as to constitute a kind of club;[7] but they were suppressed in 1590 for commenting too directly on ecclesiastical politics. The theatre of the hall i.e. that of great households, colleges, Inns of Court, choristers, schools, was theatre of privilege, but on that account it was vulnerable when authority frowned. The earliest surviving secular play, given between intervals of feasting in the hall of Cardinal Morton at Lambeth, could be prolonged only 'when my lord shall so devyse', but

It is the mynde and intent
Of me and my company to content
The least that stondeth here
(Prologue, Part 2, *Fulgens and Lucres*, 1497)

Accordingly a debate was 'interlaced' with clowning from actors 'planted' in the audience.

One of the plays at St Paul's specifies the dilemma of the actors by the mid-sixteenth century:

The proverb is, how many men, so many minds...
No play, no party can all alike content.
The grave divine calls for divinity,
The civil servant for philosophy,
The courtier craves some rare sound history,
The baser sort for knacks of plesantry.
(Prologue, *Contention between Liberality and Prodigality*, 1565)

One of the readiest ways to unite a small group is to join in mockery of a common enemy. From the time when Wolsey was lampooned at the Inns of Court to 1624, when Spain was mocked in the record success of the Elizabethan stage, Middleton's *Game at Chess* (1624), libel ranged from indirect 'glancing' to open mimicry in the victim's own apparel. It was calculated to attract and hold an audience, perhaps all the more since the savage penalties incurred turned it into a sort of Russian roulette.

Conversely, celebration of good fellowship might provide positive incentive to the social art of playing, strengthening collective identity. This was especially developed in London. (But here also the contractual element appeared when the new theatres imposed a fixed, regular price to see plays, which thereby became 'wares' for sale – 'show business'.) In *The Book of Sir Thomas More* (1590) Tudor household players of 'My Lord Cardinal' are shown offering their services to More at his Sheriff's feast. He is prepared to help them out with improvising, but their entertainment is of little more significance than 'background music' would be today. Although they are rather prematurely cut short, the customary reward is given, in spite of a dishonest servant's attempt to pocket a share. This play, itself the product of five hands, and fated never to reach the boards at all, shows that a lively sense of their own history animated the players of Shakespeare's day, even as part of a great Londoner's life story. The merry jests of More persist after the final tragic turn of Fortune's wheel (the cause of his death is naturally unexplained and he remains a popular hero).

Extemporal jesting continued on the public stages, chiefly in the afterpieces of the clowns. Harvey accused Spenser in jest for casting him as a clown and setting him on a 'painted stage' as an object of mirth; Nashe thought his pleading would make more sport than 'old *Mother Bombey*' did at Paul's.[8] Extemporal jesting could easily turn into a scolding match and so demanded skilful handling of the audience by the clown. Fighting among the audience was the chief civic risk at plays.

In the 1580s Lyly and the first play of Peele, *The Arraignment of Paris* (1581), were presented by the Children of the Chapel at court and in the Blackfriars Hall theatre. Centring on compliment to the Queen, the action is directed to the one Lady, who herself becomes the chief actor when the golden apple is delivered into her hands. Here Peele was relying on a commonplace – the same triumph over the three goddesses was depicted by 'H.E.' in the painting now at Hampton Court,[9] and it might have formed part of any triumphal entry to London or any public pageant. The legend of the Queen absorbed older religious symbols and classical grandeur or pastoral familiarity with equal ease, so that all Lyly's plays were offerings of this kind.

Whenever the Queen was seated on the stage (being of greater interest to the spectators than the show, even if she were not its subject), audience and players would become united in the common rite of homage. The public theatres, lacking such a focus, more slowly built up popular forms, evolving under workshop conditions. Shifting relations of actors and audience were stabilized by the growing power of dramatic poetry – poetry as communal action, words with a sub-text. Forms ultimately derived from particular combinations of actors and poets, working in certain playing places; to these the classical names of 'tragedy' and 'comedy' became attached, as the classical name 'theatre' had become attached to the game place or playing place. These were conventions but 'a convention has a history, it changes in time and in response to social pressures of various kinds'.[10] They were not prescriptive.

The plays survive only in haphazard, confused, sometimes non-sensical printed texts, of indirect relation to what must have been the original compositions of Peele, Greene, and Marlowe. The oral nature of the art meant that, to the public and the actors, 'the book' was susceptible to variation. Moreover, collaboration between a group of writers (as between groups of actors) was accepted; so little was the author's identity a part of the tradition that Kyd's name does not appear on the title page of *The Spanish Tragedy*, nor Marlowe's on *Tamburlaine*, nor Peele's on a number of his plays.

'Is not a comonty a Christmas gambold or a tumbling trick?' asks Sly, in the Induction to *The Taming of the Shrew*, to which the answer comes, 'It is a kind of history.' Peele's *The Love of King David and Fair Bethsabe with the Tragedy of Absalom* (1587) includes a comic drunken act (for Uriah), some delicate songs, a spectacular death for Absalom; the chorus then offers a third 'discourse', but what follows is not at all what they promise:

> Now since the story lends us other store
> To make a third discourse of David's life...
> Here end we this, and what wants here to please
> We will supply with triple willingness.

This looks forward to the epilogue to *Selimus* (1592):

> If this first part, Gentles, do like you well,
> The second part shall greater murthers tell.

Like a minstrel, he is offering another 'fitte'. *King Edward I* (1591) includes some chronicle material with some from popular ballads. It attacks the common enemy, in the person of the wicked Spanish Queen, and exalts London. Comedy provides the King's clever judgement against his Queen, the flailing match between the Friar and the Potter; Tragedy, the murder by the Spanish Queen of London's Lady Mayoress – by tying her to a chair and giving her a serpent to suckle – followed by the spectacular sinking of Queen Eleanor into the earth and her emergence at Potter's Hithe. These 'activities' achieve the same kind of unity as the street pageants which Peele, like his father before him, devised. All the marvels are familiar and traditional marvels, all the characters are animated images, and their 'discourse' more resembles proclamation than dialogue. What is being communally enacted is the solidarity or unity of the 'mere English'; even where the material is not so popular and customary it takes on the colouring. The atrocities are no more blood-chilling than beatings in a popular farce are supposed to hurt the victim. This is in a very direct sense a play world, all the more so since London or Respublica no longer appears as a character but is represented by the audience. So the English chronicle history emerged in its festive form – it had several others. Confused as he is the seeds of development lie with Peele rather than in the entirely well-planned *True Chronicle History of King Leir* (1590), which is indeed, in conventional terms of planning, more rationally motivated than Shakespeare's tragedy.

Form and identity came to the popular stages at the end of the 1580s with those two tragic masterpieces, *Tamburlaine* and *The Spanish Tragedy*. Both were imitated and affectionately parodied for years; they remained models into Jacobean times. 'Tragedy' was loosely used in the playhouse to mean 'death scene'; a death speech was the big finale for any actor, demanding complete identification. Marlowe's combination of intellectual fire and primitive violence satisfied all tastes; his professed contempt for 'jigging veins of rhyming mother wits' was justified by his own superb achievement. Kyd's play is set in an entirely evil and treacherous court, where the one just man is himself finally driven to treachery and gratuitous crime. There was no need of direct contemporary reference to this Evil Kingdom, the equivalent of the nightmare kingdom of Shakespeare's *Richard III*. All the actions are linked; an intricate pattern of interlocked betrayals and counterminings effectively cuts out spontaneous death, such as that of the poisoner in *Selimus*, who, offered the fatal cup by one of his destined victims, drinks it off farcically with the reflection:

> Faith, I am old as well as Bajazet
> And care not much to end my life with him.

The Spanish Tragedy is self-conscious about dramatic forms – witness the superb play-within-play that concludes it. Nashe in an early pamphlet proved plays to be 'a rare exercise of virtue' and no mere pastime, since 'for the most part...borrowed out of our English Chronicles' they revive the past so it lives again. Thus in *I Henry VI* 'brave Talbot the terror of the French' revives and dies on the stage, 'embalmed by the tears of ten thousand spectators, at least' – at several times, Nashe prudently and hastily adds (*Pierce Pennilesse* (1592); *Works* (1:212)). But these 'tragedies' succeeded as independent dramatic events.

Whether or not, as F. P. Wilson suggested, Shakespeare's are the first English history plays, he alone evolved an interpretation of the course of history continuous with the old craft cycles.[11] A providential pattern linked events, so that prefiguration implanted the events of that day within the still living past. In *3 Henry VI* (1591), Richard of Gloucester stabs Henry VI with a direct recollection of the role of the Prophet in the older cycles:

> Die, prophet, in thy speech.
> For this, among the rest, was I ordain'd.   (v.vi.57–8)

Richard is nevertheless always conscious of himself as an actor – Edward Hall has the common people compare the King's 'games' to stage plays.[12] A series of great death scenes pile up on each other. The prologue of Rutland's murder leads to the grand death scene of Richard of York, with its ritual of contempt and tremendous lament. This is followed by the death of his enemy Clifford, Clifford's by the death of the Prince of Wales, so that when finally King Henry VI greets his murderer, Gloucester, with the line

> What scene of death hath Roscius now to act?   (v.vi.10)

the audience's expectation must have been gratified by this acknowledgement of the climax.

Yet Shakespeare was also uncomfortably aware that an audience might fail to respond sympathetically; in *King John*, the citizens of Angiers mock the combatants ranged below:

> As in a theatre, whence they gape and point
> At your industrious scenes and acts of death   (ii.i.375–6)

And before many years had passed, the set death scene of older plays was parodied, in its proclamatory discursiveness, by the death of Pyramus:

> Now am I dead,
> Now am I fled;
> My soul is in the sky.
> Tongue, lose thy light,
> Moon, take thy flight, (*exit Moonshine*)
> Now die, die, die, die, die.   (v.i.293–8)

Death in a very different key concludes Nashe's *Summer's Last Will and Testament*, which in the late autumn of 1592, when all public theatres were closed because of the plague, was given for the Archbishop of Canterbury 'on the tilestones' of his palace at Croydon. This is 'no play but a show' – consciously nostalgic and at the same time critically balanced between lyric and paradox, jest and lament. The pageantry and speeches are controlled by two figures – Will Summers, the Jester of Henry VIII's court, who opens with what appears to be extemporal jesting, who constantly breaks the illusion to mock players and audience with ever-varying fluency; and the silent or almost silent figure of the dying King Summer, the 'beautiful and death-struck year', supported on the shoulders of his two heirs, Autumn and Winter. The procession of the seasons is embodied in traditional rustic ceremonies – harvest games, dancing, dubbing of knights with the blackjack, inter-mingled with cosmic figures like Sol and Orion the Hunter, with scholarly paradoxes, and a mock sermon or two such as Nashe might have used in his college plays at Cambridge. The medley is bound together by the audience and the players being almost in-distinguishable; it sustains the feeling of an impromptu sport rising out of the company's after-supper jests and songs. (This element of the play can be revived if it is performed in the right surroundings, for instance, in a college hall.) It is directed toward the Archbishop himself by his tenants and servants; in the words of the prologue, 'No man pleaseth all; we seek to please one.' Archbishop Whitgift was said to love mock debates with his household of young clerks; but almost the entire company might at some point have moved from the audience into the play group and back again. The circling of time and seasons, planets and feasts, ends with the arrival of the savage and poet-hating Winter and his sons, a miserly Christmas and a hostile January (or 'back-winter'). Summer, having called all his household to account, bequeaths the remnant of his good days to 'Eliza, that most sacred dame'. The concluding songs, which are litanies, lead out from the play world to the plague-stricken city beyond the rustic safety of Croydon, whence the Archbishop had come, with his train and sojourners who may have included Nashe himself:

> Adieu, farewell, earth's bliss,
> This world uncertain is...
> Lord, have mercy upon us...
>
> Autumn hath all the summer's fruitful treasure,
> Gone is our sport, fled is poor Croydon's pleasure...
> London doth mourn, Lambeth is quite forlorn,
> Trades cry woe worth that ever they were born...
> From winter, plague and pestilence, Good Lord, deliver us....

Yet this household 'show' – a nostalgic revival of old hospitality – is modernized by the built-in satire of the jester Will Summers, who breaks the illusion, comments and mocks, mines and counter-mines with his jests; for though he is also a ghost from a departed kingdom, like Yorick, he is very much a professional player.

Nashe, throughout his writings, sustained a jester's role – the semi-dramatic style of his pamphlets belongs with the games of Tarlton and Kempe, though crossed with the learning of which he was so proud. It has a Shakespearean copiousness and natural abundance, a mixture of sophistication and the natural and direct ease of common life. He raises the language of customary festive sports toward art; he does not achieve 'a pleasant comedy' for the *public* playhouse. Indeed, Nashe's public comedy, *The Isle of Dogs* (1597), was so far from pleasant that it caused a general closure of theatres, drove him to take refuge in Yarmouth, and gave his young collaborator, Ben Jonson, first taste of a situation that in future years was to recur quite frequently. This play contained too much of the invective traditional in the privileged theatre of the hall. Even at Cambridge Nashe had got into trouble for playing the 'Knave of Clubs' in the scurrilous *Terminus et Non Terminus*. There is something of the perpetual undergraduate about Nashe.

It was by combining novelty with 'the whole complex of metaphors relating man's life to the cycle of days and seasons... metaphors already just *there* for everybody'[13] that the folk elements are caught up and preserved in his show.

Love's Labour's Lost (1594), perhaps also written in some country house, ends similarly with a dark death-shadow falling, and a final contest between winter and spring, the owl and the cuckoo. In the self-consciousness of its linguistic art, it could have originated for a private audience (and some of its private jokes remain incomprehensible), but it is also a true play, shaped to the needs of the public stage; the contrast with Nashe is powerful. For Shakespeare, the different levels of playing had by now themselves become the subject of banter, in a more sophisticated yet more humane spirit than Will Summers's jest. It is not to be expected that the King of Navarre should make a good player, but the show of the nine Worthies was a loyal offering from the tenantry, and 'to dash it like a Christmas comedy' merits the rebuke – 'This is not generous, not gentle, not humble' (v.ii.627). Later, that more assured performer, Signior Cesario, defended himself in advance, saying 'Good beauties, let me sustain no scorn; I am very comptible, even to the least sinister usage' (*Twelfth Night*, I.v.164–66), but he refused to be deflected from delivering the speech which had asked such pains in the study – 'and 'tis poetical'.

Parody or burlesque is the surest measure of social change, and Shakespeare in both comedy and history not only developed a sense of form but displayed an easy, masterful ability to toy and play with different sorts of dramatic experience, to project it in plays-within-the-play, or to frame a comedy with an induction. Such ability to separate levels comes only with professional engagement – for 'perfect use worketh mastery' while Art without Exercise is as barren as Nature without Art.[14] In a play where he reached out to break and re-mould tradition – a play almost at the frontiers of drama – Shakespeare later defined the basis of his own art in the image of a triumphant Entry, made under the flashing steel of a raised portcullis. A noble civic welcome for a hero (which itself is a form of new creation of the 'deed' such as Nashe had envisaged for Talbot at the playhouse) unites with images of applause and the reverberation of a lofty speech, as if for a 'well-grac'd actor':

> No man is the lord of anything,
> Though in and of him there be much consisting,
> Till he communicate his parts to others;
> Nor doth he of himself know them for aught
> Till he behold them form'd in th'applause
> Where th'are extended; who, like an arch reverb'rate
> The voice again; or like a gate of steel
> Fronting the sun, receives and renders back
> His figure and his heat.

(Troilus and Cressida, III.iii.115–23)

With this may be compared the 'barbaric' treatment of the defeated Richard as if he were an actor to be 'scowled' on with 'contempt' and pelted with rubbish (*Richard II*, v.ii.23–36) as he follows the victorious Bolingbroke into London.

Since the significance of Shakespeare's idea of the play has been fully developed by Anne Righter (Barton),[15] I shall not now expatiate on it; I would suggest, however, that the varieties of audience for which he wrote, the versatility of his approach, may be to some extent disguised by the dignity of the First Folio, with its tripartite plan of Comedies, Histories, and Tragedies. Sometimes perhaps Shakespeare was able to call on a troupe of choristers; at other times he may have had to adapt a play for the Inns of Court or the court itself; he may have penned pageant speeches, or given other additions than those surviving in *Sir Thomas More* – the additions for *The Spanish Tragedy* have sometimes been claimed for him. Hamlet calls for a play 'extempore' – which seems to mean without rehearsal, for later he objects to clowns extemporizing. His own court entertainment, *The Murder of Gonzago* – a wedding offering from the heir apparent to the reigning sovereigns – was staged in the Great Hall where later Claudio sets up another show, a Royal Palace. In the Sonnets, there is a lament against the need to wear the motley and 'gore my own thoughts'; another sonnet protests against the shame of 'public means' to earn a livelihood.

The usual target for general mockery was not Shakespeare, but Anthony Mundy, a pageant writer to the city, who was ready to write plays, to make them, and to act (and whose share in *Sir Thomas More* brought him once in collaboration with Shakespeare). His *John a Kent and John a Cumber*, once part of the same volume as *Sir Thomas More* – which can be dated 1590[16] – shows a country troupe of tenants led by one Thomas Turnop, who present various shows at a noble wedding. They give a pageant in honour of the two bridegrooms, a serenade to the two noble brides, and in a Morris flout and jest at one of the two rival magicians, dressing him in a fool's coat; but the plot recoils so that they inflict mockery on their own ally. These country players discuss their own acting programme, and though little more than clowns, they serve to show how country sports were seen by one who himself was to be depicted in much the same way seven years later by the young Ben Jonson. By this time visits to provincial towns by actors almost ceased.[17] In *The Case is Altered* (1597) Antonio Balladino, 'pageant poet to the City of Milan', defends extemporizing: 'No matter for the pen, the plot shall carry it.' Then another character praises the fencing matches of 'Utopia', which are played in the public theatres where 'Plays, too, both Tragedy and Comedy (are) set forth with as much state as can be imagined.' Being asked 'And how are their plays, as ours are, extemporal?' he denies it: 'O no, all premeditated things, and some of them very good, i'faith' (II.vii.35–6). A more lengthy and embittered satire both of Mundy and of a hastily assembled troupe of tradesmen players was given by the young John Marston in his first play, *Histriomastix* (1599), as part of the Christmas revels of the Middle Temple.[18] The pot-poet Post Haste (to his many other occupations Mundy added that of pursuivant) assembles them in an inn (by now no place for regular players):

> For we can all sing and say
> And so with practice soon may learn to play.
> *Belch.* True, could our action answer your extempore.   (I.i)

This company runs from one patron to another, with a few old plays such as *Mother Gurton's Needle, a tragedy*, and gives such a shabby performance before an Italian lord that they are dismissed as 'trash'.

The parody of professional forms was by now taken up by

gentlemen amateurs – though this particular parody is set in a very old-fashioned pageant morality framework, organized to show the revolution of time and seasons in their social and political aspect, culminating in the triumph of Queen Elizabeth, patroness of the Seven Liberal Arts. The effect therefore is itself near to Nashe's ritual abuse of his enemies, though much sharper; and the end of Mundy's unlucky troupe is to be impressed for military service – 'Look up and play the Tamburlaine', cry their tormentors, 'Now we are the sharers and you are the hired men.' The subject of the theatre became increasingly an analysis of theatrical life and the theatrical experience itself. Social relations were analysed by analysing plays.

The much discussed question of whether Elizabethan acting was by modern standards conventional or naturalistic may be put in a different way: did the poets succeed in giving the players a language which allowed the development of sympathetic audience-identification, which replaced 'discourse' and proclamation by the subtler form of introjective and projective art? The audience had taken this attitude when at *Henry VI* they lamented 'brave Talbot, the terror of the French'; but in the English histories a tragical series was succeeded by a comical group. In 1599 Shakespeare's company put on *A Warning for Fair Women* where the Induction presents a debate between Comedy, History, and Tragedy, with Tragedy protesting to Comedy and History:

> 'Tis you have kept the theatre so long
> Painted in playbills upon every post,
> Whilst I am scorned of the multitude.

Variety was still a prime demand of the public stages, however; the inclusiveness of Shakespeare's comical histories culminates in *Henry IV*.

About this time, possibly for the Children of St Paul's, someone, possibly Rowley, rewrote an old play of *Wily Beguiled*. At first the stage bill proclaims that the play is to be *Speculum* – that is, some grave moral – but after various adjurations from the Prologue –

> For shame, come forth; your audience stays so long
> their eyes grow dim with expectation

– *Speculum* is whisked away and *Wily Beguiled* appears in its place. So in more complex change King Henry V appears at his coronation as his father's true heir,

> With his spirits sadly I survive
> To mock the expectation of the world.

(2 Henry IV, v.ii.125–6)

The keyed-up spirits of the playhouse are suggested by the Choruses to *Henry V*, where those in the audience are urged to 'work their thoughts' like a glowing forge. This apology is not so much intended to decry the players as to compliment the audience, who themselves supply the living re-embodiment of Henry's London: 'Now sits Expectation in the air' (Prologue to Act II,l.8) not only for Agincourt but for the triumphant return of the Earl of Essex from Ireland – an expectation that was to be sadly mocked in the event. When his faction hired the players to put on *Richard II* on the eve of the Essex rising, they were offering a mirror for deposition of the sovereign; the Queen asserted it had been played 'forty times' in streets and houses.

Whatever the reason, at the end of the century the English history play suffered a sudden and almost total eclipse. It had been the main means of transferring to the Elizabethan stage that providential linking of past and present, which enlarged the dramatic experience into something like a social ritual and which had been the shaping force of the older craft cycles, thus uniting it with a new professional dramatic art. But customary tradition was giving way to contract and a mood of critical questioning informed both tragedy and comedy.

The reopening of theatres of the hall in London in 1599–1600 by the Children of St Paul's and the Chapel boys meant that identification between audience and author replaced identification between audience and players. The 'little apes' could be admired for their precocious ability – but as Heywood noted later, they were used as a screen for satiric abuse directed at the city in general and also at particular individuals. St Paul's was restarted with the financial backing of the Earl of Derby and later attracted William Percy; it may have been run much more as a club, with a nominal admission charge for 'choice selected influence'.[19] In Marston's induction the little players came on before *Antonio and Mellida* and criticized their own performance in a preview of their own technique. One has a stock part, which another characterizes 'Rampum, scampum mount tufty Tamburlaine' – no boy could hope to rival Alleyn. Another uses euphuistic balance for his apology, and is maliciously twitted for it 'Whoop, in the old cut?' The peculiar mixture of violence and self-righteousness which made his verse satires so vulnerable gives way in Marston's plays to a greater uncertainty, a kind of protective prickliness; arrogance is tempered with apprehension. Fashions veered quickly; even in 1601 Marston was objecting to overconfidence and 'bubbling wit' in his audience at Paul's – the 'best seal of wit is wit's distrust' – and yet

> Music and Poetry were first approv'd
> By common sense; that which pleased most
> Held most allowed pass...rules of art
> Were shap'd to pleasure, not pleasure to your rules
> (Induction to *What You Will*, 1601)

He numbers up all the species of play, by this time well established, but concludes this one is 'perfectly neither, but even What you Will' – a disclaimer of the accepted modes which became increasingly fashionable. They include 'Comedy, Tragedy, Pastoral, Moral, Nocturnal and History'. Marston's address to his audience varied from self-depreciation to defiance, but was always more or less one of discomfort.

Ben Jonson, who moved from the public to the private theatres and back again, and whose 'humours' set the fashion, adopted every kind of attitude to his audience – but he never ignored it. In *The Case is Altered* he had objected to the pretensions of the vulgar:

But the sport is at a new play, to observe the way and variety of opinion...a confused mixture of judgment, poured out in the throng there, as ridiculous as laughter itself. One says he likes not the writing, another likes not the plot, another not the playing; and sometimes a fellow that comes not there past once in five years, at a parliament time, or so, will be as deep mired in censuring as the best. (II.vii.40–8)

He ended a play for the Chapel boys with a flat defiance 'By God, 'tis good, and if you like't, you may' – yet at other times he wooed his audience, bullied it, praised the judicious element, or defied the lot. Wit consists of 'scouring' folly and for this he assumes attentive auditors. The 'gull' who affected judgement became a figure of fun not only for Jonson but for his enemy Dekker, who drew such a figure in *The Gull's Horn Book*, displaying himself on stage as if he were the Lord of the troupe and leaving ostentatiously with a derogatory exit line.

The epilogue to *Epicoene* (1609), written for another troupe of boys, is more accommodating, at the expense of other authors (one consequence of the author's new prominence was this public quarrelling):

> Of old the art of making plays
> Was to content the people; and their praise
> Was to the poet money, wine and bays.
> But in this age, a sect of writers are
> That only for particular likings care,
> And will taste nothing that is popular,
> With such we neither mingle brains, nor breasts:
> Our wishes, like to those make public feasts,
> Are not to please the cook's taste, but the guests'.

Jonson recognized eventually that the contractual part of the bargain must be respected; on several occasions he drew up mock conditions with the audience which allowed 'censure' to be related to the price of seats – he was particularly severe on judgements exercised by the penny stinkards in the public playhouse. He wrote inductions with such characters as Tattle, Expectation, Mirth, and Curiosity (*The Staple of News*, 1626) – the last coming to see 'whose clothes are best penned, whatever the part be; which actor has the best leg and foot; what king plays without cuffs and his queen without gloves; who rides post in stockings and dances in boots'. He also wrote inductions for ideal spectators and in his last play (*The Magnetic Lady*, 1633) makes one judge say 'We come here to behold plays as they are made, and fitted for us; not. . .as we were to mould every scene anew. That were a mere plastic or potter's ambition, most unbecoming the name of a gentleman' (Chorus after Act IV). But his bitterest contests were to rise over precedence in the composition of court masques, where in one case he shows a poet in a debate with a cook, describing himself as 'a kind of

Christmas ingine; one that is used, at least once a year, for a trifling instrument of wit or so'.

Shakespeare's response to his larger audience was at once more sensitive and less obtrusive. In the 'problem plays' he tested and sometimes disclaimed old conventions. *Henry V* and *Troilus and Cressida* display opposite sides of one coin – the bright and dark aspects of war; the general view that the second was written for a private audience has recently been challenged.[20] On the other hand, *The Merry Wives of Windsor*, if it were really produced at speed for a court performance, also achieved a popular success.[21] *Hamlet* 'represents an enormous effort to move forward to the heroism of the individual, without abandoning the older social and religious framework of external action';[22] this came at least in part from the challenge and stimulus of the theatre itself, including the rival playhouses. In *King Lear* the archaic splendours of the King and Fool are joined to the bravura role of Poor Tom, described on the title page of the Quart as a 'sullen and assumed humour'.

Because of Shakespeare's sophisticated treatment of the conventional and the popular, his company dominated the public theatre. As we might expect, the company now reached out to the best of the new in the private playhouses. Eventually, it absorbed their themes, their playwrights, and finally the Blackfriars playhouse itself.

If, as a song of the time put it, 'Grief and joy and hope and fear / Play their pageants everywhere', those of the children's theatres were more self-consciously literary. The prologue to Marston's *Antonio's Revenge* (1600), the promised sequel to *Antonio and Mellida*, dismisses anyone afraid to see 'what men were, and are' and demands a mood, sensitive, emotional, and introverted. This mood is nearer to Henryson's

> Ane doolie sesoun to ane cairful dyte
> Suld correspond and be equivalent
> Richt as it wes when I began to wryte
> This tragedie

than it is to the opening scene of *Hamlet*. It begins:

> The rawish dank of clumsie winter ramps

The fluent summer's vein; and drizzling sleet
Chilleth the wan bleak cheek of the numb'd earth,
While snarling blasts nibble the juiceless leaves
From the nak'd shuddering branch....

In the private theatres, tragedy was not fully dramatic (the best was Chapman's). When Marston turned to the black comedy of *The Malcontent*, Shakespeare's company thought it worth appropriating (and Marston seems to have cooperated). The 'select' audience, aggressively superior and even anti-social in some moods, supplied a better seedbed for City Comedy, whose themes were cheating and the power game among London citizens and in the London underworld. This kind of comedy soon evolved its own conventions.[23] Even here, however, the masterpieces – such as *The Alchemist* – belonged to the men's playhouses.

The exclusiveness of the select audiences becomes most entertainingly explicit in Beaumont's burlesque, *The Knight of the Burning Pestle* (1607). The theme is obsolete theatrical demands put forward by a good citizen and his wife who somehow stray into the private playhouse. There they behave as if they were at a City Feast in Sheriff More's day, and in perfect good nature they take over the show, assigning the leading part to their 'prentice. The kind of play they are expecting is a mixture of impossibly heroic adventure interlaced with direct presentation from scenes of city life; the sting lies in the fact that it is a fairly close parody of a recent success, *The Four 'Prentices of London*, which had enthralled a city audience at the Red Bull.

Unlike the upstart gallant, who misbehaves in the theatre, the Citizen and his Wife are engaging characters. Like Bottom, the Weaver, they want everything to be put into the play, and, also like Bottom, they enjoy a big death scene:

Citizen's Wife: Now, good husband, let him come out and die.
Citizen: He shall, Nell. Ralph, come away quickly and die, boy!

Entering promptly 'with a forked arrow through his head', Ralph dies at great length with extracts from *The Spanish Tragedy* to help him out. But it is significant of the limitations of the select audience that this burlesque did not succeed on the stage (although it may have given Ben Jonson ideas for some of his later inductions). Ben Jonson's more critical scrutiny of society withdrew the audience from the 'game' of comedy, imposing on them a measure of detachment. It may be that a measure of detachment also enabled him to fill out his crowded canvases with such a full picture of society. His comic world was meant to be looked at and not lived in; in the subhuman zoo of *Volpone*, the animals may be observed as if they were caged.

Though he abandoned the peremptory tone of his earliest comical satire, Jonson remained always present in his work. According to Dekker, after a play he would come on stage 'to exchange courtesies and compliments with the gallants in the Lord's Room' (*Satiromastix*, v.ii.305).

Jonson's affiliations with the older drama were with 'morals teaching education' rather than with the civic pageantry that Marlowe and Shakespeare drew on. It is significant that Aubrey reported he 'was never a good actor, but an excellent instructor' – especially, it might be hazarded, of the boys. He expected his plays to be judged by 'those Comic Laws / Which I, your Master first did teach the age', and which he expected pupils like Dick Brome 'to observe'. When accused of writing only one play a year, he retorted ''Tis true. I would that they could not say that I did that' (Prologue to *Poetaster*).

Only in his court masques does he introduce playfully and with freedom old customs, rural sports; only here could he escape the need for judgement not only to be applied, but to be seen to be applied. Masques became the one cohesive social rite as audiences grew more diversified; for the ten years following Shakespeare's death, Ben Jonson too had withdrawn from the public stage, writing only for the court.

In the best of the public theatres, playwrights achieved something like the feat of conducting an orchestra as they wove together the variety of demands that a mixed audience exacted. Some were theatrical, some purely social. In the Prologue to *No Wit, No Help, Like a Woman's* (1613), Middleton runs through a 'naming of parts' which implies that everyone accepted an obvious diversity.[24] Education was not one of the objects:

How is't possible to suffice
So many ears, so many eyes?
Some in wit and some in shows
Take delight, and some in clothes.
Some for mirth they chiefly come,
Some for passion – for both, some;
Some for lascivious meetings, that's their arrant;
Some to detract, and ignorance their warrant.
How is't possible to please
Opinions toss'd on such wild seas?
Yet I doubt not, if attention
Seize you above, and apprehension
You below, to take things quickly,
We shall both make ye sad, and tickle ye.

Middleton's favourite solution was the multiple or composite plot. Shakespeare's experiments continued throughout the group of his latest plays, although in modern times an underlying recurrence of certain themes has tended to mask their differences. They belong to quite different theatrical species, yet each could be given in diverse surroundings. The appeals to the audience in *Pericles* are deliberately archaic; it became a great popular success, yet was also acted at court. *Cymbeline* is far more courtly in tone and complex in plot; it includes one purely spectacular triumph which is poetically a blank (the descent of Jove's eagle) but which could not easily be cut. *The Winter's Tale*, like *Pericles*, drew snorts from Ben Jonson, but its two halves are beautifully balanced. *The Tempest* bears many marks of a courtly masque, yet it combines old romances and a recent adventure from the Virginian voyages. Shakespeare, equally with Marston, might have disclaimed the usual definitions and subtitled all his later plays 'What You Will'.

Webster, to judge from the Address to the Reader prefixed to *The White Devil* (1612), cherished some rather simple-minded hankering for a Nuntius and Chorus, yet he knew that in the theatre, 'the breath that comes from the uncapable multitude' would forbid them. Although the season had corresponded with his tragic theme, this had in his case proved disastrous 'since it was acted in so dull a time of winter, presented in so open and black a theatre, that it wanted (that which is the only grace and setting-out of tragedy) a full and understanding auditory'.

Yet in this play, and still more in *The Duchess of Malfi* (1614), which appears to have succeeded rather better (Burbage took the lead), Webster himself 'plays over the whole gamut between firm convention and firm realism' – but 'the balance is held by poetic means'.[25] Shakespeare had combined his memories of naive early romances with a lifetime's experience of the stage's variety; the 'impure art of John Webster' achieved at its greatest a similar balance. This represents the recovery (or continuity) of popular traditions, along with a great deal taken from the 'black comedy' of the private theatres, which itself had been based on rejecting popular forms. It is a feat of synthesis.

The fourth act of *The Duchess of Malfi*, as Inga-Stina Ekeblad (Ewbank) has so brilliantly shown,[26] presents her death scene as beginning with an antimasque of madmen drawing on the folk tradition which inflicted social insults on a socially rejected bridal. This folk game in its popular form could be savage and primitive as the game with which Margaret of Anjou humiliates Richard, Duke of York, before killing him, in *3 Henry VI*. Here simulation of some of the forms of legal execution follow, adding evil magic to gruesome mockery.

The music which accompanies this 'device' is sophisticated in its discords; the songs are not folk songs. The gifts presented to the bride and chief spectator, who is to be the chief actor, include a shroud and a crucifix; and the art of the Duchess's death is an art of performance. With a macabre social jest she addresses both her murderers and the theatre at once:

> I'ld fain put off my last woman's-fault:
> I'll not be tedious to you.

For Webster, however, there was a second audience to be reckoned with, for he looked forward to readers, publishing his text 'with divers things printed that the length of the play would not bear in the presentment', and thereby asserting his independence as an author, in the manner characteristic of Ben Jonson.

If the conditions determining the splitting and cohesion of

society are among these reflected in drama, the significance of the madman's role on the Jacobean stage – one both split from society and split within his own identity – concentrates the tremendous effort needed to mirror and reflect back those conflicts, 'like a gate of steel / Fronting the sun'. It is unlikely that *The Duchess of Malfi* could have been accepted or acceptably produced except by the company in whose repertory stood 'kind Lear' and 'the grieved Moor'. The supreme figures of this kind are Poor Tom and Lear's Fool (both added by Shakespeare to the original story). They are close enough to the audience to indulge in direct address – Poor Tom's momentary removal of his mask would hardly be playable today. But here perhaps for the Elizabethans, the triple bond was asserted in its darkest, most chthonic aspect.

The masque at court had replaced the street theatres or Royal Entries or rural Welcomes. Monarchs themselves played in masques but shut away from their subjects. Charles I positively refused a Royal Entry to London, and the city pageants, half-built, had to be dismantled. The citizens developed their own pageantry, the Lord Mayor's Show, a real street theatre. It still survives today, the last of the old social rituals, which has suddenly become relevant again. Street theatre can still be found in the City of London.

3

SHAKESPEARE'S HISTORIES AND THE STRUCTURE OF TUDOR SOCIETY

A structure – according to the psychologist Jean Piaget – is a series of transformations which, insofar as it is a system, follows certain laws, being preserved and enriched by its own self-generated process. It is characteristically a whole (*totalité*); it is transformational and it is self-regulating (*autoreglé*). Although it may exist within a larger structure and contain substructures, their interactions are the result of confederation, not annexation. An analysis which produces a model will of necessity be reductive; thus several models may be extracted by theorists from the one structure. Linguistic structures are relatively unstable while in the fine arts *Gestalt* (structure) is stabilized. The tension between an ideal or Platonic view of structures and an empiricist view is stressed by Piaget, who comes down on the side of the empiric and the dynamic, that which is concerned with the 'genealogy of structures'.

In one word, the permanent threat to structuralism, if one attempts to create from it a philosophy, is that one may so quickly arrive at the reality of the structure as to forget its unification with the process from which it emerges. On the other hand to the degree that one recalls that the structure is essentially a cluster of transformations, it becomes impossible to dissociate it from those processes, whether physical or biological, that are inherent in the object, or, from effective processes conducted by the subject, of which the structure itself merely represents to us the laws of composition or internal equilibrium. It is not a pre-existing or superior entity upon which the object or the subject of inquiry depends.[1]

It is obvious that, since the theatre is the most social of arts, the interaction of playwright, actors, and audience constitutes a triple bond. The dynamics of such a complex structure are particularly significant both for the theatre's evolution and for its survival. The dramas of Shakespeare shaped and were shaped by the popular actors of his day, by the social expectations and unfulfilled needs of the audience which they satisfied. They have survived and have been found viable in all parts of the world because of their unique flexibility as well as their representative qualities. Shakespeare's dramas evolved during a period of rapid social and linguistic change. That they represent a triumph of the English language will not be contested, but the narrative poems of Shakespeare also survive to show how much lesser a poet he would have been (though still a great one) if he had not been offered the chance to write for the public theatre, as one deeply involved in its fortunes, himself a working actor in a team. The Sonnets, it is true, represent a far greater achievement, but one which is dependent on the dramatist's mastery of his own art, for they differ from other sonnets of the time precisely in those qualities that bring them near to drama.

It is generally recognized that the Elizabethan drama developed its literary powers in the last quarter of the sixteenth century from the growing professionalism of the London stages. It grew from a matrix of undifferentiated seasonal games, craft shows, and public entertainments, civic celebrations, private festivities, and polemics on social and religious questions. These earlier performances were not autonomous but continuous with the life of the community: the play was often 'exploded' at the end in an act of homage, a presentation or compliment to the person in whose honour it was staged.[2] The audience expected not only to attend but to participate.

It is by now accepted that the social, political, and religious changes of the mid-century left gaps in English social structure which playing helped to fill. The religious imagery and symbolism of the Catholic church were utilized in the service of the monarchy – an art of adaptation to which both Henry VIII and Elizabeth I lent themselves. The public image of a Joshua or a Moses, a Solomon or a Deborah, a star-crowned Virgin with the globe under her feet, filled a need and represented a strengthening of national identity. As A. L. Rowse wrote:

It is difficult for anybody without a knowledge of anthropology to appreciate fully the astonishing audacity, the profound disturbance to the unconscious levels upon which a society lives its life, of such an action as the substitution of an English liturgy for the age-old Latin rite of Western Christendom.[3]

The work of Sydney Anglo and of David Bergeron has shown how traditional images and emblems were scenically used, particularly in London, a city which enjoyed greater national predominance than most European capitals, and where civic display had long been used as an instrument of government.[4] The conflation of religious and political motifs can be illustrated from the sister kingdom, in William Dunbar's poetic account of the welcome of Queen Margaret to the Burgh of Aberdeen in the year 1511,[5] but such displays could be put on most readily in the capital city, the residence of the monarch, his 'City and chamber' (to use the traditional phrase). Although the independence of the City of London with its gild structure was a strong constitutional point, and in the next century was to produce national opposition to the monarch, London's civic coronation procession was an essential part of that rite, and constituted the 'showing' of the monarch to the people.

It is therefore perhaps no accident that one of the tableaux from the coronation of Anne Boleyn – the presentation of Paris' golden apple to the Queen – should have been revived by Peele for her daughter in *The Arraignment of Paris*, where (as already stated p. 16) the apple of gold is finally delivered to 'the nymph Zabeta', *exploding* the play. When Queen Anne received the same tribute, she was visibly pregnant with the future Queen Elizabeth; according to one account, her coronation procession was not devoid of satiric interludes from the crowd. In restaging it for his last and most spectacular history, Shakespeare carefully avoided any such reminiscences and made *King Henry VIII* a supreme example of pageantry and monarchical fervour.

The image of Queen Elizabeth as Astraea has been developed by Frances Yates, but this image belonged to pageants, and pageant-like plays (such as those of George Peele) or to prologues and epilogues. It could not be used in the drama of the public stages, because it was essentially a static image. In poems addressed directly to the Queen, in works given to be performed in her presence, such images could be evoked, but the direct use of the Queen's own story would not have been acceptable to the Censor.

Shakespeare's one reference to Queen Elizabeth in his early plays (the description in *A Midsummer Night's Dream* of the 'fair vestal throned by the West') offers just such an image. *The Merry Wives of Windsor* carries a compliment, in the speech of the Fairy Queen (v.v.61–80) during the final masque in Windsor Forest; both of these could have been spoken in the Queen's presence. But the oblique and tragic reflection of the image of Astraea in *Titus Andronicus*, when Titus, despairing of justice, shoots his arrows against the heavens, indicates that Shakespeare could not use this kind of image as part of the dynamics of a play for production in a public theatre. Instead of using the images of pageantry, of the Accession Tilts or the lyric poets, Shakespeare evolved a counter-image, an evil figure with every quality opposed to Astraea. Richard III, in a demonic energy that anticipates Milton's Satan, steals the show.

The Wars of the Roses showed the troublesome times from which England had been rescued by Queen Elizabeth's grandfather; the tragic history was a natural beginning to a process which Shakespeare carried forward into a great variety of drama.

There was also, of course, the possibility that English history might be used for interludes of a private sort. A medieval High Table had often been enlivened by a battle scene staged in the hall. 'Go and make your lively battle' might describe knights assaulting a portable 'castle' defended by ladies. It may be that the apocryphal *King Edward III*, as suggested below (Chapter 13, p. 233) was such a play. Mention has also been made below of the Whitsun Tilt of 1582, in which Queen Elizabeth successfully defended with her ladies the Fortress of Perfect Beauty against the assault of Sir Philip Sidney and his friends (Chapter 4, p. 53). Ten years later, in 1592, the history plays of Shakespeare were the means by which he established his reputation. *Henry VI* excited the jealousy of Greene in the first clear reference to Shakespeare (who 'with his tiger's heart wrapped in a player's hide, thinks himself the only Shakescene in the country') as well as the admiration of Nashe (see p. 19).[6]

The transformation of civic pageantry into drama, spectacle into art, was achieved by the power of language – by Marlowe's mighty line and Shakespeare's more flexible style, joined to the histrionic powers of Alleyn and Burbage. Too often the history plays have been seen simply in terms of Holinshed or Hall, but the ordinary playgoer would be no peruser of the Chronicles, and the powerful influence and source provided by street pageantry and triumph should count for at least as much. It provided a sub-text or substructure on which the formal plays evolved, which insured their recognition as part of a social inheritance and possibly helped to persuade civic authority to tolerate them. A single company of players of course could not hope to rival in splendour the re-sources of the city gilds or the royal wardrobe, but their sump-tuous apparel, so often complained of by their detractors, and the large amounts disbursed for costuming by Philip Henslowe, show that they did their best.

It was once suggested by the late F. P. Wilson that 'for all we know, there were no popular plays on English history before the Armada and that Shakespeare may have been the first to write one'.[7] This seems to me to go rather far; before 1588 there were Bale's *King Johan* and perhaps *The Troublesome Reigne*, Tarlton's play on Henry V, and almost certainly some Peele. Peele, who started a decade earlier than Shakespeare and Marlowe, was the son of a pageant writer, and his work for the City of London and for the court provides a transitional form, halfway between shows and full drama. In later civic pageants, Anthony Mundy revived the figures of the celebrated lord mayors, Walworth and Farringdon, who appeared in effigy ('as they were living'), and Webster pre-sented Chaucer, Gower, Lydgate, Sir Thomas More and Philip Sidney as 'worthies' seated in a Temple of Honour. 'These make societies and cities live.'[8]

On two occasions Shakespeare incorporates such moments of pageantry into his histories. The first is the triumphant entry of Bolingbroke into London contrasted with the crowd's scorn of the deposed Richard (*King Richard II* v.ii); the other is the coronation entry of Henry V so rudely interrupted by the motley group of Falstaff and his train, who receive on the spot a spectacular dismissal. It is, I think, no coincidence that this play ends with the staging of civic triumphs. No small part of the transformational qualities of the history plays was due to the way in which the past was seen as prefiguring the present. This both asserted national solidarity and identity and insured the relevance of an old story, as when the prologue before Act v of *Henry V* expresses the hope that the Earl of Essex will return from Ireland as triumphantly as Henry is shown returning from France. After the ignominious end of his Irish campaign, Essex's friends paid the players to stage *Richard II* as a curtain-raiser to his unsuccessful attempt to win control of the City of London on 8 February, 1601, but they had miscalculated the effect and the City remained totally unmoved by the dramatic entry and appeal of the former favourite.

In its pageantry and emblematic development of poetic images, *Richard II* shows a new, more conscious and 'artificial' relation with the ceremonies and ritual of royalty (as in the emblematic scene between the Queen and gardeners, based on a tableau familiar at coronations).

The chronicle history play, the predominant 'dramatic' form of the last decade of the sixteenth century, probably did more than any other to shape and give structure to popular drama. Its patriotic appeal worked for every class of society, and the vividness of presentation owed as much to poetry and plot as to staging. Peele's writing had presented speeches to accompany pageantry, many of which had the style of proclamation or direct address, but Shakespeare's Talbot had impressed the spectators because he seemed revived and the spectators, 'in the tragedian that represented his person, imagine they behold him fresh bleeding', as Nashe reports. In the phrase of Hamlet, Burbage later could 'suit the action to the words and the word to the action'; his acting was integrated, and Shakespeare's whole conception achieved a unity which captivated the audience. 'Attentiveness' and 'expectation', common words in the prologues of the time, witness to the power by which playwright and actor gained ascendancy over the audience. At the same time, of course, they were dependent on the audience's favour; their aim was to please. If, by the end of the century, the various dramatic genres had evolved and 'comedy, history, tragedy, pastoral' were recognizable, each with its own conventions and its own appeal, these were workshop definitions, not dependent on any external code of rules. The ideal code of classic drama as developed by Italian critics, though disregarded, prevented development of alternative theory. The use of classic names for different genres was honorific. Sir Philip Sidney in his *Apology for Poetry* had promulgated Castelvetro's doctrine of the Unities (supposedly Aristotelian). The popular use of 'tragedy' and 'comedy' differed from his (see pp. 17–19 above), but by the turn of the century even the private theatres were defying the 'rules of art' also (see, for Marston, p. 8 above), and Jonson lent his powerful advocacy to experience, as against theory.

Workshop conditions may well have depended partly on the specific type of audience and occasion from which the various 'kinds' or genres originated; that is, the poetic and dramatic structure emerged from a substructure of events. The close links between history and tragedy have been studied by many historians of the drama, most notably by Wolfgang Clemen,[9] a common root in civic display has been very suggestively traced. Festive comedy, originating in seasonal games and courtly compliment as C. L. Barber has demonstrated,[10] can be seen subjected to critical parody in the plays-within-the-play of *Love's Labour's Lost* and *Midsummer Night's Dream*. As theatrical performance became more of an independent, autonomous activity, audience intervention was courteously frowned upon. Satiric, admonitory, or polemical plays belonged to the privileged theatre of the hall, with its private audience – a type of theatre represented in London chiefly by the Inns of Court and later by the 'little eyasses'.

By the mid-1590s, the conventions were sufficiently formed for parody, a self-regulating and self-correcting device widely used. 'A convention has a history, it changes in time in response to social pressures of various kinds'.[11]

The theatre became aware of its own evolution, as in the presentation of old-style acting in *Sir Thomas More*. By the end of the century *The Spanish Tragedy* (*c.* 1589) was being both parodied and revised, and the 'second wave' of revenge tragedy profoundly modified this most popular 'kind'. Shakespeare's *Hamlet*, based on an older play, produced a new crop of imitations and parodies; although the chronology is confused, the revenge plays of Marston, Chettle's *Hoffman*, such a piece of mockery as *The Wisdom of Dr Dodipoll* with its mad young man, or Dekker's *Honest Whore* with its melancholy prince, testified to the professional, theatrical autonomy of the play world.

By this time also the personalities of famous actors and the names of the best known playwrights had become factors in the entertainment. According to the prologue to *A Warning for Fair Women* (1597), Comedy and History were more popular than Tragedy. It was in this year that the very scurrilous (lost) play *The Isle of Dogs* caused the imprisonment of actors and authors and a much stiffer attempt at control of the playhouses. In a recent volume,[12] 1597 has been mentioned (see above, p. 5) as a dividing line between relatively free unlicensed playing in London and a strong regulative system that, by reducing the number of play troupes, made for greater professionalism and closer connexion between the players and government (see also p. 5, above). The constant fear of riot and tumult in the theatres is an indirect index to the extent to which they promoted social activism – a function well understood in political theatres today!

At the same time, it is clear that provincial playing on an amateur basis was fading out, and that professional touring of the kind that had been common in the 1580s and early 1590s suffered a sharp decline.[13] Soon afterward, the English chronicle history suddenly ceased to be a predominant kind. It survived only in minor playhouses;[14] a much more critical, questioning, and probing sort of play came into prominence elsewhere. *Henry V*, the last of Shakespeare's history series, is at once a celebration and a deeply disturbing study of the problems of rule and government. The speeches of the common soldiers to the disguised king raise issues which Henry does not pretend really to answer. In other plays of this time, Shakespeare questioned old patterns of heroism, old conventions of stage action, while from 1600 his younger contemporaries, Jonson and Marston, assumed attitudes much more critical and prescriptive in their writing for the newly revived 'private' stages of St Paul's and Blackfriars.

Without the transforming power of Marlowe's and Shakespeare's poetry, the social and customary forms might have vanished relatively unobserved. Country pastimes too might have vanished ('For O, for O, the hobby horse is forgot') and the temporary unification of court and city faded, leaving no signs other than those to be disinterred by the social historian. The scenic fecundity of the early stages was transferred to Shakespeare's vocabulary. Ben Jonson thought Shakespeare was carried away by his own facility; 'His wit was in his power; would the rule of it had been so too.' From the perspective of our structural analysis, we may say that the transformational qualities of spectacle fed into a dynamic way of writing where crowded images, as Dr Johnson remarked, are mingled with endless variety of proportion and innumerable varieties of combination. Charles Lamb noted more approvingly, 'Before one idea has burst its shell, another has hatched and clamours for expression.' Coleridge described how Shakespeare's imagery itself, by 'the constant intervening and running comment by tone, look and gesture of the actor' becomes 'a series and never broken chain …always vivid and because unbroken, often minute', but these are 'organically related because modified by a predominent passion'.

One of the outstanding features of Shakespearean tragedy is the series of iterative images, whose presence has been so thoroughly analysed by Wilson Knight, Caroline Spurgeon, and Wolfgang Clemen; these present an alternative structure to that provided by the plot. This imagery derives its emblematic force from the tradition of unified themes in public pageantry which was characteristic of earlier street theatre. It is not an accidental outcrop of Shakespeare's idiosyncratic development, but an emblematic, verbal statement of familiar themes. As such, it could have been recognized, and indeed the imagery of revenge plays constitutes a structure which is relatively independent of individual authors, although characteristically modified by Shakespeare, Tourneur, and Webster.

These formal structures were judiciously fitted to special occasions. Robert Greene called Shakespeare a Johannes Factotum, and an abusive term for players was 'Chameleons' because they would take on the colour of their background. The conjunction of *Henry V* with Essex's Irish expedition has already been noted. Part of the pleasure might lie in the dexterous application of some familiar stage property to the exact needs of a given occasion – as when for a lord mayor called Harper the gilds brought out King David and Arion. So the twin images of the faded and flourishing tree of commonwealth lurk obscurely in *Macbeth* behind the blasted heath and the green boughs of Birnam Wood.

By the beginning of the seventeenth century, when a relatively stable structure of metropolitan playing had emerged, Shakespeare's company was settled in its own new playhouse, the Globe, and Alleyn's at the Fortune; old playhouses like the one at Newington Butts were demolished, and the Boar's Head in Whitechapel had fallen on evil days, but still housed Heywood's experienced London troupe. The new 'private' playhouses offered a different kind of play, appealing to what Marston termed a 'choice selected influence'. In other words, different kinds of play were being devised for different kinds of auditory, and in different acting conditions. Substructures developed.

The refinement of acting was also leading to a closer delineation of characters. Andrew Gurr has pointed out that the term *personation*, which came into use about 1599, suggests the same developments that made the two great tragedians succeed the extemporizing clowns on the pinnacle of theatrical fame.[15]

Certainly those 'interlocutions with the audience' that had been typical of Tarlton in the 1580s and of Kempe later were among the features that Shakespeare would banish, if Hamlet's advice to the players may be taken as reflecting the author's views. 'Gentle' Shakespeare was not given that title for mildness of manner but for courtesy (gentility), and his comedies were obviously educative. Young gallants copied witty passages into their tablets and a decade later, in his *Apology for Actors*, Heywood virtually repeats Hamlet's definition of the player's art, and adds:

Our English tongue, which hath been the most harsh, uneven and broken language of the world....is now by this secondary means of playing, continually refined...[16].

44

The degree of self-correction or self-regulation in *Hamlet* is obvious not only in Hamlet's own constant inspection of his motives and words but in the balance of tragedy against comedy, lyricism against satire, irony against tenderness in the play itself.

The history of *Hamlet* epitomizes the history of the English stage from that date; it has acquired a geological deposit of accumulated experience. As I have already written at length on this topic,[17] I shall now only briefly recall that it has been adapted as well as parodied, that each generation from Betterton to Gielgud has modified the play according to its own needs. The nineteenth century produced parodies, *Hamlet Travestie* and W. S. Gilbert's *Rosencrantz and Guildenstern*, which by their mere existence witness to its unassailable position. Tom Stoppard's more recent fantasia, the numerous film versions, and the ballets, from Helpmann to Marowitz, show that the play can generate new forms and structures. If, as structuralist critics have urged, the enjoyment of literature is an act of continuous re-creation in which the reader brings his own knowledge and social reading to join with the original work, this is even stronger in the case of drama where the collaborators include producers, actors, and spectators. The freedom of the modern stage has by now made some new approach almost obligatory on each occasion. Shakespeare is in some danger of being crowded off by those who are more intent on display than collaboration, but the texts survive for reinterpretation in other societies, in accordance with different structures. I have seen *Hamlet* produced in Hiroshima – the Japanese understand the Ghost extremely well, but not the Gravediggers – and I have seen the Princess Lalla Fatima of Morocco amused by a presentation of *The Merchant of Venice*, from which an earlier royalty would have stalked out when the Prince of Morocco was hopelessly guyed. The manner of presentation being a matter of adjustment, it is the elasticity of Shakespeare's work which guarantees its universal appeal. This elasticity must in part be attributed to the original 'open' conditions of production, the absence of prescriptive codes, and perhaps to the rapidly changing and expanding nature of the language itself, particularly during the crucial decade of the 1590s when Shakespeare's dramatic style was formed.[18]

The Jacobean Shakespeare developed new forms which reflected a new social structure. I shall not enlarge on this beyond saying they increasingly led to transformation of earlier forms. F. P. Wilson summed up the gulf that separated the Elizabethan from the Jacobean Shakespeare: 'The histories are tragedies of a divided state; the tragedies are tragedies of a divided mind.'[19] Meanwhile the common stages, which had evolved by trial and error and with such workshop forms as the Medley, the Chronicle History, the Tragedy of Revenge, the Nocturnal, were receiving some pre-scriptive justification from Ben Jonson; spectators were invited to make judgements upon performance, no longer simply to lay wagers on an actor's part, as had been done in Alleyn's day when plays alternated with cockfighting and bearbaiting in the public game place. The very form of the new closed theatres imposed a closer attention, a more concentrated and sophisticated audience. In *The Knight of the Burning Pestle* (1607), Beaumont satirized the old kind of audience expectation in the figures of the Grocer and his wife.

Meanwhile, although at the Boar's Head or later at the Red Bull the conservative Heywood was placidly continuing with what he called 'domestic histories', he was aware of the *effects* of acting. Even Jonson scored his greatest triumphs in the public theatres, and in his openness of approach he offers the happiest contrast to the classicism of Robert Garnier, whose talent was circumscribed by the French dramatic situation, where there was no continuity with the medieval tradition and where standards were imposed by external critical rules inhibiting dramatic action. Garnier was a favourite of English adherents to the rules (see p. 41 above) and was translated by the Countess of Pembroke.

In many ways the Spanish national stage may be held to resemble the English. The physical conditions are not dissimilar; *comedias* were given in open courtyards surrounded by galleries, the companies were directed by the leading player, and they played to a mixed audience in the principal cities and also occasionally at court. Grand processional shows still continued at seasons of religious festivity (*autos*) with occasional university drama. Although the first were far more splendid than England had known, these represent a structural division similar to the English. From the late fifteenth century, strolling companies moved to the principal Spanish cities, but by the later sixteenth century, Madrid, like London, had taken the lead. When the great Lope de Vega, two years older than Shakespeare, began to write *comedias*, the principal *corral* of Madrid had opened, two years before Burbage's Theatre (in 1574). More significantly the Spaniards, like the English, rejected prescriptive rules. In his *New Art of Making Comedies* (1609), Lope says that he composed from his tenth year onward, and that although he knew the rules of art he wrote according to custom, for anyone who wrote according to art would die without fame and without reward:

> Que quien con arte ahora escribe
> Muere sin fama y galardin.

So he locks up all the precepts with three keys and casts Terence and Plautus out of his study. True comedy shows the action of men and reflects the customs of the age. With this ironic disclaimer, Lope proceeds to give a workman's advice to his fellow workmen. The length of a play must be carefully worked out, but put in what you like as long as it is skilfully compounded. Under his mock apologies he shows a superb assurance and ends by defending his popular plays, since what is written against the 'right' sometimes satisfies just for that very reason:

> Porque a veces lo que es contra lo justo
> Por la misma razón deleita el gusto.

This would seem to represent a triumph of empiricism against Platonic structure. When the polymetric freedom of the Spanish plays is added, it might be assumed that a comparable verbal freedom could also be claimed. The great variety of speech in the most famous of Lope's dramas, *Fuenteovejuna* (*c.*1611), ranges from the farcical to the horrific. The vile noble who rapes the village bride and the collective vengeance wreaked by her community upon him is followed by a scene in which the villagers of Fuenteovejuna are tortured to make them confess the identity of the killer. From the child of ten to the oldest inhabitant they all declare 'Fuenteovejuna did it'; finally the comedian offers to confess, but only varies the declaration: 'Little old Fuenteovejuna did it!' The heroics of the play at times touch great splendour, as in the military processional scenes; at other times the villagers hold improbable debates on love. The delicate balance is resolved when the decision rests with the King; the code of honour, though in an unorthodox way, is reasserted. It is at this point that the greater rigidity of social structure in Spanish as compared with English drama becomes explicit.[20]

In the majority of Lope's plays action follows the code of honour and the Catholic faith. As has been said:

We are not dealing with class conflict but with class relationship, within an accepted social structure. The structure and the social differences which it involves are never called into question, but only the way the classes deal with one another – the conduct of individuals is evaluated in terms of whether they observe the duties and obligations incumbent upon them.[21]

In short, there is none of the probing of Shakespeare's later histories.

In the plays of Lope, honour acts as a code which is sometimes flouted and sometimes tragically maintained, as in the great tragedy of his latest years, *Punishment without Revenge* (1631). Since there is apparently no national possibility of a social development such as Shakespeare experienced, the dynamics of Lope's structure are dependent on confrontations, such as that between the heroic peasant and the evil nobleman. The final dilemma is often summarized in a judgement scene; the response is Brechtian rather than Shakespearean. There is no simple assent; the audience is left with a paradox sharply defined. Some plays approach satire rather than tragedy; others, like *Punishment without Revenge*, achieve indictment rather than catharsis; therefore the great Spanish theatre, though it has been transmitted, has not been adapted. Comparison with Marlowe or with Kyd rather than with Shakespeare brings out the balance of strict control and primitive violence, of noble and peasant (in *Tamburlaine*); or comparison with the tragedies of Webster and Middleton brings out the underlying fatalism.

The thematic structure which is found in Kyd, Marlowe, Shakespeare, and Webster has been found also by E. M. Wilson in Lope de Vega,[22] but Lope's plays (often based on ballad and chronicle) appeal to an innate conservatism, a popular insistence on order and degree. The insistence on order and degree in Tudor England was largely theoretic; society was more fluid,[23] and Shakespeare's stage, set amid the shifting populace of London, reflects a mobility in vocabulary and larger structural elements that has permitted many later transformations. This, however, does not apply in at all the same degree to other Tudor dramatists. Comparison with Marlowe, Webster, or Heywood shows the diversity of achievement produced by an environment which may have nourished Shakespeare's art but does not explain it.

4

SOCIAL CHANGE AND THE
EVOLUTION OF BEN JONSON'S
COURT MASQUES

THE BACKGROUND TO THE JACOBEAN MASQUE

In his masques, Ben Jonson speaks with a voice very different from that of Ben Jonson, playwright and satirist. The one voice is silken, idealizing, jocular; the other stern, authoritarian, critical. The second Ben Jonson consistently condemns romance, as primitive, stale, and unnatural;[1] yet some of his best masques are based on romantic motifs, and the tradition of the masque drew largely on the assumptions and conventions that had sustained the romance as recited in the hall.

Constant invocation of the pleasures of 'strangeness' and 'variety'; grotesque absurdities of the antimasque set among stately splendours; enlargement of the central figure beyond the confines of humanity, and apparent suspension of the laws of nature are common to masquing and romance.

In a romance, the hero often journeys from the familiar local setting in which he is born, and after strange adventures returns at last; the combination of monstrosity and familiarity enthralled the audience, charming them out of the monotonous round of daily existence. Total absorption, variously described as 'delight', 'rapture' or 'wonder', is essential to a meeting with or identification with the uncanny, exotic, or other world of the romance. In his *Art of Rhetoric* (1553) with a certain condescension, Thomas Wilson described the sort of festive game that developed between reciter and audience:

If there be any old tale or strange history well and truly applied to some man living, all men love to hear it of life. As, if one were called Arthur, some good fellow that were well acquainted with King Arthur's book and his Knights of the

Round Table would want no matter to make good sport, and for a need would dub him knight of the round table, or else prove him to be one of his kin or else (which were much) prove him to be Arthur himself.[2]

Don Quixote himself could have asked for no more.

The game or sport of identifying with some hero of romance provided a ritual of celebration. The public triumphs offered by the City of London to the ruler made use of historical and allegorical figures as well as figures from romance, as a tribute or offering which glorified the realm as well as its ruler. Sometimes a jest would be incorporated to set off the magnificence.

Masquing or mumming at court was of a more intimate character, but was still designed to honour one person, and to maze or delight his company. It too joined the near and the far, the past and the present. Conventionally it was a surprise; the initial advent of masked or vizarded strangers, accompanied by a dazzling torchlight procession, gave a *frisson* or feeling of the uncanny.[3] The mummers danced in silence and never spoke.

The masquers bore gifts; after they had danced, they would take out members of the audience to dance with them. These final dances, known as 'revels', were the chief purpose of the entertainment. The strange visitants and the company unite, the unfamiliar turns into the familiar as the dancers unmask. Finally they withdraw, though a banquet may follow.

The drama also grew out of processional shows in the great cities and out of festal interludes in the hall; but the masque is not the ancestor of the play, nor a derivative from it. The masque and the play are alternative forms, since their aims and purposes are different, their developments, though parallel, distinct, and their mutual influence, though powerful, oblique. The two forms might be thought mutually exclusive, since the masque existed to merge the performers with the audience as both united to honour their lord or lady. This was a triumph, a wooing, a serenade. Drama on the public stages evolved, on the other hand, by establishing a firm degree of distance between the spectators and play; imaginative participation precluded physical intervention or intermingling.[4]

The form of courtly sports would vary with the tastes of the ruler. Henry VIII gave and enjoyed magnificent entertainments, at which he appeared disguised. He introduced Italian customs into the masquerade, yet the popular traditions also remained – at the end the audience could despoil and loot freely and at one masque their rich habits were torn off the masquers' backs and their pageant car broken up. Yet Henry turned all this to 'largesse' and sport, and retired to make a jest of it, rather as King Arthur made a jest of the Green Knight. These elaborate and active shows were replaced during the reign of Edward VI – whether to please the boy king's sardonic humour or that of his court – by such grotesque mimes as a drunken masque, a masque of covetous men with long noses, a masque of cats, a masque of bagpipes, and a masque of medyoxes (half men and half death's heads). George Ferrars, Lord of Misrule at Edward's court, seems to have stressed the kind of sport which issued in mockery and scorn.[5]

Elizabeth rapidly shed this tone in entertainment. May Day or Whitsun Summer Lords and Christmas sports developed into a regular form of homage. The masque at Christmas was traditionally fixed for Epiphany, the Feast of the Three Kings – an appropriate time not only for the incursion of rich strangers bearing gifts, but for an epiphany of the glory of the court to visiting foreigners. It was the climax and end of the Twelve Great Days of Christmas; and though shows might be revived or a new masque presented at Shrovetide, when all revels ended and Lent began, yet when King James wanted to move the masque back to Christmas he was firmly told that it was not the fashion.

Sir Philip Sidney, the perfect courtier, reformed the conventions of courtly games and ceremonies; his sister's sons, the Earls of Pembroke and Montgomery, strongly influenced the early years of James. His *Arcadia* written for the Countess of Pembroke and her circle, was meant to be 'applied' to various members, yet the undeviating nobility of the chief characters or rôles would prevent any simple identification; Sidney himself was famed for his witty 'ironia' or self-mockery. Such sports, like the earlier recitals of dreams or visions, might conceal courtly hopes or pleas; they were part of the 'Game of Love' as it has been traced from medieval times by John Stevens.[6]

While the note of banter may be thought to sound sometimes behind the superlatives of this high romance, Sidney was a student of Castiglione, and believed in the lifting of the mind to virtue 'with the end of well doing, and not of well knowing only'.[7] The ascent of the Platonic ladder from earthly to divine love came through the practice of the nobler arts: yet poetry, like modern advertising, implanted an impulse to action which was the more effective because it did not appear to aim at instruction or conversion. 'With a tale forsooth he cometh unto you', says Sidney and yet may 'intend the winning of the mind from wickedness to virtue.... Truly, I have known men, that even with reading *Amadis de Gaulle*, which God knoweth, wanteth much of a perfect poesy, have found their hearts moved to the exercise of courtesy, liberality, and especially courage.' There is a certain note of condescension when Sidney refers to the old Arthurian stories – 'I dare undertake, Orlando Furioso, or honest King Arthur, will never displease a soldier: but the quiddity of *Ensa* and *Prima Materia*, will hardly agree with a corslet.'

Yet Ben Jonson, who censured Sidney for making all characters speak as well as himself, told Drummond of Hawthornden that there was not better ground for an heroic poem, and that Sidney meant to transpose his *Arcadia* into Arthurian form.

Sidney found his own heart stirred 'more than with the trumpet'[8] by the popular minstrel's ballad of Percy and Douglas; he thought that in drama, romance was out of place, as 'the whole tract of a comedy should be full of delight, as the tragedy should be still maintained in a well raised admiration.' The audience, that is, should be captivated, as he and his companions depicted themselves captivated by the invincible beauty of Queen Elizabeth and her maids of honour in the famous Whitsun tourney of 1582, *The Four Foster Children of Desire*, where, after an unsuccessful siege of the Fortress of Perfect Beauty, they all yielded themselves prisoners to Beauty. In another May-time masquing for the Queen, of a much simpler and more private kind, his pastoral *Lady of May*, Sidney at the end 'exploded' the game. The Queen judged a wooing contest – and her judgement did not go the way the poem suggests it was meant to go.

Throughout her long reign, Elizabeth showed great tact and skill in meeting the offers of homage and praise with some ready gesture. Her power to respond was part of her art of government; on her progresses she played her part superbly. But as she did not choose to dance in public (except during Alençon's wooing) her courtly revels and masques took on a literary character, which persisted into the reign of her successor. King James was probably too severe a pedant to believe in Sidney's play-way of education (he had himself been severely beaten by his schoolmaster, Buchanan); but though it finds little support in *Basilikon Doron* (his plan for a princely education) the effectiveness of poetic inculcation in the virtues was by then well established.

Although the materials of masques and welcomes became conventionally set – the processional entry led by Mercury or Cupid, occasionally a prophet or sybil – their 'application' gave scope for ingenuity and wit. The occasion was what counted. When Wyatt wrote

> My days decay, my grief doth grow,
> The cause thereof is in this place,
> ('Since you will needs that I shall sing', ll. 14–15)

it was intended to be sung in a room with many ladies present, and (as C. S. Lewis observed[9]) it was not written for those who would sit down to *The Poetical Works of Wyatt*. The dimension of 'activity' or 'application', is essential to the masque; a well-turned compliment should utilize the most familiar in a surprising and delightful way. When Dame Peggy Ashcroft received an honorary degree at Cambridge, the Public Orator quoted Shakespeare's lines about Dido with a willow in her hand, and Desdemona's song of the willow to illustrate Dame Peggy's passion for playing cricket.

It is generally recognized that the masque of *Proteus and the Rock Adamantine*, written by Francis Davison and Thomas Campion and performed by the Gentlemen of Gray's Inn before Elizabeth at court on Shrovetide 1595, supplied the prototype for the Jacobean masque. Here the ritual of the Queen's epiphany achieved a final simplicity more telling than the profusion by which Tudor festivities, like Tudor farthingales, were apt to be decorated. Protean variety is ordered and controlled by the Lady of the Masque, the 'true Adamant of Hearts', who has drawn the masquers to her, whose presence solves a paradox by providing an attractive power, stronger than the loadstone, that releases them from the rock where they are imprisoned. The simple act of approach, like the physical power of the loadstone, is transmuted to represent homage and loyalty; while the Queen reciprocated by extending her hand to be kissed. The little masque turns on a quest, expressed by motion and revelation; this, and not a story line, was to be the form or plot of the Jacobean masque. It is essentially an activity; it culminated in revels (and next day, in the military team-game played on foot, of fighting at Barriers, as did some of the Jacobean masques).

A year after this production, in his *Orchestra* – also a product of the Inns of Court, though perhaps owing something to Gager's Oxford play *Ulysses Redux* (1595) – Sir John Davis showed how the figures of a dance could embody cosmic harmony. This is traced through the creative dance of atoms, the movement of heavenly bodies, the growth of plants, the loadstone, and finally to the chaste Penelope, the heroine of the poem. In a magic perspective glass she is shown the moon with the stars dancing around her, and then the mortal moon, Queen Elizabeth, surrounded by her court:

> Like sight no mortal eye might elsewhere see,
> So full of state, art, and variety,[10]

Having brought its action to bear, and persuaded Queen Penelope to rise and dance, the poem breaks off. The attractive virtue which surpassed the adamant, which subdued all Protean variety, was revealed – *Semper Eadem*.

The elaborate figure-dances of the masque sometimes spelled out the name of a person to be honoured. Their hieroglyphics might be mathematical and vaguely magical. The dance separated off the noble masquers from their attendant torchbearers and musicians, who merely stood by to assist. It was an assertion of hierarchy as well as of harmony.

In the century and a half that separated the accession of Henry VII from the last masque of Charles I, court ceremonial changed greatly in response to changing social conditions; but the element of continuity was also strong, and in his latest works of this kind, Ben Jonson recalls old customs and the ancient writers, the founders of this order of things.

JONSON'S EARLY JACOBEAN MASQUES, 1604–08

When his long dream of succeeding to the English crown came true, James VI and I was thirty-six years old, and enjoyed a wide reputation as a poet. His *Essayes of a Prentise in the Divine Art of Poesie* had appeared when he was only eighteen; the introductory sonnets invoked all the gods from Jupiter downwards.[11] He became the centre of a little poetic circle, was known variously as 'the whistler Pan' or 'Willie Mow', in stately or in scurrilous verse; in a wedding masque which he wrote for the Marquis of Huntley's marriage in 1588, the court of Scotland was compared to Arthur's court, the proximity of Arthur's Seat (the hill near Holyrood Palace) lending colour to this claim of its attraction for knights errant.

The hopes of English poets must have risen high at his accession, for they too had been dreaming dreams. In *Cynthia's Revels* (1600) Ben Jonson, after drawing a most unflattering picture of the Court, imagined a poet with a strong likeness to himself authorized to expose all the vices in a Revel that ends in penance. The play was not favourably received, Cynthia showing no interest in this dream of power that was joined to an attack upon the Queen's festivities and nearly all her court.

Like his own Macilente, Jonson was soon to be purged of his humour by Jacobean favour, and found himself involved in rituals of magnificence and festivity which the sober, black-clad Arete of *Cynthia's Revels* would have abjured. The rejoicing was general; in the coronation ritual rose a nationwide sense of relief that sovereignty had passed peaceably to a Protestant monarch who would unite the kingdoms, who could supply an heir to the throne, who appeared to have controlled his turbulent Scottish kingdom with skill. In the many splendid pageants that the City erected for James's Coronation Entry to the capital on 15 March

1604, peace was the predominant theme. Three of these pageants were devised by Jonson; in the one at Temple Bar, Peace sat throned in the very Temple of Janus, while beyond, in the Strand tableau, a rainbow shone.

> Thy court be free
> No less from envy, than from flattery;
> All tumult, faction, and harsh discord cease,
> That might perturb the music of thy peace.[12]
> (*Part of the King's Entertainment*, ll. 750-3)

The welcome to James's Scottish followers was less cordial, as with him they swarmed over the border to plunder the land of milk and honey. In the autumn of 1605 Jonson was in prison for libelling the Scots – including King James – in *Eastward Ho!* and the first of the magnificent Twelfth Night masques had already gone to Samuel Daniel, Jonson's rival, a protégé of the Sidneys.

Daniel's masque is worth consideration, not merely as a contrast to Jonson's but as the first in which royalty participated since the days of King Henry VIII and one which contained the governing idea by which Jonson was to give a 'soul' to the masque. *The Vision of the Twelve Goddesses*, given in Hall at Hampton Court on 8 January 1604, is explained in Iris' concluding speech. Pallas herself, 'the glorious patroness of this mighty monarchy' (l. 407)[13] descending upon a mountain had found there 'the best (and most worthily the best) of ladies' (ll. 409-10) disporting with her chief attendants, where she and other goddesses had taken upon them these forms 'and in them vouchsafed to appear in this manner, being otherwise no objects for mortal eyes' (ll. 412-13). Queen Anne represented the incarnation of the tutelar deity to the throne, which because of the efficacy of her prayers will ever more be graced 'with the real effects of these blessings represented' (ll. 417-18).

Pallas Athene, the Virgin Goddess, had been the archetype for Queen Elizabeth; however unsuitable the Virgin Goddess of Wisdom as a role for Anne of Denmark, she was partly following precedent as she descended the Mountain with her ladies, three by three, all clad in the spoils of Elizabeth's wardrobe, and the meanest covered with jewels worth £20,000.[14] The rite might be considered a sacramental one, in terms of Christian Platonism; the Olympians descended and in the Temple of Peace laid their offerings which were mere insignia of the blessings attributed to the new reign.

The experienced observer, Sir Dudley Carleton, thought the descent from the mountain made 'the best presentation'. The Mountain was at the lower end of the Hall, facing the King's chair of state at the upper end; beside him was the Cave of Sleep, and the Temple of Peace, at first covered with a veil. Night and Sleep produce the Vision for, Daniel said, 'these apparitions and shows are but as imaginations and dreams that portend our affections' (ll. 126–7); yet the overwhelming effect of the Vision was intended to sink deep into the minds of all, with an impress that would not pass away. However, the stateliness did not persist; when the young Prince, aged ten, was taken out to dance he was 'tossed from hand to hand (among the ladies) like a tennis ball'.[15] Then, too, the pacific theme was flatly contradicted by the live drama involving the audience.

The King's presence was always the real focus; the seats near him belonged to Ambassadors by protocol. If the King could not attend, the masque could not be performed,[16] but his presence with the Ambassadors made a visible rite of pacification, the role for which he had cast himself; in *Basilikon Doron* he had told his son that the moment to look gravely is when majesty is sitting in judgement or receiving ambassadors.[17] Every royal masque throughout James's reign caused ambassadorial disputes and conflicts. They offended by not arriving in time, they refused to go away so that others could be asked, or they threatened to ask for recall when they had been insulted.

Queen Anne had invited the Spanish Ambassador to her masque. The French Ambassador, deeply offended, was offered several pacifications by James, including an invitation for Twelfth Night, but when he came to court it turned out he saw a play and a Scottish sword dance; the Queen's masque had been cunningly postponed for two nights. She then not only took out the Spanish Ambassador to dance, but wore his colours as a favour. Later James was to be so infuriated by his Pallas' display of partiality in

The Masque of Beauty that he himself departed the next day without seeing her.

The simple rite of descending the Mountain into the Hall, a mimetic recollection of James's descent from his northern mountains to the English plain, was preceded by a speech from an aged Sybil who, with the aid of a perspective glass, described the goddesses before they appeared. This both helped to identify the goddesses and emphasized their celestial origin. The 'mortal shapes to the gifts...of an eternal power' (ll. 262–3) would 'work the best motions' (l. 268) but would 'bereave' the onlookers 'of all save admiration and amazement' (l. 276). Or so Iris said in her prologue. Nevertheless, this device to heighten expectancy, which might recall the old Prophet's speech in medieval drama, was much derided, as a way of joining the near and the far.

Jonson, far from the depreciatory attitude of Daniel towards his own 'dreams' and 'shadows', succeeded not only in outdistancing his competitors, but, in collaboration with Inigo Jones, in evolving a new form which integrated poetry and other activity into a specific 'genre'. Even so, it may be that spectacle and dance remained for most of those present the potent elements in the rite. King James, who did not participate but remained fixed as the object of homage and the 'cause' of all (a masque cost him about £4,000) was certain that what he came to see was dancing, as on occasion he made explosively clear to all. The action or plot of a masque consisted not of a story line (though Jonson developed it) but of a traction movement which drew together masquers and audience in homage to the throne and in celebration of unity, concord, or harmony.

The first of Ben Jonson's masques established the new spectacular form; the second made explicit his unifying conception, a Christian Platonic celebration of harmony or concord, whereby the joining of two separable and divided worlds displayed the organic harmony of the whole frame of things entire. This can be embodied and fixed only in poetry, where it becomes the 'soul' of the masque diffused through and uniting all the senses, of sight, hearing, motion. The show, the song, the dance, were knit together by the poet's 'conceit'. Here lay the germ of Jonson's future quarrel with Inigo Jones, who gave artistic precedence to the visual aspect of the masque.

Jonson's first performance, certainly, owed its greatest effects to Inigo Jones, for in place of the dispersed scene of ordinary masques and shows, he introduced the revolutionary principle of concentrating the scene, throwing it into perspective, and thus producing an effect analogous to the modern unified stage. At the end of the hall hung a curtain, depicting scenes of the King's favourite sport, hunting. At one stroke Sidney's objection to the old stage 'where you shall have Asia of the one side and Africa of the other',[18] was swept away. The garden, rock, cave, and pitched field which Sidney goes on to enumerate were the common elements of the masque or the city triumph, but henceforth they were shown in order, as a grouped unity, or later as a series of transformation scenes.

The curtain dropped – although in other accounts a traverse is drawn back – and between the turning cranks of a wave machine, appeared a huge sea-shell brilliantly lit, in which sat the Queen and her ladies. It was then drawn forward by two sea monsters ridden by Oceanus and Niger, surrounded by other sea monsters sporting and writhing, on which rode the torch-bearers; while six tritons and two mermaids, also riding fishes, provided the music. The effect of complex motion and dazzling colour must have held the eyes with the compulsion of a flickering neon sign, as 'the Queen's masque...or rather her pageant'[19] moved forward towards the throne. Jonson stressed the effect as 'an artificial sea was seen to shoot forth' (*The Masque of Blackness*, ll. 26–7). The perspective was centred on the royal seat, but the whole stage was on wheels.

But Jonson was posed a problem. Queen Anne had announced that she wished to appear as a negress; and this, though not an unheard-of thing in a masque, yet for a queen was considered a great indecorum.[20] Her costume too was 'light and courtesan-like'.[21] Indeed, the courtiers noted the danger of disfigurement to the Spanish Ambassador, as he was taken out to dance by the Queen and kissed her painted hand, 'foot[ing] it like a lusty old gallant', and that strangers should see the court so strangely disguised was felt to be a disgrace, as well as 'a very loathsome sight'.

Jonson did his best, inventing a riddle that the daughters of the Niger were in quest of a realm where a milder sun would bleach their skins. The King was thus put at the centre of the masque and the new name of his kingdoms – Britannia – which he was endeavouring to unite in one – gave the answer to the riddle. The attractive virtue of the throne was explained by the moon goddess, who appeared in the heavens (thus perhaps recalling to the English their divine Cynthia) as the whole platform stage creaked forward to loud music, the sea monsters rising and falling as the cranks turned, till the shell deposited the ladies for their dance. Still, some were determined to be unimpressed; as one historian has observed, where Jonson saw a vast sea flowing forth, disenchanted Carleton saw 'a great engine at the lower end of the room which had motion' but which was 'all fish and no water'.

In the manner of a romance, the story was resumed three years later, when in *The Masque of Beauty* (10 January 1608) in the new Banqueting Hall the nymphs reappeared, seated on an island throne in a calm sea, which 'shot itself to the land' (ll. 264–5). The throne was composed of two revolving circular platforms, which turned in contrary directions, the masquers being on the higher one and their torch-bearers on the lower one. This double movement, brilliantly lit, contrasted the movement of the planets with that of the earth, and as the transformed ladies moved forward, a double echo invoked the music of the spheres:

> When Love, at first, did move
> From out of Chaos, brightened
> So was the world, and lightened
> As now! *Echo:* As now! *Echo:* As now!
> Yield, Night, then, to the light,
> As Blackness hath to Beauty.   (ll. 281–6)

But the Queen, still showing herself like a Spaniard, as the French Ambassador said, was insisting on inviting whom she pleased; the newly united kingdom was being wooed, through its rulers, by most other European powers. The rest of Europe had perhaps formed exaggerated expectations of the island kingdom, with some idea that in addition to the obvious strategic advantages its striking power had also been tripled. In the early years of his reign,

James received overtures from all parties, and the myth of a re-united kingdom, restoring the ancient kingdom that Brute had founded, became prominent in pageantry and masque. (At the court of England, as at Shakespeare's Elsinore, the balance of compliment and Machiavellian movement might lead judicious spectators to watch the royal family rather than the show.)

In between these twin masques came the occasion when Jonson, in more complete control of his design, could enshrine his pro-founder 'conceits'. While all three taken together enabled him to establish a new form as surely as Marlowe and Shakespeare had established a common form for the public stages, in *Hymenaei* (Twelfth Night, 1606) he gives his fullest statement, defended by an elaborate preface.[22] The match celebrated, between two young creatures thirteen and fourteen years of age, was made by King James, in an effort to pacify two great families. A pageant was followed by a double masque of men and women; then on the second evening, 'all mention of the former being utterly removed and taken away' (ll. 679–80), a contest at Barriers was held, with fifteen a side contending on behalf of the Bride and Groom for Virginity and Marriage. Whether intentionally or not, this reflects the order at the wedding masque which James himself had com-posed for the Marquis of Huntley, where the masquing had been followed by the antiquated sport of tilting at the ring.

A contemporary correspondent noted Jonson's symbolism; 'the poet made an apostrophe to the union of the kingdoms',[23] for James himself, as Elizabeth had done, used continuously the image of a marriage to his realms. The opening pageant, at Juno's altar, shows the ancient Roman marriage rite, whose queer properties of fleeces, woollen girdles, and little wicker flaskets, were no queerer than the actual ceremonies often observed at weddings of the great involving 'bride-cakes, points, garters and gloves; and at night... sewing into the sheet, casting off the bride's left hose, with many pretty sorceries'.[24]

Hymen greets the King and Queen, and the anagram Juno/Unio is expounded after which the nobler shows begin. Eight humours and affections of men, revealed in a turning globe, inharmonious at first, are reconciled by Juno's servant Reason, and by the descent of her heavenly powers. The lady masquers and a full choir appearing in a cloud machine, far from dropping 'like a bucket into a well…came gently sloping down'.[25] As they had 'hired and borrowed all the principal jewels and ropes of pearls both in court or city', the 'Spanish ambassador seemed but poor to the meanest of them', but they had to represent the summit of the Platonic ladder of being;

> Such was the golden chain let down from Heaven;
> And not those links more even,
> Than these.   (ll. 320–2)

They ended with the circle dance, and a prayer for the union of the kingdoms, which James had not yet succeeded in imposing on his unwilling subjects:

> Long may his union find increase
> As he, to ours, hath deigned his peace.   (ll. 429–30)

The Epithalamium, as Jonson admitted, was too long to be performed, notwithstanding that in traditional manner it asks for haste. King James's own 'Epithalamion upon the Marquis of Huntley's Marriage' had also been both lengthy and learned, dropping occasionally, however, into broad Scots:

> O Venus make them broodie als for to produce with speed.   (l. 15)

Though Spenser had celebrated marriage harmony in full Platonic splendour, Chapman's continuation of *Hero and Leander* came nearest of all to Jonson in contrasting the 'things of sense', momentary though attractive, with the 'things of understanding', which impress more deeply and persist. 'Else the glory of all these solemnities had perished like a blaze, and gone out, in the beholder's eyes' (*Hymenaei*, ll.4–6). Princes and great persons who are the 'personators in these actions' (ll. 11–12) seek themselves some way in which 'the present occasions' (l. 17) should lay hold on 'more removed mysteries', grounded on 'antiquity and solid learnings' (l. 16), so 'these transitory devices' (l. 21) give 'nourishing and sound meats' (l. 27). With a final snarl at Daniel, Jonson ends his not very concordant introduction; but in his publication of the next wedding masque he makes full acknowledgment to Thomas

Giles and Hierome Herne for the dances, Alfonso Ferrabosco for the music, and Inigo Jones for the setting.

Composite yet balanced use of every resource demanded team-work; and the large number of courtiers involved (among the gentlemen at the barriers being Sir Oliver Cromwell, the uncle of the Protector, and Donne's patron, Sir Robert Drury) meant that while James was receiving a tribute of enhanced magnificence, the professional advisers and stage managers had a correspondingly intricate task.

Hymenaei, the most classical and explicit of Jonson's masques, sums up the convention of cosmic harmony evoked in sacramental rites, as in *Orchestra*, and in *The Vision of the Twelve Goddesses*. But Jonson gave no concession to such as Daniel who 'squeamishly cry out, that all endeavour of *learning*, and *sharpness* in these transitory *devices*…is superfluous' (ll. 19–23). Perhaps he was ritualist enough to believe that something was truly effected by a properly based ceremony; perhaps as a poet he knew that poetry can com-municate without being fully understood. In a later masque, *The Vision of Delight* (1617), a song instructs the whole company:

> Let your shews be new, as strange,
>   let them oft and sweetly vary;
> Let them haste so to their change,
>   as the seers may not tarry. (ll. 15–18)

The glories of Spring are offered by the figure of Wonder; Nature's body 'set in art' (l. 161) charms all the senses together: 'we see, we hear, we feel, we taste / We smell the change in every flower' (ll. 136–7).

At this time Jonson could certainly vary, and though the next marriage masque, *The Haddington Masque*, used both the cloud chariot and the turning globe, the activities were playful, in parts even grotesque and antic. A lucky Scot, James Ramsey, Viscount Haddington, was marrying a great heiress, one of the prime beauties of the kingdom; the French Ambassador was invited, and to his delight, his little daughter danced with the little Duke of York aged eight. Although Jonson supplied much learned detail, his tone is quite different from that of *Hymenaei*. Cupid here is

1 Exterior of the Curtain Theatre, identified in the only known copy of *The View of the Cittye of London from the North towards the Sowth, c.* 1600. University Library, Utrecht, Ms. 1198, fol. 83 (detail)

2a   The Children of the Chapel, from drawings of Queen Elizabeth's funeral procession, probably by William Camden. Department of Manuscripts, British Museum, Additional Ms. 35 324, f. 31v

2b   Drawing, attributed to Henry Peacham, of a production of *Titus Andronicus*, c. 1595. Collection of the Marquess of Bath

3 Engraving by William Kip of the 'Nova Felix Arabia' from Stephen Harrison's *Archs of Triumph* (1604). This arch was one of six built by Harrison in the streets of London for the Coronation Procession of James I in 1604. Department of Prints and Drawings, British Museum

4   Drawing, by Inigo Jones, of 'a Daughter of the Niger' for Jonson's
Masque of Blackness (1605). Devonshire Collection, Chatsworth

'Venus' runaway' (l. 92), pursued by his mother with disciplinary intent. Coming as it did less than a month after the stately *Masque of Beauty*, Jonson must have found himself hard pressed. He contrived a lighter effect for this non-royal masque; Inigo Jones thriftily re-used some of his machines, so that the chief effect was made by the splendid costumes of the masquers, dressed as the signs of the zodiac. It cost them some £300 apiece, yet the French Ambassador thought the revels 'assez maigre'.[26]

The arrival of a new courtly form had strong repercussions in the theatres. Actors who took the speaking parts and directed the professional aspect of rehearsal, in all probability, incorporated some elements into their own plays for general display. In the private theatres, gentlemen who sat upon the stage imitated Kings and Ambassadors by dressing splendidly, arriving late, departing with haughty comments, while in the public theatres, the Machiavellian intrigues and by-play that accompanied masques offered material for tragic and satiric plots. True, John Marston, writing strictly for the private stages, praised Italian drama in terms that his enemy Jonson would have accepted:

> In honour of our Italy we sport,
> As if a synod of the holy gods
> Came to triumph within our theatres,[27]
>
> (*Histriomastix*, II.i)

but a commoner attitude to the masque was Tourneur's

> Last revelling night,
> When torchlight made an artificial noon...
> O, vicious minute,   (*The Revenger's Tragedy*, I.iv.27-8, 40)

or

> music, sports...
> Nine coaches waiting – hurry, hurry, hurry –
> Castiza: Ay, to the devil!   (*The Revenger's Tragedy*, II.i.199, 202-3)

The murders in a masque with which revenge tragedy is filled magnify the horrid contrast between the stage and what happens off-stage. More realistic is the ironic use of the wedding masque in

The Maid's Tragedy (1610). It is cynically introduced: masques 'must commend their king, and speak in praise / Of the assembly, bless the bride and bridegroom, / In person of some god; they are tied to rules / Of flattery' (I.i.8–11). Here the songs make all the usual assumptions about bridal chastity and royal nobility, so that the revelation of how the bridegroom is being used by the King to provide security for his mistress comes as a violent dramatic reversal.

An account of Jonson's first royal masque gives a sufficiently cynical account of what happened backstage:

> The confusion in getting in was so great, that some ladies lie by it and complain of the fury of the white staves. In the passages through the galleries they were shut up in several heaps betwixt doors and there stayed till all was ended. And in the coming out, a banquet which was prepared for the king in the great chamber was overturned table and all before it was scarce touched. It were infinite to tell you what losses there were of chains, jewels, purses, and such like loose ware. And one woman among the rest lost her honesty, for which she was carried to the porter's lodge being surprised at her business at the top of the Taras.[28]

Jonson himself said in his introduction that he sought to preserve the 'spirits' of this masque because of the 'rage of the people, who, as a part of greatness, are privileged by custom to deface their carcases' (*The Masque of Blackness*, ll. 7–8).

Six months after *Hymenaei* was performed, Jonson wrote a welcome for the Kings of Britain and Denmark to the Earl of Salisbury's house at Theobalds. This visit saw the performance of an entertainment of which Sir John Harington left a devastatingly mocking account. The Queen of Sheba, as she mounted the steps of the dais, spilled her offering of wine cream and jelly into the royal lap; the King of Denmark, as he rose besmeared to dance, collapsed and was taken away to bed. Faith and Hope were both sick and spewing in the lower Hall, Victory was led away 'a silly captive' and put to sleep on the steps, but Peace 'most rudely made war with her olive branch...on the pates of those that did oppose her coming'.[29] Yet the Earl of Salisbury, on whom lay the main task of running the government, commented coolly on the habits of his guests, 'God forbid that this Dane should think the English did anything but drink'.

Social change and Ben Jonson's court masques

Jonson's firm classical conception of the masque began to modify almost as soon as he had formed it. Popular and romantic elements in his third masque for the Queen, given at Candlemas 1609, recall the older English pattern. In accordance with the Queen's wishes for 'some dance or show that might precede hers and have the place of a foil, or false-masque' (*The Masque of Queens*, ll. 12–13), Jonson devised an antimasque of 'Hags or Witches' (l. 17) which offered a 'spectacle of strangeness' (l. 20). The company, set 'in full expectation' (ll. 23–4) of a royal spectacle, suddenly found before them Hell opened on the stage, flaming and smoking 'unto the top of the roof' (ll. 25–6) – and this on one of the four nights of the year when charms were at their most powerful. The eeriness, the *frisson*, had returned. From this time, the antimasque became increasingly for Jonson the inventive part of the action.

The antimasque was of course nothing new. One of Henry VIII's early masques had been preceded by a dance of wild men or Woodhouses, who interrupted a combat between two teams of knights.[30] Queen Anne's *Masque of Blackness* might have been considered an antimasque to her *Masque of Beauty*. Certainly, the Contrary Winds that introduced *The Masque of Beauty* and the antic Cupids of *The Haddington Masque* already suggest development of the antimasque. But the twelve witches who appeared as the antimasque to *The Masque of Queens* introduced new and complex features into the Jacobean masque.

These picturesque witches in their incantations and wild dances not only contrasted with the 'white witchcraft' of masquing but would surely recall the Witches of Berwick who had raised a great storm when James prepared to cross the seas to bring back his bride, Anne of Denmark. They were part of the romantic royal life story. James himself was extremely interested in demonology, and his book of that title had appeared in 1597. Therefore, when Jonson fully annotated the antimasque for publication, with all the classical evidence for his devices, he probably had his sovereign's interests in mind, as much as those of Prince Henry, who was said to have asked for this information. (Henry's role was perhaps no more active than that of Queen Anne in devising the whole masque; the attribution was a form of compliment.)

The twelve witches or hags would be enacted by professional players; they had speaking parts. The 'story line' of future masques included a kind of poetic transformation, allowing some grotesque fancy to be developed (and Drummond of Hawthornden was later to observe that Jonson was 'oppressed with fantasy, which hath ever mastered his reason').[31] Yet unlike the attendants of earlier masques, the torch-bearers, musicians, and truchman or 'speaker', the figures of this antimasque vanished and played no part in the full revels. They did not join the dance. To the audience, waiting to see their partners, and hoping perhaps to be invited out by the chief masquer, the antimasque must have served only to raise expectation and eagerness. The introduction of the anti-masque in its Jacobean form produced a theatrical element in the performance, an alien 'foil', which broke up the classic simplicity of Jonson's initial idea.

At the moment of transformation, as loud music sounded, the witches disappeared into Hell's mouth 'and the whole face of the scene altered: scarce suffering the memory of any such thing' (ll. 357–9). In place of it, 'circled with all store of light' (l. 363), appeared Chaucer's House of Fame, with the twelve queens seated in pyramid shape upon the upper part. The apex was 'Bel-Anna, Queen of the Ocean' who appeared in her own person. Each was identified by a speaker who, in the form of Perseus, represented Heroic and Masculine Virtue, and who proclaimed himself also the only begetter of Good Fame. Bel-Anna's assumption of the chief place was intended only as a tribute to the King:

> And to that light, from whence her truth of spirit
> Confesseth all the lustre of her merit.   (ll. 430–1)

It was impossible that Fame herself should in any way augment the glory of King James.

Then, disguised by more loud music, the House of Fame creaked round, so that Good Fame herself was revealed, while behind the scene the twelve queens filed down into three chariots, symbols of regal triumph, which were drawn through the portal of the House, each with a sufficient number of hags bound captive before.

The Queen was doing her best to be polite to the French Ambassador, his wife, and family; she had waited till the Spanish Ambassador Extraordinary had left the country; and when the Venetian Ambassador complained, the Queen, he said,

let me know that she regretted I had not been invited and pleaded that, as the King paid the bill, he desired to be the host. She says she is resolved to trouble herself no more with masques.[32]

Ben Jonson was gratified by the figures of ancient poets who were set round the lower level of the House of Fame, while above were the heroes they had sung (Inigo Jones had varied them from Chaucer). The House of Fame provided apotheosis and so Jonson had to justify putting a living queen among the great queens of history, for this was felt by some to be lacking in decorum. Queen Anne had to be praised and defended, and perhaps it was not wholly inappropriate that Webster put the recollection of this masque into a scene of trial before Lieger Ambassadors, when his heroine cried:

> my defense of force, like Perseus,
> Must personate masculine virtue.
>
> (*The White Devil*, III.iii.135–6)

As his dedication suggests, Jonson, like many others, was now turning towards the heir apparent, Henry; perhaps it is not without significance after all that he placed Anne among the queens of the past. She danced in one more masque of Jonson, and one of Daniel; but the young prince's energy, his taste for martial sports, his patronage of Chapman's Homer, made him a much more sympathetic image for the centre of a masque. However, next year's sports took the form of Barriers, in which the sixteen-year-old Prince, under his Arthurian name of Meliades, the lover of the Lady of the Lake, issued his general challenge and kept his tent in the field. Jonson wrote the speeches where the stellified Arthur, the Lady of the Lake, and Merlin, as prophet, greeted the young prince whose warlike tastes contrasted so sharply with his father's pacifism.

> Let him be famous, as was Tristram, Tor,
> Lancelot, and all our list of knighthood: or

Who were before, or have been since.

(*The Speeches at Prince Henry's Barriers*, ll. 86–8)

So prayed Arthur, the presiding star, under whose light the Prince, with six companions, met the assault of 58 defendants and 'did admirably fight his part, giving and receiving that night, 32 pushes of pikes and about 360 strokes of swords'.[33]

Prince Henry's Barriers inaugurated the year of his solemn investiture as Prince of Wales; the ceremony, with many surrounding masques and triumphs, took place in June. The Prince would have liked a show on horseback next revelling season, but his father would not agree. Henry appeared therefore as the principal figure in Jonson's masque of *Oberon, the Fairy Prince* (New Year's Day, 1611), a complete capitulation to romance. The first curtain depicted the three kingdoms; behind it was 'a dark rock, with trees beyond it; and all wildness, that could be presented' (ll. 2–3). The playful, mocking, young satyrs of the antimasque with Silenus, their 'grandsire', celebrate the coming of Oberon, who surpasses Bacchus, Phoebus, and Mars. The rock opened to reveal the fairy palace, translucent, 'with countless lights and colours all shifting, a lovely thing to see'.[34]

Its guardians are asleep, wakened only by the satyrs with a gay catch, a nonsense song of Ben Jonson's lightest fancy. The satyrs sing again, mockingly to 'my cunning lady, Moon' (l. 261), begging for a share in her pleasures; they perform an antic dance. This ends the antimasque, for the fairy hill opens (and in how many old romances had not the hill opened to admit the mortal hero, Orfeo or True Thomas, to the fairy realm?). Within were discovered the 'nation of Fays' (l. 291) (noble children including little Charles, Duke of York), the knights masquers afar off in perspective, and 'At the further end of all Oberon, in a chariot...drawn by two white bears' (ll. 294–7). Whether these were the usual traction devices, or masquers with the heads of bears, like the lions of the later *Tempe Restored*,[35] Oberon, being at the farthest end, would at first be visible only to the King, who sat directly in front of the opening. Expectation would therefore be further raised in the audience, till to 'loud triumphant music' the chariot rolled forward towards the opening of the palace (which was only nine feet high by five feet wide), but one spectator – who perhaps sat obliquely – did not see it at all. The full rite was therefore shared only by the King and his son who descended from his chariot to greet his father humbly on foot.

The song that accompanies this approach, so fully built up as climax, mounts through the elements to the Fairy Throne, then it descends again to the organs of sense, all of which are to be struck by wonder, as the Prince of Wales offers homage to the real sovereign. Yet by a pun in the word 'desire' love and ambition are both suggested:

> Melt earth to sea, sea flow to air,
> And air fly into fire,
> Whilst we, in tunes, to Arthur's chair
> Bear Oberon's desire;
> Than which there nothing can be higher,
> Save James, to whom it flies:
> But he the wonder is of tongues, of ears, of eyes.   (ll. 300–6)

The sylvan guardians disperse the satyrs with their 'light, and skipping sport' (l. 321) for this is

> A night of homage to the *British* court,
> And ceremony, due to Arthur's chair,
> From our bright master, Oberon the fair.[36]
>
>   (ll. 322–4)

If Henry is an ever-increasing Spring, James 'stays the time from turning old' (l. 350) and 'holds his course, as certain as the sun' (l. 353) so that the moon, who has hitherto presided 'now borrows from a greater light' (l. 390). His masque must *not* be taken as the inauguration of an alternative power – although that is what in human terms it was.

It has been suggested that James was far too earthly an object for the fairy quest, and that thus incorporated in the masque, 'the unfortunate monarch may remind us of Bottom'.[37] Certainly Jonson has concentrated all his erudition on the opening sequences; he may also have seen himself in the role of Silenus, as tutor to the youthful sports of the young Prince. The dances of the satyrs were incorporated by the King's Men into their popular play, *The Winter's Tale*, for the sports of Prince Florizel. Jonson himself was never more Shakespearean than in the satyrs' catch 'Buz, qoth the blue fly' (l. 210); this bantering tone revives at the end, when the dancers are drawn away from the ladies of the court:

> Here be forms, so bright, and airy,
>   And their motions so they vary,
>   As they will enchant the fairy,
>   If you longer, here, should tarry. (ll. 429–32)

The like bantering tone comes in *Love Freed from Ignorance and Folly*, the last masque to be danced by Queen Anne, which after various delays was performed on 3 February 1611. As in *The Masque of Blackness*, the Queen and her ladies are released by guessing a riddle, designed to honour the King. The machine and the pyramid grouping of the ladies on it recalls *The Masque of Queens*. Inspiration derived from both Anne and James was waning.

The Masque of Oberon formed the climax and culmination of the year's festivities, which had included the solemn Investiture of the Prince, of which it provided a shadow or mirror image. On 30 May, Henry came down the Thames from Richmond to Chelsea, where he was received with a city pageant of Neptune and Corinea, Queen of Cornwall, played by Richard Burbage and John Rice. Salutes and a 'triumphal noise of drums and trumpets'[38] followed as the Prince and the Lord Mayor 'came altogether rowing down the proud river' to Whitehall stairs. On Monday 5 June, Henry entered the Houses of Parliament, made his obeisance to the King, and knelt before him while the Earl of Salisbury read the letters patent. Then James and two assistants put the robes on the Prince, girded him with the sword, invested him with the rod and ring, and set the cap and coronet on his head. After his father had taken him by the hand and kissed him, he was escorted to his seat in Parliament.

The Prince set up his own household at St James's Palace where he celebrated with feasts and martial sports. Innumerable books were dedicated to him. Sir John Davis who devised a second edition of *Orchestra*, praised him as

> both loadstone and the star
> Of hearts and eyes
>
> ('The Author to his Muse', ll. 7–8)

and

> The fairest flower of noble chivalry,
> And of St George his band, the bravest knight.
>
> ('To the Prince', ll. 7–8)

Henry lent his patronage (but not his active participation) to the Twelfth Night masque of 1612, *Love Restored*, which is described as given by Gentlemen the King's Servants but in *The Book of the Revels* is referred to as 'The Prince's Mask'.[39] Robin Goodfellow, a servant of Oberon, and Masquerado play in the antimasque where it is rumoured that there will be no masquing. The difficulty is Money who has got himself into the show disguised as Love, but who is banished by the appearance of the true Cupid, wrapped in furs like a Muscovite. The masque was indeed a very modest affair, but it was the latest one with which the Prince of Wales can in any way be connected.

Jonson was abroad when, in November 1612, the sudden death of Prince Henry dashed the hopes of all the court, as well as Jonson's own aspiration to use the masque in Sidney's manner to raise the mind to virtue. As the Prince was buried, and the officers of his dissolving household broke their staves of office over the coffin, Chapman wrote a funeral song and dedicated it to a poor friend. The vision had ended and the scene closed:

> Heaven opened, and but showed him to our eyes,
> Then shut again, and showed our Miseries.
>
> ('A Funeral Song', ll. 13–14)

Jonson, who so movingly mourned his own son:

> Rest in soft peace, and ask'd, say here doth lie
> Ben Jonson his best piece of poetry,
>
> ('On My First Son', VIII, 41)

lost the impulse to produce masques at once fantastic and learned. James did not know how to respond to public gestures of loyalty and praise, those reciprocal gestures of affection in which Elizabeth had been so skilled. Moreover, complaints against the extravagance of court masques had begun to mount; the King himself had tried without much success to impose a limit on the cost. The sumptuous masques for the wedding of the Princess Elizabeth which followed two months after her brother's death were presented by noblemen and by the Inns of Court; the most successful of the antimasques was again incorporated by the King's Men into a public play which enabled the general population to see it. *The Two Noble Kinsmen*[40] may have been Shakespeare's latest work, but in *The Tempest* he had also reflected the court masque clearly within another mode; masques play an important part, too, in *King Henry VIII* where the earthly masque in which the King woos Anne Boleyn is contrasted with the heavenly masque that comforts the dying Katharine.

THE LATER JACOBEAN MASQUES, 1613–25, AND CAROLINE EPILOGUE

> With you, lucky bird, I begin; let me see,
> I aim at the best, and I trow you are he.
> Here's some luck, already, if I understand
> The ground of my art. Here's a gentleman's hand.
> I'll kiss it for luck's sake; you should by this line
> Love a horse and a hound, but no part of a swine.
> – – – – – – – – – – – – – – – – –
> You are no great wencher, I see by your table,
> Although your *Mons Veneris* says you are able.
> You live chaste and single, and have buried your wife,
> And mean not to marry by the line of your life.
> Whence he that conjectures your quality, learns
> You are an honest good man, and have care of your bairns.
>
> (*The Gypsies Metamorphosed*, ll. 275–80, 287–92)

The Marquis of Buckingham, disguised as a gypsy, is telling the King's fortune. The lines are part of the most successful entertainment Jonson ever devised. A decade after *Oberon*, in the summer and autumn of 1621, it was performed three times during the King's progress – the last performance being at Windsor – and it was said that James wished to bestow a knighthood on Jonson for his pains.

Since 1616 the poet had been recognized by a small court pension; he had given up writing for the public stages altogether. The masque had settled down in a conventional form, with Jonson's fertility of inventions being expended on the antimasque, where he could introduce the note of satire that had been heard in *Love Restored*, or indulge his fantasy; but the image of harmony and unity was becoming impossible to sustain, to fulfil the hopes of court and nation. By the last decade of the reign, things grew very different. After the death of Robert Cecil, the Earl of Salisbury – which almost coincided with Prince Henry's – the King assumed personal responsibility for much of the work that he had previously left in those experienced hands; and his personal predilections became a serious consequence.

The masques of James's final decade reflect a greater intimacy and daring on the part of Jonson, with a closer grip on his monarch's character. Deeply deprived in childhood, and deeply insecure, James demanded a mixture of boisterous familiarity and grandiloquent adulation. His insecurity fed on compliments, but he craved affection. His personal language, like his habits, was filthy ('I kiss your dirty hands',[41] wrote Buckingham), and his temper explosive. He struggled with a feeble body and a bad inheritance, but his weakness for handsome young men betrayed a mixture of the idealizing and the gross.

On his first arrival, he had succumbed to Philip Herbert, Sidney's nephew and namesake, whom he created Earl of Montgomery. At Herbert's wedding at Christmas 1604, the bride was led to church between the Queen's brother and the Prince of Wales, to be given away by the King, who swore 'that if he were unmarried he would keep her for himself....Bride and groom were lodged in the Council chamber where the King in his shirt and nightgown paid them an early visit next morning before they were up', and, according to Dudley Carleton, 'spent a good time in or upon the bed, choose which you will believe'.[42]

In the Christmas season of 1613 Jonson wrote a *Challenge at Tilt* to celebrate the second marriage of the girl for whom he had earlier written *Hymenaei*, but two years later, in publishing his *Works*, he expunged the names of bride and groom from both masques. The scandal of Lady Frances Howard's divorce from her first husband and her marriage to the King's favourite, Robert Carr, Earl of Somerset, ended with a trial for murder. Lady Frances was accused of poisoning Sir Thomas Overbury, and she and her husband were both condemned to death. The King was widely believed to be involved; he waited in horror for news from the trial 'but at last one bringing him word he was condemned, and the passages, all was quiet'.[43]

From a position where he had disposed of 'all courtesies and places' Somerset fell to oblivion, but he had already been succeeded in the King's favour by George Villiers, Earl, Marquis, and eventually Duke of Buckingham, whom the King first met in the autumn of 1614. Villiers was more charming, more dangerous, and far more absolute than Somerset. Among his accomplishments was dancing, so he appeared to advantage in Jonson's masque of Christmas 1614. By the spring of 1616 he had become Master of the Horse and a Knight of the Garter. He was effectually to govern the kingdom, not only during the remainder of James's reign, but under Charles, until his death by assassination in 1628. He disposed of all offices and ruled arbitrarily and irresponsibly. In his letters James was Buckingham's 'purveyor', 'dear dad', and 'husband'.

Given the grounds of Buckingham's favour, his complimenting the King upon being 'no great wencher' must be taken as a rather salacious joke; at Windsor, too, Lord Pembroke, the brother of James' first favourite and Jonson's patron was complimented:

> You never yet helped your master to a wench.
>   'Tis well for your honour, he's pious and chaste,
>   Or you had most certainly been displac'd.   (ll. 695–97)

Equally impudent are the allusions to the predatory habits of Buckingham's family. The gypsies prepare to steal the great offices of state: 'There's a purse and a seal / I've a great mind to steal' (ll. 228–9) – the Great Seal being at this time in the keeping of a nominee of Buckingham, one reputed to be the lover of Buckingham's termagent mother.

This masque was a family affair, the novelty being of course that the talented Buckingham was prepared to take a speaking part of the kind usually reserved for the common players: some of the gypsy songs are charming, but the most famous, Cock Lorell's Song, is very dirty. The whole affair dramatized the intimacies of King James while contriving also in the usual way to compliment him and all the members of Buckingham's family who were not actually playing at gypsies. When the masque was produced at the Marquis' seat at Burley, the old King himself was moved to write some verses complimenting his host on his entertainment and expressing hopes for the arrival of an heir:

> This goodly house it smiles, and all this store
> Of huge provision smiles upon us here.
> The Bucks and Stags in fat they seem to smile,
> God send a smiling boy within a while.[44]

Jonson's writing is light and his wit in exploiting the situation is adroit; but the attempt to reach a lofty tone at the end exposed him to parody, from none other than his friend and former host, Drummond of Hawthornden. The final song is a blessing on the King's five senses: his sight is blessed from gypsies and the Evil Eye, drunkards and 'a smock rampant' (l. 1335), his hearing from lawyers and Puritans 'Or a long pretended fit, / Meant for mirth, but is not it' (ll. 1349–50), and his other senses from James's known dislikes and afflictions, tobacco, pork, and gout. Drummond began his parody, 'The Five Senses'[45]

> From such a face, whose excellence
> May captivate my sovereign's sense,
> And make him Phoebus-like, his throne
> Resign to some young Phaeton,
> Whose skilless and unstayed hand
> May prove the ruin of the land.
> – – – – – – – – – – – – – –
> Bless my sovereign and his seeing.
>
> (ll. 1–6, 14)

From profane jests 'bawdy tales, and beastly songs' (l. 16), forbidden fruit, Jesuit baits, Italian salads, Roman drugs, 'From such a smooth and beardless chin / As may provoke or tempt to sin' (ll. 45–46), in short, from 'a Ganymede' (l. 61) protection is plainly and piously invoked. The verses end with a stinging 'abstract':

> Then let him hear, good God, the sounds
> As well of men as of his hounds....
> Give him a taste, and truly too,
> Of what his subjects undergo.
>
> (ll. 71–4)

With the growing impoverishment of the court, and failure in royal interest as James lost his grip, the court masque had become less sumptuous and less serious; but as an alternative channel for magnificence, setting forth the 'body and soul ' of the state in pageantry and verse, the annual city procession for the Lord Mayor could now rival it. As the split between court and city widened, the Lord Mayor's pageants concentrated rather on the history of the city itself than on the glories of a united monarchy. After the triumphal entry of James, there had been such shows as *The Triumphs of Re-united Britannia* (1605); and some of the pageants seem to model themselves on court masques. Jonson would occasionally contribute, but for the most part the authors were writers for the common stages – Dekker, Heywood, Mundy, Middleton, and Webster. Gerard Christmas, the city's substitute for Inigo Jones, devised quite elaborate machinery for chariots drawn by unicorns, lions, and ostriches; also fountains, arbours, gardens, mountains. The Ironmongers' pageant of 1609 with its ocean and mermaids recalls *The Masque of Beauty*; Virtue and Good Fame in 1612 recall *The Masque of Queens*. In Dekker's House of Fame can be found Henry, Prince of Wales, who in 1624 again occupies an honourable place in a pageant written by Webster for the Merchant Taylors, where he is placed in the Monument of Gratitude. Perhaps the city knew how Henry had opposed the King's favourite, Somerset (or Rochester, as he was at that time). Its tribute to Henry in 1610 was one of the last occasions of a double celebration by court and city.

Middleton likens the Lord Mayor to a bridegroom who is wedded to the city; and this use of what had been a favourite royal metaphor stresses that the affection and obedience of the city could lie primarily to its own officers. Glynne Wickham noted 'a similarly dangerous and aggressive spirit beneath the theatrical cloak of these festivities at Court and in the City', which by Caroline times have become 'two faces of a coin which had parted company'.[46]

In court masques, Jonson might banter city feasts, as in the genial *Christmas his Masque* (1616), when Venus appears a tire-woman from Pudding Lane, and Cupid as prentice to a bugle-maker 'that makes your bobs, and bird-bolts for ladies' (l. 120) with suggestions that he might join Master Burbage (who was probably speaking the lines). Later, at the first masque in the New Banqueting Hall of Inigo Jones, he was to show a lighterman and a bear-ward as antimasque (*The Masque of Augurs*, Twelfth Night, 1622) who came 'hearing the Christmas invention was drawn dry at court, and that neither the King's poet, nor his architect had wherewithal left to entertain so much as a baboon of quality, nor scarce the Welsh Ambassador [the cuckoo] if he should come there' (ll. 84–89).

Joviality, whether of the city or of courtly favourites, gained no support from the new heir to the throne. In 1618, the sober, formal, young Charles, now Prince of Wales, had appeared for the first time as chief masquer in *Pleasure Reconciled to Virtue*, where Comus, the god of good cheer or the belly, led the antimasque. Hercules, whose choice of Virtue before Pleasure set a good example to the young Prince, was softened by Mercury and the presence of Hesperus (or King James):

> Pleasure, for his delight,
> is reconciled to Virtue; and this night
> Virtue brings forth twelve princes have been bred
> in this rough mountain, and near Atlas' head,
> the hill of knowledge. (ll. 200–4)

Throughout the evening James had been confronted by his 'brother' Atlas, the dominating feature of the scene – a mountain formed in the likeness of an old man with a long white beard, who, according to a Venetian present, could roll his eyes very cleverly. But the court was cool – 'there was nothing in it extraordinary but rather the invention proved dull'; 'a poorer was never seen'.[47] As the Venetian gleefully records, the King himself at one point had cried out furiously 'What did you bring me here for? Why aren't you dancing? Devil take you, dance!' Buckingham leaped forward and, by cutting a score of very elegant capers, restored the monarch's temper.

To compensate for the lack of success, for a repeat performance Jonson wrote a new antimasque, decrying the masque to follow, and utilizing the rustic loyalties, quarrelsome vivacity, and the innocent perspectives of some Welsh countrymen to give the King the kind of banter he enjoyed:

Go to, see him once upon a time your own sellive, is more good mean you, than is aware of: By got 'is very hard, but s'all make you a Shestice of Peace the first daies you come; and pershance (say nothing) Knight o'the S'ire too; 'Is not Worcesters, nor Pembrokes, nor Mongymeries s'all carry him from you.

(VII, 498, ll. 29–34)

He could celebrate the King's birthday with *Pan's Anniversary*, where James was deified among the shepherds, with his poetry and his hunting praised equally with his arts of government. Kept firmly in his country houses, remote from government, James became more and more helpless in the hands of Buckingham and Charles (who had grown intimates) till he abetted their own masquerade, the incognito visit to Spain in pursuit of the Spanish marriage, himself writing a familiar set of verses, lamenting their absence from 'Arcadia' under their assumed names of Jack and Tom, 'his sweet boys and dear venturous knights, worthy to be put in a new romanzo'.[48]

Neptune's Triumph, which Jonson wrote to celebrate the return of Charles without a Spanish bride in the autumn of 1623, was kept from performance by the protests of Spain. The common players exploited the national relief with the most popular play of the age, *A Game of Chess*. In Jonson's masque the Prince escapes from enticing 'sirens' and reappears under 'the tree of harmony' on a floating island; but as the concluding sequence celebrates British naval power, the mood is not entirely pacific. In a particularly self-conscious antimasque, in which the poet appears in person, the masquers are openly referred to as such; yet, as the image of an important historic event, it looks back to *Oberon* and the investiture of Henry. Although he affected to despise ballad-makers, Jonson is for the last time celebrating a nationwide sentiment.

The King was tiring; in a bad-tempered little epistle addressed to country ladies he orders them home from London where 'You …dream on naught but visars, masques and plays',[49] and in an even worse-tempered attack, asserts his godlike supremacy over his complaining subjects, in *An Answer to the Libel called 'The*

Commons' Tears'. James's ill health caused the last two masques of his reign to be postponed, though in *The Fortunate Isles* it was bravely asserted that in Britain 'There is no sickness, nor no old age known / To men, nor any grief that he dares own' (ll. 507–08).

But Jonson dared to bring his personal quarrel with another poet into an antimasque and this presumption caused much displeasure. In the last year of James, he wrote a country welcome for the rising sun, Charles, when he visited Kenilworth; this sounds a note both nostalgic and disillusioned. It is in very sharp contrast to *The Gypsies Metamorphosed*. *The Masque of Owls* presents the tragi-comic figures of six 'owls in an ivy-bush' – a term for bankrupts in hiding. These 'unlucky birds' include both London and Coventry traders, all presented by the ghost of Captain Cox, captain of the militia, who at Queen Elizabeth's Princely Pleasures nearly fifty years before had led the revels.

> This Captain Cox, by St. Mary,
> Was at Bullen with King Harry;
> And (if some do not vary)
> Had a goodly library,
> By which he was discerned
> To be one of the learned.[50]   (ll. 24–9)

Country entertainments were to provide the best products of Jonson's later years. At court he was not in favour, for his smouldering quarrel with Inigo Jones broke out; he caricatured Jones in a play, but the caricature was censored by the Master of the Revels.

Charles I succeeded on 27 March 1625. It must have been clear that Jonson was out of tune with the times. In the antimasques to *The Masque of Augurs* and *Neptune's Triumph* Jonson had nostalgically discussed the antimasque as a genre, looking back to the old days of 'disguising': in the latter he had ironically satirized himself by engaging a Poet in debate with the Master Cook who provided the banquet, and assured him that 'Either's art is the wisdom of the mind' (ll. 43–4).

Jonson had been given the post of City Chronologer, and though he steadfastly refused to produce anything of the complimentary kind looked for by the Aldermen, they paid him at least as regularly as did his royal master. He had attempted to return to

the public stage; but had not found favour there. His epilogue
to *The New Inn* (1629) was apologetic:

> All strength must yield.
> Yet judgment would the last be, in the field,

but unsubmissive:

> had he lived the care of king, and queen,
> His art in something more yet had been seen;
> But mayors and shrieves may yearly fill the stage:
> A king's, or poet's birth do ask an age. (ll. 11–13, 21–4)

It was followed by an angry 'Ode to himself', denouncing 'that
strumpet the Stage' and appealing to his powers of praising
Charles, 'raising Charles his chariot, 'bove his Waine' (l. 60), presumably in masques. Jonson in old age reflected some of the quality
of the King he had served; his absolute claims and his irascibility.

Charles and his Queen were both masquers, so the sovereign
now re-entered the masque world, with, however, none of the
'astonishment' and 'wonder' of former days. No longer an act of
homage but, as Jonson himself said in the preface to *Love's
Triumph through Callipolis* (Twelfth Night, 1631), 'the donatives
of great princes, to their people' (ll. 5–6), the ritual celebrated the
virtues of royalty, which diffused greatness upon the audience.
Instead of the coupling of heaven and earth or past and present, it
became almost a political challenge. Charles, like Sidney, sought
a lofty and known tale to 'shadow' his own life but not with the
purpose of arousing to noble action. What has been termed the
'trammelled frivolity' of Charles' elegant court found this game
better played among the family of courtiers, and for five years the
powerful and increasingly opinionated old man who had served
James' court so long was not called upon. In 1631 he wrote both
the King's Twelfth Night masque and the one which the Queen
offered in return at Shrovetide, *Chloridia*; this introduced a notion
to be developed in one of the most ambitious of Caroline masques,
Carew's *Coelum Britannicum*, where the English court represented
a stellified and already deified society. Chloris, nymph of the
flowers, is to be made a goddess by decree of Jupiter 'who would
have the earth to be adorned with stars, as well as the heavens'

(ll. 11–12). However, a fresh quarrel with Inigo Jones broke out, and in his *Expostulation* Jonson exclaimed bitterly:

> O Shows! Shows! Mighty Shows!
> The eloquence of masques! What need of prose
> Or verse, or sense, t'express immortal you?
> – – – – – – – – – – – – – – – – – –
> Painting and carpentry are the soul of masque.
> Pack with your peddling poetry to the stage,
> This is the money-get, mechanic age.[51]   (ll. 39–41, 50–2)

He did not insert Inigo Jones' name on the title page of *Chloridia*. But he was never asked for another masque for court and one of his friends told him candidly the King was not pleased with his verses. Some of his old friends offered him the writing of country entertainments, the last of which contained a final jest against 'Iniquo Vitruvius'.

Years before, in *Hymenaei*, Jonson had distinguished between 'magnificence in the outward celebration or show' (l. 13) and 'the most high and hearty inventions, to furnish the inward parts' (ll. 14–15). This high invention he had not been able to sustain. Charles (who had refused a triumphal procession through the city and forced the City Fathers to dismantle their half-built pageants) wanted a fastidiously formed ritual, a revival of courtly games. The masque became a counterworld, like the world of Don Quixote. In the last masque of all to be performed at Charles' court (by Davenant and Inigo Jones), the Queen appeared as an Amazon, surrounded by her martial ladies, but the final song reasserts 'All that are harsh, all that are rude / Are by your harmony subdued' (ll. 455–6). These regal harmonies are not presented as part of a divine order; they are themselves that order – although the aftermath was as it had always been, disorder.[52]

The city was still holding its rival pageants of which the last, Heywood's *Londoni Status Pacatus: or, Londons Peaceable Estate* (1639) had celebrated a harmony greater than the music of the spheres; so this final pageant of war and peace shows how the same emblems could be used by both parties. But in 1640 it is recorded in the city that 'there is no public show, either with pageants or upon the water'. The citizens were at grimmer sports in the Artillery Yard.

5

JONSON AND THE
IMAGE OF JACOBEAN LONDON

Seen against the ritual of the court masque, the ritual of London's government and gilds might seem only a mirror image, the Lord Mayor's pageant reflecting the masquing, Gerard Christmas, the city pageanter, imitating Inigo Jones, Heywood and Middleton understudying Ben Jonson. Yet a powerful image of the unified city emerged, most splendidly in Jonson's own comedies, where satire counterbalanced the official ritual of praise, yet did not exclude admiration. Descended from the early Tudor moral play, but crossed with many other traditions from Aristophanes to the *commedia dell'arte*, after a decade of lively and varied contest between the private and public theatres, a new sense of the metropolitan community established itself, closely joined to a new self-consciousness about the nature of theatrical experience. These two kinds of awareness developed together.

The playwrights chiefly concerned were Marston, Middleton, Jonson and Dekker; the genre has been studied by Brian Gibbons in *The Jacobean City Comedy*.[1] Over thirty plays are listed here, of which ten belong to the public stages, the rest to the choristers' troupes, ranging in date from 1599 to 1616 – coinciding therefore with the transfer of the Theatre from Shoreditch to Bankside.

From this genre Shakespeare withheld himself, unless certain aspects of *Coriolanus* or *Timon of Athens* may be influenced by it. *The Merchant of Venice* offers an earlier study of the most heavily satirized aspect of city life, in the figure of Shylock, and several plays in the Shakespeare Apocrypha come close to the predominant model.

Early in the sixteenth century, the Scot, William Dunbar, in praising the 'flower of citties all' had specified as its wonders the Bridge, the Tower and the stately splendour of the Lord Mayor.

The annals of London had been compiled, and John Stow, the London tailor who gave his long life to the study of its antiquities, brought out his great *Survey of London* in 1598, enlarging it in 1603; this helped to build in the public mind an image of London's greatness in terms of her topography.

London predominated over other cities of England more completely than any other capital city of Europe. If, in the years between 1525 and 1660, the national population almost doubled, that of London rose from around 50,000 to a quarter of a million. Men were constantly driven to the city, as economic change decimated the small-holders of the countryside; London itself was decimated by plague[2] but as constantly replenished from the rural areas, especially during the disastrous harvests of the 1590s. London was the only English city which knew an underworld, and a quarter recognized as lawless; it also developed a hinterland which sent in supplies and offered recreation.

From the first, the image of London was as likely to give warnings as flattery; satire on city cheats is as old as Chaucer and Langland, but 'estates' satire preceded the specific identification of the cheats with London.[3] Chaucer's city group – his Merchant and Shipman, his gildsmen and his Sergeant – already show the leading types. As in the mid-sixteenth century, social moralities began to replace theologically based studies of evil;[4] Avarice became Usury, Pierce Pickpurse and Cuthbert Cutpurse made their appearance. In the opening years of Elizabeth's reign, popular treatises on knavish tricks, set in familiar parts of London, exposed the kind of fraudulent begging that could flourish only in cities.[5] In the seventies and eighties, with jests and jest books, the dramatic writers Tarlton and Peele brought the merry London rogue nearer to the Comic Vices of the interludes as a character who might be condemned for his cheating but must also be admired for his agility and the success of his lawlessness.

During the eighties, Robert Wilson, in *Three Ladies of London* and *Three Lords and Three Ladies of London*, intermingled moral vices (Fraud, Dissimulation, etc.) with merchants and lawyers;

the second play began with a triumphant procession in which the figure of London appeared, guarded by angels. These two plays represent the dark and bright mirror of city life. Peele's pageant for Wolstan Dixi showed 'lovely London rich and fortunate' as the figure of a woman crowned with towers, the royal arms over her head, and a variety of trades and inhabitants offering their services.[6]

Robert Greene, who developed the 'coney-catching' pamphlets, took a more ambiguous stance, which culminated in his repentance. In the city, players had to meet the open hostility of the citizens, but their mockery was supported by the young gentlemen of the Inns of Court, where as they prepared themselves to administer their country estates as Justices of the Peace, they would meanwhile frequent the court, and run into debt in the city. The Presence Chamber, the Royal Courts of Justice, the Exchange were three magnets that drew all.[7]

As Queen Elizabeth passed Temple Bar on her way to thanksgiving at St Paul's for the defeat of the Armada, the road was lined on one side by lawyers, on the other by the liverymen; young Francis Bacon observed as the courtiers came in view, 'If they bow to citizens, they are in debt; if to us, they are in law'.

Janus-faced images became familiar; Spenser, in *Colin Clout's Come Home Again*, first depicted the court as the seat of all virtues, then as the haunt of all vices. In the Shakespearean play of *Sir Thomas More*, the hero, a London worthy famed both as a lawyer and a jester, is shown in the opening scene inciting a pickpocket to take the purse of Mr Justice Suresbie (who has just sentenced him); in return for this jest, he promises to obtain a pardon. At the same time, there evolved a pattern of cautionary tales which persisted until the age of Hogarth and Goldsmith, of the innocent country maid seduced, the innocent country youth cheated of his inheritance by 'ingrossers', usurers, dishonest traders, confidence men, alchemists, projectors, card-sharpers, pickpockets, bawds and whores. At the end of every rake's progress stood the London jails, whose horrors were separately portrayed in pamphlets and on the stage.[8] Two hundred years of slow preparation suddenly flowered in the popular writings of the last decade of Queen

Elizabeth. Shakespeare's variation appears in the history of Prince Hal and Falstaff.

The cheats, whether condemned or only half condemned, whether covertly admired or merely displayed, were placed in a special milieu. Greene exploited their private language. He mentions the three chief haunts of the 'nips' and 'foists' (cutpurses and pickpockets) as St Paul's, Westminster Hall and the Exchange. It is to these three that Nashe sends his suppliant Pierce Penniless in search of a messenger to the Devil, to whom he wishes to offer his soul. After visiting the Exchange and the Law courts, a minor devil is located by Pierce in St Paul's, in the guise of a professional perjuror or 'knight of the Post'. But Nashe expressly defends the Theatre of Burbage on highest political grounds. This newest focus of social life, though akin to the festivities of the alehouses and inns – where players sometimes stationed themselves – offered less temptation than any other haunt,

For whereas the afternoon being the idlest part of the day; wherein men that are their own masters (as Gentlemen of the Court, the Inns of Court and the number of Captains and Soldiers about London) do wholly bestow themselves upon pleasure, and that pleasure they divide (how virtuously it skills not) either into gaming, following harlots, drinking or seeing a play; is it not then better (since of four extremes all the world cannot keep them but they will choose one) that they should take themselves to the least, which is plays?

(*Works*, ed. McKerrow, i, 211–12)

Nashe, having created for himself the persona of Jester-General to the City of London, was prepared to turn his talents to any form of journalism from defence of episcopy to bawdy celebration of the stews (see Chapter 2, p. 21). His caricatures, drawn on the page in racy absurdities, bring him close to the language of the coterie dramatists; his vocabulary, though not his structure, displays the rhetorical flourish of the stage poet. His is the first example of that ability to cross the barriers of different genres which nourished the later literature of London life.

From jest books and prose pamphlets it passed at the end of the nineties to verse satire, in the work of Donne, Marston and Hall, thence into the private theatre and, after a brilliant run, into the public theatres, where as the national vision of the chronicle history faded, comedy gained new depth and resonance in the masterpieces of Jonson and Middleton.

Both popular and 'private' theatres varied the balance between a traditional 'frame' for the plot and fresh local detail. Henslowe's theatres saw such works as William Haughton's *Englishmen for My Money* (1598) where three Englishmen steal the three daughters of a rich city man from their foreign rivals; the next year Dekker's *The Shoemakers' Holiday*, most festive of all city plays, interwove an idyll of true love with the humours of 'mad' Simon Eyre, the merry Lord Mayor who built Leadenhall. Only the location is exact, the rest is legend.

These local legends enhanced traditional certitudes and promoted a stable society; they could have given to the drifting population of London an illusion of rootedness, in the tales of a grandam. A feeling of solidarity and neighbourhood could spring from these 'games' and jests, where kings consorted with their subjects in holiday mood. Satiric comedy, on the contrary, required the audience to pass judgement on the city, from a point of view privileged and detached; the theatre itself and the activity of the play was included in the judgement. Middleton and Jonson, by developing complex plots, were able to make irony pervasive, moral implicit.

Dekker knew his London, street by street: Heywood, another popular writer, tended rather to send his 'prentices off on long voyages of discovery. Youth is menaced by tight-fisted age, but more and more the prodigal is required only a summary act of repentance and reformation, after enjoying a reckless career; *The London Prodigal* (1605) offers pieties and humours of the same undisturbing reassuring model as *Sir Thomas Wyatt*, or Heywood's historical plays featuring Jane Shore, or the building of the Royal Exchange by Sir Thomas Gresham. *The Fair Maid of the Exchange* extols 'the valiant cripple of Fenchurch Street'; *The Boss of Billingsgate* presumably celebrated the fishmongers' fountain. But in 1603, in *The Old Joiner of Aldgate* a notorious scandal was dramatized by Chapman for St Paul's Boys.

Nashe had been the first to put on paper the full exuberance of Cockney wit, as in his search for a messenger to the Devil:

But written and all, here lies the question; where shall I find this old ass, that I may deliver it. Mass, that's true; they say the lawyers have the devil and all; and it is like enough he is playing Ambodexter among them. Fie, fie, the Devil a driver in Westminster Hall? It can never be.

Now I pray you, what do you imagine him to be? Perhaps you think it is not possible that he should be so grave? Oh, then you are in error, for he is as formal as the best Scrivener of them all. (*Works*, ed. McKerrow, i.162)

At the Exchange he meets

an old, straddling Usurer, clad in a damask cassocke, edged with fox fur, a pair of trunk slops, sagging down like a Shoemaker's wallet, and a short threadbare gown on his back, faced with motheaten budge; upon his head he wore a filthy coarse biggin and next it a garnish of night caps, which a sage button cap, of the form of a cow sheard overspread very orderly; a fat chuff it was, I remember, with a grey beard cut short to the stumps and a huge worm eaten nose, like a cluster of grapes, hanging downwards. (*Ibid*, 162–3)

The monstrous figure is clearly related to the more unsavoury of Chaucer's portraits, on the one hand, and to the satiric characters of Ben Jonson on the other.[9] He would serve for a procession of the seven deadly sins, and is fully realized in that style. But the devil is finally located in church – at St Paul's. (cf. below, p. 93 and p. 98).

Only a few years ahead, the *Satires* and *Elegies* of young Jack Donne, son of a wealthy London tradesman, Warden of the Ironmongers' Company, and of the dramatist John Heywood's daughter, were to anatomize the follies of the courtiers. At Lincoln's Inn, Donne played in the Christmas sports; and although he satirizes a young lawyer (Satire II) and a citizen who is destined to be a cuckold (Elegie XIV) with long extracts of their characteristic speech, his models are hardly specifically from London: the city may appear as backdrop.

> He them to him with amorous smiles allures,
> And grins, smacks, shrugs and such an itch endures
> As prentices or schoolboys which do know
> Of some gay sport abroad, yet dare not go   (Satire I).

Donne, however, as a great frequenter of plays, supplies a glimpse of the inner constitution of that witty, select audience which supported the chorister's theatres, and the outburst of city satire in the works of Marston and Jonson. The neat epigrammatist can be met in the 'characters' of the persons prefixed to Ben Jonson's *Every Man Out of His Humour* (1599), dedicated to the Inns of Court, for whom it was written for that season when 'the cap and gown is off and the lord of liberty reigns'. Courtiers, citizens and citizens' wives, with other estates are crisply defined, but the Induction affirms a moral purpose.

> To strip the ragged follies of the time
> Naked, as at their birth.

Comment and debate on the way the play works is provided in the intervals. The third act is set in the middle aisle of St Paul's, where the bills of those who sought service are posted; other scenes are at the Mitre tavern, on the Palace stairs, finally to reach the Counter prison. *Cynthia's Revels* satirizes the court, whose fashionable courtiers, fine ladies and hangers-on are ruthlessly exposed by the God Mercury, and a wry personification of the presentor, Crites. This combination of witty discussion and detachment with lively parody recalls the Revels of the Inns of Court, with their large elements of parody, but adds much more sophistication (see below, Chapter 6, p. 108 and Chapter 11, pp. 213–14). However, Jonson and, following him, Marston, in their satire indulged in medieval attitudes of moral superiority, joined with and reinforced by the ancient satiric right to give chastisement to drive out evil habits. It was this therapeutic harshness which exposed them both to ridicule.

> I bear the whip of just Rhamnusia
> Lashing the lewdness of Britannia.

In this claim of the wealthy young lawyer, John Marston who, surprisingly, took to the stage before, like his contemporary Donne, ending in the church, assumed a *persona* much angrier than that of his predecessor Nashe.

Vicious, harsh, lascivious and utterly merciless, the satirist attacks others, partly out of moral outrage and desire to correct, partly out of the pleasure to be derived from whipping...He concentrates his attention in an obsessive way on the shocking, the lurid, and the sexual; seeks out unerringly the scandalous, the abnormal and rotting; and denounces these in a 'stuttering' style, mixing the

crude and the sublime, now as vulgar as a fishwife, now as lofty as Cicero.
(Alvin Kernan, *Revels History of Drama*, iii.391)

Following on Middleton and Dekker's *The Honest Whore* of
1604, a sentimental study of low life in Bedlam and Bridewell
(though ostensibly set in 'Milan') came the realistic and stinging
first play of Marston which exploited the London scene, *The Dutch
Courtesan* (1605) – a Blackfriars' play – where the vivid portrait of
a whore and her bawd is set in a frame of jests perpetrated by
Cockledemoy 'a knavishly witty City companion', at the expense
of the tavern-keeper, Master Mulligrub. This high-spirited play
was followed the same year by the more famous *Eastward Ho!*, for
which the authors were imprisoned. The latter is a parody of the
Idle and Industrious apprentice, in which the scene is set in Cheapside; and here Chapman, Jonson and Marston collaborated to mock
broken gentry and city pretensions; yet gullible city dames and
the riotous prentice Quicksilver are so much more entertaining
than their virtuous counterparts, that the effect is highly sub-
versive. Like its predecessor, *Eastward Ho!* followed the tradition
of the popular theatres, where *Westward Ho!*, a much more conventional work, had been put on the previous year by Dekker and
Webster. Marston's two plays remain actable today: both have
been revived at the Mermaid Theatre.

These Jacobean years are crowded with plays and counter-
plays on London themes, the novelty being a frank treatment of
wifely infidelity, and of the trade of prostitution (including
prostitution of their wives by unscrupulous husbands); the growing city ambition to marry into the gentry yields a means of
satirizing both.

Thomas Middleton (1580–1627), another Londoner (and, like
Jonson, the son of a bricklayer?) began, like Marston, to write very
young, and by 1601 was reported to be 'daily accompanying the
players'. Having married Mary Marbeck, daughter of a famous
musician and sister to an actor, and served his apprenticeship with
Dekker, Middleton went on to provide the private theatres with a
group of satiric comedies, very closely related to London's underworld, although the framework is often that of the moral play,
whilst the ingenious detail of the plots recalls the trickery of the

commedia dell'arte. Middleton moved on from the static analysis of the early comedies of Jonson, with their parade of fools, gulls and knaves, selected with punitive intent. From

> the time's deformity
> Anatomized in every nerve and sinew,
> (Induction to *Every Man in His Humour*)

he developed sinewy plots, whose fast-moving intrigue revealed an underlying irony. He was given to satirizing lawyers as much as usurers; as his audience was largely composed of law students, this might represent the young men's protest against the habits of their elders, the students' own interests in dispute and debate, or simply the general move towards a legal rather than a theological approach to the problems of society, which has been already re-marked upon.

Middleton's young prodigals take to the cheating tricks of the town as does his Country Wench.[10] Whilst Marston played the rôle of a poetic protesting moralist, Middleton's ironic prose avoided the heightened vocabulary of caricature; he reduced the issues to the city level, leaving judgement to be contributed by the audience. The evil characters are left to wreak vengeance on each other. 'Is't come about? tricks are repaid, I see', is the cheerful comment of young Follywit on finding he has married a whore. Other plays end more darkly than this. The character too, is no longer described, but implied through his activities. Thus, old Hoard, who has been brought by trickery to marry another whore, in the belief that he was robbing his enemy's kinsman of the match, soliloquizes:

What a sweet blessing hast thou, Master Hoard, above a multitude, Wilt thou never be thankful? How dost thou think to be blest another time?...to ride to her lands in state and order following; my brother and other worshipful gentle-men...to ride along with us in their goodly decorum beards, their broad velvet cassocks and the chains of gold twice or thrice double...the sight of which will so vex my adversary Lucre – for we'll pass by his door o' purpose, make a little stand for the nonce, and have our horses curvet before the window – certainly he will never endure it, but run up and hang himself presently.

(*Trick to Catch the Old One*, IV.4)

Middleton's is a thoroughly secular world; the detail is sometimes fantastic, as if the extraordinary features of some leading case were being enlarged, but law is often successfully defied by aggressive individuals. The action is highly patterned and symmetrical; characters fit in with each other because they are all seen from a consistantly ironic point of view, whilst they remain recognizable figures from city life. At the same time, they may be also seen to be descended from the evil tempters of the moral play: Jonson was to define the position in one of the critical discussions that form part of *The Staple of News* (1626). Tattle complains that there is no fiend in the play and that 'she would not give a rush, for a Vice that has not a wooden dagger', to which Mirth, her gossip, replies

That was the old way, gossip, when Iniquity came in like Hocus Pocus, in a juggler's jerkin with false skirts, like the Knave of Clubs; but now they are attir'd like men and women o' the time, the Vices, male and female; Prodigality like a young heir, and his Mistress Money (whose favours he scatters like counters) prank't up like a fine lady, the Infanta of the Mines!

Clara Aurelia Pecunia may be descended from Wilson's Lady Lucre, indeed from Langland's Lady Meed, but the name carries a broad hint of that corruption which pervaded the court of James. (The Queen herself was supposed to receive money from the Spanish Ambassador.)[11]

Satire of the city, first drawn from the small in-group of the Inns of Court, expanded upon city and court alike. Middleton added to the traditional pamphlets on roguery with *The Black Book* (1604) and, with Dekker, provided a somewhat romanticized version of the life of a celebrated London transvestite, Moll Frith, in *The Roaring Girl* (1607). For this play, Moll, a tobacco-taking virago, appeared on the stage of the Fortune in person. Dekker added in pamphlets new accounts of London prisons, and satirized young gallants with his *Gull's Horn Book* (1609).

These works all depict a society in a state of mutual hostility and exploitation. The assumptions issue from a secular and predatory world, closely inter-related and functioning like clockwork. Here, Hoard and Lucre can spend their time cutting each other out; old and young are set against each other; kinsmen against kinsmen; much turns on court judgements, signing of bonds, personal credit, legalized fraud. Middleton offers a reductive vision of the city; Hobbes was later to assert that 'Force and fraud are in war the two cardinal virtues', but in the close-knit society of London a state of something like war already prevails. This is revealed by the multiple plots by which Middleton links different groups, generating the dynamics of a mobile society. His masterpiece, *A Chaste Maid in Cheapside* (1611), written after an interval for Lady Elizabeth's Men, far exceeds in complexity of plot the earlier group of comedies. It may owe much to the fact that Jonson had also returned to the popular stages, with *The Alchemist* (1610).

In these plays, together with *Bartholomew Fair* (1614), which was also produced by Lady Elizabeth's Men, the long development of City Comedy reached its triumphant conclusion. It then disappeared with the completeness that the chronicle history had evinced at an earlier stage. After 1613 Middleton became a writer of city pageants and City Chronologer – perhaps the burgesses thought him worth buying off. Jonson put his vitality into masques; and to the court, in *The Gypsies Metamorphosed*, he even transferred the traditional tricks of roguery. Not, however, before he had added to Middleton's complex plots and contrasted groups a new dimension, which makes his greatest comedy also the most powerful image of Jacobean London.

In *The Alchemist*, Jonson creates within the one house in 'the Friars', a whole little world. Like Langland's 'fair field full of folk' or his own *Bartholomew Fair*, it is complete, rounded within itself. The shop of cheating and roguery sells everyone's dreams and hopes and fantasies. Thus the story draws in the audience, as witness to the power of illusion that is in art itself. Here, there is no overt discussion, as in the earlier 'critical' plays. In Middleton's manner, comment is implicit, and once the action is warmed up, the whole collection of fools and knaves is used to help cheat each other.

The Alchemist differs, however, from the reductive works of Middleton in that each of the victims is himself engaged in a passionately active pursuit of some hoped-for greatness, so that the total effect is explosive, covering all the various aspects of city life and much that lies beyond it, from the Faustian expansiveness of Epicure Mammon's imaginings to poor little Dapper's dream of being loved by the Fairy Queen. He emerges finally as the only one who gets an illusory fulfilment, in the brief glimpse of divinity provided at the very last moment by Doll Common – this in exchange for all his ready money, including his sweetheart's love-token, and two acts' imprisonment in the privy.

Mammon's old iron, bought for transmutation, is sold to the Puritans; the Spanish Count in search of a whore is brought to court the widow in search of a husband; the little tobacco seller who covets her is sent to fetch the disguise by means of which she is to marry someone else; her brother's lesson in quarrelling is used to get rid of the man who has penetrated all the cheating; then, just when all these people have been played off successfully by the trio of cheaters, the master of the house returns. The cheats double-cross each other but Jeremy, the clever ancestor of all amoral servants, down to Figaro and the butler of *You Never Can Tell*, finally escapes scot free, by offering his old master the enormous bribe of the wealthy young widow, whom Lovewit weds and beds at top speed, as he exultantly declares:

> Well fare an old harquebusier yet,
> Could prime his powder and give fire and hit
> All in a twinkling! (v.ii.56–8)

The jargon of *The Alchemist* is used with all the gusto that Chaucer had displayed in *The Canon's Yeoman's Tale*, perhaps one of the play's originals. The shock and clash of two worlds coming to-gether can be felt from the plot action (as when Dapper's cries from the privy interrupt the butler's assurances that no one is in the house), and penetrates down to the details of language:

> You will not come then, punk devise, my suster,

shouts Kestrel, the Angry Boy, but the Puritan Ananias reacts at once in the religious terms of the 'separated brethren' of Amsterdam:

> Call her not, sister; she is a harlot, verily.

The opening quarrel between Subtle, Face and Doll, with the minimum of set explanation, tells the audience at once who they are. Coupled with the natural vigour of the language, the action runs on in a surge of raucous eager life – all set in the theatre district, but in plague time, when death lurks behind, making the extremes of absurdity the more violent by contrast. The play itself was put on when the theatres opened after a closure for plague. Lashing of religious hypocrisy, if the severest part of the play, is also the funniest; in one of her rôles Doll Common plays a religious maniac, spouting passages from a contemporary religious ranter.

In his earlier plays Jonson had depicted a relatively static scene, with characters engaged chiefly in talking and only occasional bursts of action. But this is a society in which not only is wealth fluid, there is also the possibility of social movement; the trades-man hopes to rise at least to the top of his trade, others hope for much more. No longer is there the insistence upon many familiar scenes of London because the life itself of London has been caught in the ceaseless pulse and flame of movement; as Dr Johnson was to say, 'He that is tired of London is tired of life; for there is in London all that life can afford.'

In *Volpone*, the great preceding comedy, Jonson had, as it were, shown a refracted and more distorted image of city corruption; the worship of gold, and the mutual trickery of Volpone and his dupes reach a more horrific scale. The deception of Volpone and of Mosca, controlled within a tighter frame, has satanic overtones of glee

> Success hath made me wanton. I could skip
> Out of my skin now, like a subtle snake   (III.i.5–6)

yet that parasite is also a Protean actor, a 'larcinous Ariel', whilst from within the curtains of his bed, his master devises a play-within-a-play, emerging to a mountebank's stage. At the end, throwing off not only his disguise but finally his rôle, he asks for judgement from the audience, not the court. But the scene was Venice, a larger London.

The shower of commendatory verses (Donne's was in Latin) included some from playwrights and one set from an actor-playwright, Nat Field, to whose troupe Jonson offered, in *Bartholomew Fair* (1614), a merrier scene with a looser web of action. The action is set out of doors, in an extended setting where many different actions can occur at once. Festive Opening Play for the public theatre, the Hope at Bankside,[12] in its Induction it reveals the old stage-keeper protesting that the author does not really know his London: 'He hath not conversed with the Bartholomew birds, as they say'. He himself would have brought a pump on the stage (like Mr Vincent Crummles at a later date):

And a punk set under upon her head, with her stern upward, and ha' been soused by my witty young masters o' the Inns of Court. What think you of this for a show now? He will not hear of this! I am an ass, I; yet I kept the stage in Master Tarleton's time, I thank my stars.

At the end of the play, wherein Justice goes disguised like 'mad Arthur of Bradley' to spy out the 'enormities' of his jurisdiction, Jonson's critical appeal culminates in the argument conducted between Zeal-of-the-Land Busy and the chief puppet on the lawfulness of puppet plays. A roaring parody of *Hero and Leander* has been staged by the puppeteer, in league with a 'civil cutpurse', who has been meanwhile taken under the special protection of Justice Overdo. Assailed by the smells of pork, tobacco, ale, urine, he fails completely to scent out the cheats, and with the other two 'governors' – Busy and Waspe – is clapped into the stocks, a familiar emblem of misrule. This little world includes the risk of death, but to draw a crowd, the ballad seller, who is also the cutpurse's receiver, strikes up a pious song:

> Youth, youth, thou hadst better been starv'd by thy nurse
> Than live to be hang'd for cutting a purse

Bartholomew Cokes, the overgrown child, loses his all, including his bride, to one of the sharp-eyed young gallants who are observing and admiring the cutpurse; the other gains a rich Puritan widow.

Bartholomew Fair comes at harvest time, and the ripeness of the late summer warms Jonson's Saturnalia.[13] At its centre, Ursula, the monstrous pig-seller (a part for a man) presides, with the outrageous fluency of a pantomime 'dame'. The play indulges both the intelligence and animal spirits, whilst subtracting from its composition personal and sympathetic feminine emotions. There is a shared perspective between the theatre audience and the various stage audiences. Though from the induction to the play-within-a-play, the perspective constantly shifts, though the Aristophanic fantasy ranges from the infantile to the manic, from parody to inflation, yet the Fair is no longer a place but a community; all are feeling the same way if not quite looking in the same direction.

The year 1616, already noted as defining the limits of City Comedy, marks a turning point for Jonson (it was also the year of Shakespeare's death). With the appearance of his collected *Works* in folio, he drew a line, retiring from the stage for a full decade, after one last play, *The Devil is an Ass*, set in a framework of the old moral interlude, inverted. Pug, a junior devil, rooked by the London cheaters, is rescued from Newgate only by Iniquity and Satan. The audience, led by Fitzdottrell, usurp the stage with new satire on projects for draining the fens and with Pirandello-like reflections on going to see *The Devil is an Ass*. London is no longer a community; rather a sort of cabaret is presented.

At court, in the antimasque of *Mercury Vindicated from the Alchemists*, Jonson began the year by showing all the labour and sweat of the forge left behind. He ended it with citizens' mumming,[14] a burlesque of old sports and pastimes, with Gregory Christmas (a surrogate for Gerard Christmas) leading in ten dancers intended 'for Curriers' Hall'. The city acquires an almost rustic innocence in the persons of 'Tom of Bosoms Inn' as Misrule and 'Clem Wasp of Honey Lane' as New Year's Gift, with their fellows. Later, a team from the brewery at St Katherine's Dock furnished an antimasque, which included also three dancing bears; city simplicity replaced the rusticity of the Welsh or Irish[15] for entertainment of the court.

In the theatre, as city and court lost contact, the conventions of city comedy were appropriated for the country gentry who increasingly flocked to town; the popular audience withdrew to its own purlieus.

At some time in the 1620s, Philip Massinger remodelled Middleton's *Trick to Catch the Old One* into a highly successful tragi-comedy, which held the stage into the next age.[16] By a pretended infatuation on the part of a rich benevolent widow, the ruined

Welborne tricks his merciless, usurous uncle, Sir Giles Overreach into advancing him money, whilst a treacherous notary razes the deed of sale of his land. The sub-plot of *A New Way to Pay Old Debts* shows the benevolent Lord Lovell assisting his page, young Frank Allworth, to steal a marriage with Overreach's heiress, under cover of taking her himself; the Lord then marries the rich widow whilst the wicked uncle, who runs mad, is committed to Bedlam.

Overreach dominates the play, though tricked at every turn. A villain of melodrama, compounded of Avarice, Barabbas, Shylock and Middleton's Lucre, he has acquired his estates by ruinous law suits, would prostitute his daughter for a peerage. His nephew, reduced to a beggar's rags and cudgel, recovers his station not by rogue's tricks but by skilled use of credit, in borrowing on confidence rather than security, clinching his advantage with a chemical conjuring trick. The simplicity of the young lovers inveigles Overreach into ordering their marriage licence, and dispatching them to a parson; so the plot turns on the triumph of virtue over vice, of country gentry over city usury; in the unfamiliar country setting of Nottinghamshire the city man is at a loss. Social decorum in two great households ensures the studiously moderate and courteous behaviour of the two leaders of society, as when the Lady ventures to advise the Lord against marrying Overreach's daughter, whilst he rebukes her dotage on Welborne:

> Think you, madam,
> 'Tis not grown public conference? (IV.ii.236–7)

His condescension in finally marrying Lady Allworth is acknowledged, but he takes her devotion to the memory of her first husband – which prompts her stratagem on behalf of his friend – as guarantee for a second marriage. Massinger contrives to establish a patriarchal kind of social credit; whilst strict legal bonds, forged in the city, work for the villain and his creatures, Marrall and Overdo, attorney and magistrate, the two young men accept the arbitration of Lord Lovell over the spoils, and both take service with him – Allworth in his household, Welborne in his regiment. The ideal of the country gentry came to Massinger from Wilton where his father had been the Earl of Pembroke's steward; he himself was a servant of the Earl of Montgomery, Pembroke's brother. Good manners are found inherent in a class, and whilst social mobility is not excluded, it must be regulated. Assumptions, intentions, audience-response in Massinger's play differ radically from Middleton's; social rather than moral values are in control. Overreach's own mixture of flattery and bullying belongs to a social rather than a monstrous being, such as the plot requires him to be.

The audience is never directly told the nature of the plots afoot, so that the final revelation of what were by now familiar stage devices would serve to gratify those able to divine the probable course of events. Dramatic irony is quiet, as in Lord Lovell's reply to Overreach's eager 'Is it a match?' 'I hope, that is past doubt, now' (IV.i.141). Nothing could be more soothing, more smoothly compounded than the dexterity of the neatly interwoven and reassuringly planned intrigue, so that the farce of Tapwell and Froth, the inflation of Justice Greedy, the wildness of Welborne might serve as serious relief to the gentry's version of *The Shoemakers' Holiday*, were not the audience also invited to detect an echo of major constitutional issues. Sir Giles Overreach inevitably recalls Sir Giles Mompessen, whose impeachment and trial in 1621 for the abuse of monopolies constituted the first great case by which the House of Commons asserted itself against the Crown. Reviving long-dormant powers, they arrested seven of the royal servants, questioned fourteen, expelled three and suspended one from the House; as Thomas Wentworth told his constituents, the censure of Mompessen had been of more good to the Commonwealth than six of the best laws made in the last Parliament.[17] Under protection of royal grants to license alehouses, these men had been feathering their own nests by legal extortion and blackmail – hinted at in the opening of the play. In return for handsome bribes, Mompessen had licensed several bawdy houses; eventually he dodged justice by fleeing the country, whilst his accomplices were all the more sharply punished by degradation and fines.

Mompessen, however, was no city usurer but himself a West Country squire, connected by marriage with the Buckingham family; indeed, the great Duke himself had begun as just such a handsome, orphaned, young page as Frank Allworth. By joining in the outcry, the Duke got off with no penalty at all, although both his brothers were deeply implicated; eventually Mompessen himself returned to live on his estates, and even to proceed in new extortions.[18]

History therefore offered a less moral conclusion to the story, but Massinger had good grounds for keeping quiet about the shady part played by the nobility in Mompessen's affairs; the heir of his patron Montgomery was married to Buckingham's daughter. Under device of transforming the courtly extortioner into a city usurer, the gentry are safeguarded; following their lead in denouncing an unsuccessful tool – in itself a highly Machiavellian procedure – the play reflected contemporary events in such a way as to stimulate the audience whilst evading the true issue. That the Overreach mentality was well established at court, that even a Villiers might attempt unsuccessfully to marry a city heiress is deceptively concealed. The audience of the private theatres was no longer prepared to be disturbed by public events, however disturbing.

The morality element in the old City Comedy was adapted by Middleton in his famous *Game at Chess* (1624) to the treatment of Prince Charles's projected Spanish marriage; this shows precisely the opposite use being made of old material from the popular stage, and, as one theory would have it, it was backed by the same noble family.[19] The theatre took to humbler scandals, such as the play by Dekker, Ford, Rowley and Webster upon another marriage hunt, *Keep the Widow Waking*.[20] When, shortly afterwards, Ben Jonson returned to the public stages with *The Staple of News* (1626), he satirized journalists and scolded his audience; for the move towards news-vending, whether in the theatre or in the newsletters, involved just that imputation of particularity and slander which he had fiercely opposed but with which he had often been charged. The integrity of satire, depending on what Dr Johnson termed 'just representations of general nature' was impugned by this new development.

Massinger continued to exploit the line he had opened, and in *The City Madam*, the villain Luke Frugal not only ruins his ambitious sister-in-law but prepares to sell his nieces as human sacrifices to some visiting 'Indians' from Virginia – the rescue team in disguise. The moral of this play is 'the distance twixt the city and the court';[21] it would find no audience among citizens. So the themes of London comedy came in Caroline times to serve a group, increasingly alienated from the city, and to reflect the isolation of wits who frequented the private houses.

City Comedy had sprung from lively interplay between private and public stages, and was designed for an audience diversified but not antagonized. It was but one of several forms, for behind it lay that little world, the microcosm of the Jacobean London theatre, which from the turn of the century had been placed by visiting foreigners among the city's wonders.

6

THE MANIFOLD THEATRES OF
JACOBEAN LONDON AND THEIR POETS

New structures out of old emerged in London in the early years of the seventeenth century; with them, and the new actor–audience relationships they supplied, new forms of interplay between these theatres became more clearly distinguishable. Playwrights as well as companies became associated in some cases with one type of theatre, or learnt to modify their approach in writing for different types, and they themselves became notable. Their names appeared on the title pages of plays[1] although not till Dryden's time were they featured on playbills.

The established companies, each with its 'now usual house of playing' publicly designated, sometimes controlled a second house; Henslowe's 'Empire' included more than one company. New theatres of the open type were built for the men, but there was a marked move from outdoor to indoor playing – even at court, tilts and tourneys were increasingly replaced by Barriers, an indoor sport which could be performed during the Christmas revels.

The closing of the London inns to players in 1597 coincided with an attempt by Burbage to open in the Blackfriars, and was followed in 1599 by the revival of St Paul's boys (see above, pp. 5, 42). In a recent paper,[2] Reavley Gair suggested that they played in a private dwelling, 'Mr Leighton's' in 'the Shrouds', built between the cathedral wall and the Chapter House in the South Cloister and lying partly below ground level. He thinks the tiny auditorium faced a stage set between two buttresses of the Chapter House; the converted dwelling shared this crowded area with other less authorized intruders – a joiner's shop stood near.[3]

In 1608, when the Burbage–Shakespeare company, now the King's Men, gained possession of Blackfriars from their tenants,

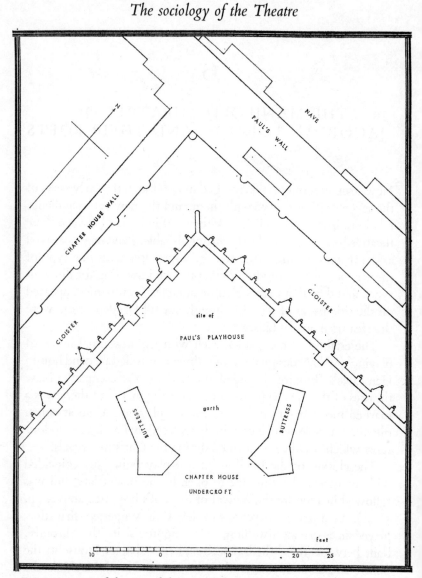

Reconstruction of the site of the second theatre at St Paul's by Professor W. Reavley Gair (tiring rooms, etc., were probably in the cloisters behind the screens)

the Children of the Chapel, several other attempts to build theatres in this south-west quarter followed; displaced from Blackfriars, a 'liberty' which included the dwellings of nobles and gentry, the remnant of the choristers' troupe moved a few hundred yards to Whitefriars. Shakespeare having elected to go and live in Stratford, in 1613 bought himself a lodging in the Blackfriars Gatehouse (but quickly let it out).

At the other end of the city and at the other end socially from the little group of playhouses round Ludgate, stood the old cluster of inn-yard theatres, one of which was renovated at this time. The Red Lion in Stepney had started up as early as the 1560s; Brayne, the brother-in-law of Burbage, who shared in the beginnings of the Theatre, had been responsible; as early as 1557 he had also worked on the Boar's Head in Whitechapel, though his third attempt in the area, the George, proved abortive.

Recent work on the Boar's Head has thrown a great deal of light on its history.[4] An old house for the wool traders from East Anglia, its rectangular yard had taken their waggons. It was slightly longer than it was wide, with an entrance from Whitechapel and an exit into a garden and back yard. The stage, a permanent structure, erected against one of the longer walls, had galleries to face it, built out into the yard, which would give sheltered standing, and open into the rooms behind. The owners lived at the gatehouse, the actors probably also lived on the spot; food and drink could be had at the ordinary table or taken to those 'secret and private chambers' so feared by the godly as 'shops of Satan'. In being less exclusively used for performances the inn would paradoxically resemble the 'private houses', for the game places in the fields had less in the way of amenities – a tap-house being the most essential, ancestor of the foyer bar.

In 1602 the Boar's Head was said to be liked best by the third London troupe (Worcester's, afterwards Queen Anne's Men) but in 1604 they moved off to the north-west, to where Aaron Hollond, an innkeeper, had converted the Red Bull, said also to offer 'a square court in an inn' with stables and other buildings ready for conversion.

In this notorious theatre an Elizabethan audience survived late into the seventeenth century. Led by a famous clown, Thomas Greene, and served by the playwright Thomas Heywood, the Red Bull troupe offered spectaculars, with sword and target fights, fireworks, plays either mockingly depicting local characters or praising London and its worthies. To other theatres, the Red Bull became a general jest. In *The Knight of the Burning Pestle* (1607) Beaumont satirized one of its recent successes – as well as using some lines from Shakespeare for his ambitious hero, the grocer's prentice, who also satirized those members of the Red Bull audience choosing to be recruited as actors. Among them was the future playwright and actor Thomas Killigrew, who later recounted his schoolboy activities:

He would go to the Red Bull, and when the man cried to the boys, 'Who will go and be a devil, and he shall see the play for nothing?' then he would go in and be a devil upon the stage, and so get to see the plays.

(Pepys's *Diary*, 30 October 1662)

Few of the Red Bull's plays reached print, although Heywood claimed to have had a share in more than 220. He was also prepared to pen a prologue 'for a young witty lad playing Richard III at the Red Bull, to encourage him' – presumably a private show.

At the other end of the town, the boys of St Paul's and the Chapel Royal choir schools gave performances that included an hour's preliminary concert of instrumental music, according to one foreign visitor to the Blackfriars.[5] Dean's Yard, Westminster, probably offers the nearest surviving model to this complex of buildings – there, a church, a school and private dwellings still share the quarters.

The Upper Frater of the Dominicans, known as the Great Parliament Chamber, had been the scene of the divorce proceedings between Henry VIII and Katherine of Aragon; its capacity would probably be less than a quarter of the Globe's. But, as has been said already (see p. 11), the closed theatre offered the form of the future; eventually it housed the proscenium stage that Inigo Jones introduced at court, which completely altered the relation of actors and audience and also the presentation of scenes. But this lay far ahead. Although the capacity of the Blackfriars was so small, yet in addition to charging much higher prices, it is possible that a roofed theatre could compensate by a much larger number of performances, extending from afternoon to late night shows; and, of course, it could remain open all the year.[6]

At Paul's which was far smaller, the address to the audience was both deferential and inviting:

What imperfection you have seen in us, leave with us, and we'll amend it; what hath pleased you, take with you and cherish it. You shall not be more ready to embrace anything more commendable than we will endeavour to amend all things improvable.

was the appeal fluted from a chorister who appeared in a suit of armour to speak the epilogue to *Antonio and Mellida*. Artifice had been stressed in the Induction where the boys had appeared to discuss their performance: 'Faith, we can say our parts, but we are ignorant in what mould we should cast our actors', observes the stage villain, who is then given the proper 'form' for 'a tyrant's vein'. Disguise was 'varied', for instead of the familiar girl-page, the hero is disguised as an Amazon. The boys' limited range distanced the extreme violence of this play and its sequel, defusing the 'passions'. The charm of the 'wrens', 'pygmies' or 'pismires' playing at affairs of love and state was both absurd and reassuring; they specialized later in old men and lechery, and replaced their old repertory by mockery of the men's professional troupes. A lyric intensity for the operatic 'arias' of passion should have fitted in well enough with the singing, musical and dancing interludes.

In Marston's best play, *The Malcontent* (?1603) the Janus-faced Altofront/Malevole allowed some talented boy to play 'two parts in one' now grown 'a common fashion'.[7] When, later, the King's Men took over this play and Burbage played the rôle, the men in turn advertised their intention in an Induction written by Webster, which has the effect of still further distancing the artifice and stressing the audience's response. But here they are not flattered. On the contrary, they are represented by two foolish gallants, one of whom has several lines stolen from Shakespeare's Osric; in the opening scenes *Hamlet* is recalled more than once.[8] Burbage blandly protests in the Induction that the play is not 'bitter', although in his dedication to Ben Jonson Marston termed it a bitter comedy. The epilogue offers another compliment to this master, as exemplifying 'art above nature, judgement above art'.

There is no agreement about the leading rôle, Altofront/ Malevole; one editor accepts the satiric aspect as predominating, whilst another will find the satirist 'kills' the moralist, who in turn is accepted as dominant by a third editor. The latest edition, by George Hunter, suggests that 'Altofront's sovereignty is a line drawn round the play rather than a vision that pervades it'. Yet 'the libertine and the moralist are not simply alternating responses (enjoyment followed by condemnation) but simultaneous aspects of a unified view of the world'.[9]

Marston's fellow students from the Inns of Court, the liveliest and most critical part of the new audience, who would be accustomed to taking alternate sides in their 'moots' would feel that the more ingenious and far-fetched the paradoxes, the more their wits would be engaged. In the sixteenth century, theological dispute had provided the chief model for play-argument; the seventeenth became the age of legal arguments about the constitution, and in London the lawyers were in the majority. The young men of the Inns were sharpening their claws in preparation for disputation. 'Any man that hath wit may censure if he sit in the twelvepenny room' was the caustic observation of the men's Induction to *The Malcontent*.[10] Marston used the techniques he had learnt in Christmas shows as a student of the Inns of Court.

The main effect of this play comes from its dizzying intrigue, its rapid changes of fortune which forbid the build-up of emotion; the intrigue unwinds in a final scene of court dancing, in keeping with what T. S. Eliot termed 'the significant lifelessness of its shadow show'. The grisly slapstick of two characters finding they are deputed to murder each other can be matched by the deflating self-consciousness of Malevole's comment to the passionate Pietro 'Let Heaven unclasp itself, vomit forth flame'.

O do not rant, do not turn player. There's more of them than can well live by one another already. (iv.iv.3–5)

For the men, extensions were made to the Polonius-like part of Bilioso, and another bitter fool, Pasarello – a part for Armin – was added to the cast. They capped the jesting both of law students and choristers.

The boys had previously appropriated *The Spanish Tragedy*, and from the way it is rehearsed by the 'pygmies' in Ben Jonson's *Poetaster*, it seems that they played it as a 'send-up'.[11] The same game is played in *The Malcontent*:

> Death and damnation!
> Lightning and thunder!
> Vengeance and murder!
> *Catzo!*
> O revenge! (I.iii.103–7)

The choristers were equally ready to burlesque one another's shows: *Eastward Ho!*, a scandalous success at the Revels, succeeded *Westward Ho!* at St Paul's; Paul's feeble sequel *Northward Ho!* aimed at the city, suggests the Christmas burlesques so popular at the Inns of Court.[12] All the brighter theatres were prepared to play theatrical 'games' with one another.

In the year that Shakespeare died, the Red Bull Company prepared to move to a tiny 'private house', the Cockpit in Drury Lane.[13] Cockpits had to be small and roofed; the London prentices ('These are the youths that thunder at a playhouse and fight for bitten apples'),[14] deprived of their most popular resort, wrecked the new theatre in a Shrove Tuesday riot, but it was found worthwhile to rebuild and the next year, 1617, the Cockpit reopened as the Phoenix.

It is difficult to imagine much interchange between the Red Bull and the Phoenix; Webster, whose *White Devil* failed at its first performance, blamed the audience of the Red Bull as well as the weather – 'most of the people that came to that playhouse resemble those ignorant asses who visiting stationers' shops, their use is not to enquire for good books but new books.' The play was afterwards put on at the Phoenix where it seems to have succeeded better.

A late account shows a popular audience hissing a play off the stage and calling for an old favourite;[15] if the actors did not comply, 'The benches, tiles, the laths, the stones, oranges, apples and nuts flew about most liberally, as there were mechanics of all professions who fell everyone to his trade'.

The Red Bull, however, was the only popular theatre that seems to have survived the Commonwealth, continuing in use throughout that period. A late record, *Historia Histrionica* (1699) declares 'The Globe, the Fortune and Bull were large houses and lay open to the weather, and there they always acted by daylight', whilst the Cockpit, like the Blackfriars and the Salisbury Court playhouse, was small.

This last, the latest theatre to be opened in pre-Restoration London, was made by converting a brick barn in the grounds of Dorset House, near St Bride's. A note for 'coals in all the rooms' suggests the private boxes had small fireplaces. Opened in 1629, Salisbury Court enjoyed a special degree of court favour and direct courtly subsidy; the Master of the Revels at one time held a share, magnificent scenes were painted for Nabbes' *Microcosmos* (1637). However, in the Prologue to Goffe's *Careless Shepherdess* (1638) a Country Landlord asks for his money back because there is no fool in the play, whilst a citizen reflects:

> I will hasten to the money box
> And take my shilling out again, for now
> I have considered that it is too much;
> I'll go to the Bull or Fortune, and there see
> A play for two pence, with a jig to boot.

Spruce, a courtier and Sparke, an Inns of Court man, remain.

In the private theatres, seats on the stage were allowed; in *The Devil is an Ass* (1616, King's Men) Jonson protested that the actors were 'driven to act in compass of a cheese trencher'. He himself wrote for every kind of stage; in *Epicoene*, a play for the choristers, he nevertheless offers to satisfy a widely drawn audience.[16] For the King's Men he produced *Volpone* and *The Alchemist*, and those stage failures *Sejanus* and *Catiline*. For his young friend Nat Field (who moved off to lead the Lady Elizabeth's Men, having been pressed for the Chapel Royal in 1600 at the age of thirteen) Jonson in 1614 wrote the festive rumbustious city play, *Bartholomew Fair*, which opened the new 'Bear's College' – the Hope on Bankside. Jonson takes full advantage of all the disadvantages of the site: 'the author hath observed a special decorum' he declares, 'the place being as dirty as Smithfield, and as stinking every whit'. Nonetheless, to please James in his unbuttoned mood, the play was taken to court – 'Your Majesty is welcome to a Fair' – and its well-known jibes at 'Tales, Tempests and such drolleries' representing banter rather than spleen, scored off other court successes. The Inns of Court also paid the compliment of parody to Shakespeare's Romances, and to Heywood also.[17]

Shakespeare, who had learnt his art in the original Theatre, shared the changes that came when his company also acquired the Blackfriars in 1608; but he did not launch into masques. He had not joined the other playwrights who penned the coronation triumphs for King James. Jonson, in addition to his court masques, wrought many poems and prose works; Chapman toiled at his translations; Daniel and Drayton used a variety of forms; but Shakespeare neither took to non-dramatic poetry nor even, apparently, wished to publish his plays. Webster (who did) classes him, however courteously, in the rear of Chapman, Jonson, Beaumont and Fletcher with the 'right happy and copious industry' of Dekker and Heywood,[18] journeymen theatre poets who never blotted a line and seldom printed one.

Recognition of the great influence upon the common stages of the street theatre, royal entries, and later of the Jacobean court masque, of tilts and tourneys, was due in the first instance to Glynne Wickham's *Early English Stages*, which brought out the implications of earlier histories, especially E. K. Chambers's. The historian of the Jacobean masque, Stephen Orgel, has termed it 'Power conceived as art'. Consequently, there is now a tendency to interpret the works of Shakespeare, especially the Jacobean Shakespeare, as if they were centred on the court. A new Jacobean Shakespeare appears, writing almost as directly for King James and his children as did Jonson in his masques.[19]

This view is not wholly incompatible with the older one that he was primarily the poet of popular morality and wisdom, the traditionalist who conformed.[20] Though, as originally stated, it was over-simplified, yet a more recent study of the profession of playwright[21] classes Shakespeare with a small group who were 'fully' professional, attached exclusively and permanently under contract to certain companies. Professor Bentley's view is that these eight men – they include also Dekker and Heywood – might be better paid than a curate or schoolmaster, but that those dramatists who made modest fortunes, as did Shakespeare and Heywood, were also sharers and actors.

The general list of plays belonging to Shakespeare's company may represent only a fragment of the repertory, but the new dramas recorded offer a wide range from citizen conformity to full sceptical melancholy.[22]

The Jacobean court did not commission plays, and in spite of the very considerable sums disbursed at special times, such as the wedding festivities of the Princess Elizabeth – when the company offered fourteen plays – such a large group could not have survived on these payments. The status of the King's Men, and their ability to produce at the public theatres some of the antimasques which they had presented as part of the court entertainment would, however, draw the London crowd. Yet any public attempt too closely to reproduce court splendour might earn the strictures that Sir Henry Wotton bestowed on the splendour of *King Henry VIII* 'sufficient in truth within a while to make greatness very familiar, if not ridiculous'.

Praise delivered *en face* constituted a form of exhortation, and a rite; attempts to reproduce this elsewhere would lack decorum and detract from the very special circumstances that royalty provided. To insert a prologue to be spoken at court or a few lines in a popular play, as Hamlet suggested to the players, would be an occasion for ingenuity in 'application'. On the other hand, if *Two Noble Kinsmen*, as I have suggested below, existed to incorporate the royal antimasque, it would be pointless to play it at court, where the antimasque was originally given.

The players' entertainment was only ancillary to the court festivities. In 1613, at Princess Elizabeth's wedding festivities, her own troupe of players and the Queen's Revels gave, presumably by request, such unfestive mockeries as *The Dutch Courtesan* and *The Widow's Tears*; whilst in addition to *The Tempest* – which had already been seen at court at Hallowmas 1611, but was revived – the King's Men presented *Philaster*, *The Maid's Tragedy* and *The Merry Devil of Edmonton*. Shakespeare's contributions were 'Sir John Falstaff', 'The Moor of Venice', *The Winter's Tale*, *Much Ado about Nothing* and perhaps, under 'Caesar's Tragedy', *Julius Caesar*.

When he had wished to compliment Queen Elizabeth, in *A Midsummer Night's Dream* or *The Merry Wives of Windsor*, Shakespeare had made it plain; the references to the Succession in *Macbeth* are also unambiguous and designed for the public stage. It would have been inappropriate and indeed insulting to play out of the royal presence anything designed especially and particularly for the royal ear. Analogies with the public images of Elizabeth (discussed in Chapter 3 above) will not hold. True it is that the coronation pageants for James offered the new myth of Troynovant, a reunited Britain that restored the ancient Trojan kingdom of Brute, divided among his three sons, but reunited under the 'second Brut'. James inscribed his first gold crowns *Henricus rosas*, *regna Jacobus* (Henry united the roses, James the kingdoms) to signify the replacement of the Tudor myth; but as King James was incapable of sustaining a public image, the British Solomon was soon rechristened 'the wisest fool in Christendom'. The relatively stable and widely accepted images of Elizabeth as Astraea, Belphoebe or Diana, which had met the specific needs of the religious–political adjustments embodied in the Elizabethan Settlement, could not be simply reproduced in another form where the conflict was to be political in a more defined manner, since the nature of the social pressures defined it eventually as one between Crown and Commons. Nor in a theatre so given to parody and mockery were royal images to be accepted with the faith of the previous generation. Chapman, the most explicit and emblematic of the dramatic moralists in Jacobean times, could mock the old cult; for the author of *Hymnus in Cynthiam* gave to his cynical hero Tharsalio a parody of a famous royal madrigal, uttered at the moment when the heroine (another Cynthia) yields to assault:

> She, she, she, and only she,
> She, only queen of love and chastity
>
> (*The Widow's Tears*, v.i.31–3)

But, in graver vein, he directly attacked the 'observance' that in England had made

> demigods
> Of their great nobles and of their old queen
> An ever young and most immortal goddess
>
> (*Bussy D'Ambois*, I.ii.II–I3)

yet pointed out that the proportion and order kept at her court was superior to that of France ('Our rooms of state/Kept like our stables'), and most significantly added that the English would shortly leave their better court habits and begin to imitate the French.

Chapman's, Jonson's and Shakespeare's 'tragedies of state' would seem to provide a better offering than romance to the grave young Prince of Wales, who alternated the most violent martial games with a sporadic study of history (see below, Chapter 9, p. 176).

The changes in the nature of poetry and the working of its images, where scepticism must be parried, mockery forestalled and wit displayed, depended on paradox of the kind defended by Donne (against constancy):

For everything as it is better than another, so it is fuller of change; the Heavens themselves continually turn, the stars move, the moon changeth...so in Man, they that have most reason are alterable in their designs and the darkest or most ignorant do seldom change...

Webster's protests that the Red Bull audiences looked only for new plays could be applied to the court masque, where 'novelty' and 'variety' were demanded. It is true that when his attempts to get agreement on the union of the kingdoms failed, James was presented by way of consolation with the show of *Britannia Rediviva*, and that the country progresses of Queen Anne evoked faded images of Elizabeth.[23] But this was less a revival than a confession of barrenness. Likewise, it is true that in France or in Florence, the Valois or Medici would use pageantry to evoke or assert a state of union or harmony, especially in times that were turbulent or insecure. None of this seems to me to justify the suggestion that in *King Lear*, whilst Shakespeare 'prudently chose to refrain' from a public declaration that the second Brutus had finally arrived in the person of King James' he is 'admitting the possibility through making Albany the agent of Lear's reunion with Cordelia'.[24]

If the icon of King Lear entering with the body of Cordelia does not suggest anything involving prudence, neither are the last plays, in spite of the temptations they seem to offer, built on cryptograms about Henry Prince of Wales or the Princess Elizabeth, or the belated placing of the body of James's mother among the royal tombs of Westminster Abbey.[25] For there is too much in these plays which would make such decoding very embarrassing; cryptograms, to work, must be exact.

Indeed, the tragedy of *King Lear* can be read in quite the opposite way in relation to the myth of Troynovant, recording the moment when it was recognized that the miracle would *not* happen.[26] It implies a shrunken reductive view of Shakespeare – even assuming these court emblems had nationwide validity – so limiting his plays, when even in his own age, open form – as defined below in Part II – was a virtue: to set the audience debating meant full houses. The usual fear, and the usual caveat entered by players, was against slander of particular individuals; but the variety of expectations which the players acknowledged they had constantly to meet would surely always include weddings. If *The Tempest* were specially adapted for the royal wedding festivities, it could have been by stressing that shadowy but insistent figure Claribel, wedded to the King of Tunis. (The departure of Princess Elizabeth for Germany, so soon after the death of the Prince of Wales, was doubly unwelcome by the fact that after her weakly second brother Charles, she was the kingdom's heir.) Her father, the king, is reminded in the play by an unfriendly courtier how

> the fair soul herself
> Weighed between loathness and obedience, at
> Which end o' th' beam should bow   (II.i.125–6)

is 'banish'd from your eye'; and if 'Tunis was never before grac'd with such a paragon to their Queen' yet she is lost to Naples

> Claribel,
> She that is Queen of Tunis, she that dwells,
> Ten leagues beyond man's life...   (II.i.236–8)

Miss Yates's recent elaborate parallel between Princess Elizabeth's cult and that of Astraea brings in all her own interests – Philip Sidney, John Dee, Bruno, the French Court and Rosicrucian science. Her speculative sallies serve very clearly to show 'the open nature of the last plays and what Frank Kermode has termed the 'patience of Shakespeare'.[27]

Henry, Prince of Wales, had only some two years of full public life, since he died at eighteen; most of the images that cluster round him became fixed after his death in November 1612. The national sentiments of grief at his death found their expression in many elegies but in the drama only indirectly. Shakespeare's contribution, as I suggest in Chapter 14, was *Two Noble Kinsmen*.

The most notable example is furnished by Webster, who produced an inferior elegy, *A Monumental Column*, which appeared bound up with those of Tourneur and Heywood. In this work, fragmented and without imaginative form, lie the sentiments that were soon built into the great ritual of mourning, *The Duchess of Malfi* (1614), a play of the King's Men. I would suggest that its great depth and its strange unity in disparity – which has been termed a 'curious wrought perspective' – derives from this root in a great public grief. It is transformational, in the Shakespearean manner.[28]

Henry, 'a perfect Diamond set in lead', brought low in all his martial promise, is an image of the world's transience.

> O Greatness, what shall we compare thee to?
> To Giants, Beasts or Towers fram'd out of Snow,
> Or like wax gilded tapers, more for show
> Than durance? (109–12)

The pageants of the snow-shapes might recall the brief glory of Henry's masques, but the elegy also directly depicts life as such a masque. Pleasure, being recalled to heaven by Jupiter, has let fall her 'eye-seeded' masquing robe, which was found and donned by Sorrow, who consequently was courted by all the world. Sorrow, that

> long liv'd in banishment,
> Tugg'd at the oar in galleys. (163–4)

showed great statesmen themselves and their fortunes 'in false perspectives.' Her 'cursed mask' lasts 'day and night'. Henry is presented on his death-bed as being like a king at a revels, impatiently wishing them over (a reminder that James himself appears not greatly to have relished the entertainments provided for him)

> It seems he lay
> As Kings at Revels, wishing the crowd away,
> The tedious sports done, and himself asleep
> ...fixing his constant eye
> Upon his triumph, immortality...   (216–17, 229–30)

and finally he felt such joy

> as great Accountants (troubled much in mind)
> when they hear newes of their quietus sign'd   (219–20)

for he was like a dial broken which is 'taken to pieces' to be 'made go true' (241–2).

These images, woven later into the web of the Duchess's tragedy at crucial points of joy or sorrow – the betrothal, the parting, the masque of death – witness to an underlying feeling behind this play to which the audience could respond intuitively without knowing its origin. In Webster, the 'perspective pictures' which 'rightly gazed upon' show nothing but 'confusion' may 'if eyed aright, distinguish form'.[29]

More than any other dramatist, Webster builds the dramatic equivalent of the masque, expressed through poetry; 'stabbing similes' or epigrammatic metaphors replace the visual splendour of its jewels and coloured lights with 'jewels five words long'. But the central figure is one who had dispensed with ceremony, whilst remaining Duchess of Malfi still. Webster has reached a stage of integration that is the opposite of Marston's 'significant lifelessness', presenting flesh and blood at its most vulnerable, yet ritualized.

> What would it pleasure me to have my throat cut
> With diamonds? or to be smothered
> With cassia? or to be shot to death with pearls?   (iv.ii.216–17)

asks the Duchess, as the masque of her death proceeds with ritual gifts of cross and coffin.

It is worth noting that, when masques are dramatically depicted in the plays of this period, they tend to reflect the public distrust of the form, suggesting that dark mood which has been briefly mentioned already.[30]

Especially in the Italian revenge plays, the tragic emblems provided by inverting the emblems of the court masque are among the most powerful and constant conventions of Jacobean plays, more especially those of the King's Men. *The Revenger's Tragedy*, another play from their repertory, develops with great poetic intensity the attack on masquing. Antonio's wife has been raped

> Last revelling night,
> When torches made an artificial noon. . .
> O vicious minute.   (I.iv.27–8, 40)

For 'the poor benefit of a bewitching minute' a man's life may be hazarded. The feverish excitement of lustful anticipation

> O think upon the pleasure of the palace
> Secured ease and state. . .
> Banquets abroad by torchlight, music, sports, . . .
> Nine coaches waiting – hurry, hurry, hurry –
>   (II.i.195–6, 199, 202)

is given different enactment as the skull of a murdered woman, decked and masked, lures the Duke to his death. This is later to put Vindice's own life 'between the judges' lips' for his revenge. The silkworm of luxury and the grave-worm are brought together; though built out of familiar materials,[31] the image is new and surprising. Vindice asks the skull as 'nine years' vengeance crowd into a minute'

> Does the silk-worm expend her yellow labours
> For thee? for thee does she undo herself?   (III.v.71–2)

The yellow silk, spun out of the worm's entrails, covers the yellow skull-bone on which grave-worms have long ago expended their labours to the undoing of the flesh. A negative sexual image leads up to the conclusion addressed to the audience:

> See, ladies, with false forms
> You deceive men, but cannot deceive worms.   (III.v.96–7)

(This oxymoron is later used to precisely the opposite end in Andrew Marvell's plea *To His Coy Mistress*:

> ...then worms shall try
> That long preserv'd virginity...
> The grave's a fine and private place,
> But none, I think, do there embrace.)

It is as part of this emblematic tradition that the final very flat couplet spoken by the White Devil, Vittoria Corombona, gains its depth:

> O, happy they that never saw the court,
> Nor ever knew great men but by report! (v.vi.259–60)

The most ironic use of masque, as already noted, occurs in *The Maid's Tragedy*, staged by the King's Men in 1610; in real life this was approached perhaps only by the fulsome praise and dark secrets that attended the marriage of the Earl of Somerset and Lady Frances Howard.

One of the defenders of this murderous pair – who remained faithful to them in disgrace – and the only dramatist who was sworn servant of Prince Henry, was George Chapman. He wrote for the men's theatre at first, but later for the boys'; tragedy put at the centre of his best works, *Bussy D'Ambois* and the two Byron plays, the incompatibility of the man of *virtù* with the life of the court. Bussy, the great swordsman ignominiously killed by a pistol shot, seems to express in his dying metaphors the kind of brevity that belonged to all court splendours:

> O frail condition of strength, valour, virtue
> In me, like warning fire (upon the top
> Of some steep beacon, on a steeper hill)
> Made to express it; like a falling star,
> Silently glanced, that like a thunderbolt
> Looked to have struck and shook the firmament. (v.iv.141–6)

This play was later appropriated by the men's theatres, and revised – inter-connexions between the characters being stressed. In general, it is never the relationships between characters that hold Chapman's plays together; the speeches are bravura pieces like operatic arias. Their fiery aspiration does not belong to that sort of 'personation' which had already been noted as characteristic of the mature actor (see above, Chapter 3, p. 44). Burbage and

Armin were not looking for a 'mould' to cast their parts in, like the boy actors who discuss their parts before *Antonio and Mellida*; rather, they sought a good 'conceit' – an integrated idea of the character *in action*. This was what Shakespeare offered; the integration of his plays reflects the integration of his company and must have promoted it further. The element of satire was reserved for the Jonsonian plays, but *Volpone* and *The Alchemist* are also written for a team, 'The Elizabethan way of making is to put things together, the Jacobean way is to fuse.'[32]

Shakespeare, by his steady devotion to his own company, and Jonson by his free-ranging and differently adapted plays, each in their different ways brought over the traditions of the earlier stages into Jacobean times. Even the Red Bull felt able to stage Shakespeare (and when the First Folio appeared, had to be restrained from doing so). The Herculean effort of making available for other playwrights many rapidly vanishing traditions, whilst keeping in touch with the new forms, is one which in the present age will be readily understood at its true worth. This is the effect of his last plays.[33]

It is by now a commonplace to observe that the modern theatre approximates more closely to the Elizabethan and Jacobean theatre than any in the intervening years; not only the return of the thrust stage, circular auditorium and multiple entry, but the audience participation derives from the interaction of scholars and theatre men, beginning with Poel and Craig. Some modern theatres built for Shakespearean productions can offer special opportunities to modern plays (as Shaw's *St Joan*, at Stratford, Ontario).

Reinterpreted in terms of other societies, Shakespeare has been played in London in such varied styles as the magnificent Zulu *Umabatha* or the Marowitz versions of *Hamlet* and *An Othello*.

The loss of a single stage-tradition of Shakespearean playing, such as older actors relied on, may lead to what can appear totally permissive freedom. Modern appeals to the cult of cruelty and violence can darken even *King Lear*,[34] and the director's theatre at its most irresponsible can suffer from the conditions denounced by Robert Brustein in *The Third Theatre*:

The democratization of art...is the inevitable consequence of a culture where everyone is encouraged to do his own thing, and excellence gives way before permissiveness. But whilst all this self expression is undoubtedly exhilarating to those who practice it, it could spell the end of history, literature and tradition whilst banishing craft and inspiration from the arts. For the arts, including the theatre, are the culmination not of self-indulgence and accident, but of discipline and imagination. What may be coming now is a theatre of liberated, arrogant amateurs – a theatre where there will be no more spectators, only performers, each tied up in his own tight bag.

Yet the director is by now very fully in touch with the history of the age, and the freedom of interpretation aims at interpretation in the light of such knowledge. At its best, it brings out a deeply creative unity of form; knowledge of the past united with work that 'sank to the depth of feeling was saturated, transformed there – "these are pearls that were his eyes" and brought up to daylight again', so that 'it gives the impression of having suffered a long incubation, though we do not know till the shell breaks what kind of egg we have been sitting on'.[35]

The director's dream has to become united with the public response, until through new intuitions a new objectivity is created – when the composite work, in performance, evolves its own laws and corrects its own mistakes. Some modern productions have succeeded as no archaeologically 'correct' play could do, because they respond to the open form which is inherent in the Jacobean drama itself. The variety of audiences, and of acting conditions in which this drama began, and the need to appeal to a diversified audience makes such re-creations valid in terms of an original invitation extended to the audience to 'work, work your thoughts'.

Shakespeare's works now supply the new universal mythology. They are adapted and rewritten in the way in which the Christian story was adapted in the late middle ages; and like all mythologies they are open to adaptation, improvisation and reformation for each individual, including, of course, the perverted and the obscene. The function of myth is to provide a common vehicle whilst allowing an individual application; the adaptable and flexible strength of the plays is improved by the removal of conventional habits and assumptions imposed on the plays by accumulated tradition, so that once again they are free to impose their own form, freshly and directly experienced in an alien world. The process may be compared with the use of modern chemicals to clean an old painting.

The English no longer feel Shakespeare their exclusive possession. Other media, too, have adopted Shakespeare. (Thirty years ago, as John Gielgud confessed, he would not have thought of a film contract.) Here the language must be translated into visual images, as the greatest of film directors, Kozintsev, has declared: 'One has to seek out and decipher the poetic signs, the code. It's in the lines, and as always happens with poetry, it's between the lines as well.'[36]

Through the poetry, if it is trusted, a sure and direct communication with the past is achieved, for 'Poetry can communicate whilst it is only generally understood.' What is to be learnt from history can best be rediscovered as art, if it is to be reanimated and made new within our own time. In Shakespeare's plays we meet 'the past that is always present'.

Part II

JACOBEAN SHAKESPEARE

7

MACBETH: THE SUBLIMATION
OF SPECTACLE

As the successor to Shakespeare's English chronicle histories, and
in particular to the first great tragical history, *Richard III, Macbeth*
blends the distant past of what to Englishmen was still in many
ways an alien country with powerful reflections of contemporary
disruption. One of Shakespeare's near Warwickshire neighbours,
the politician Fulke Greville, had written sombre political plays
(unacted) and was to proclaim his faith and his disillusion to John
Coke in the paradox: 'I know the world – and believe in God.'
Shakespeare's English Histories had turned towards the comical,
and then with *2 Henry IV* back towards a darker colouring and a
more Machiavellian scene, but they were to remain a standing
dish for playgoers, recited by prentices[1] and recalled up to the time
of the Civil War, when an old lord boasts of his household:

> These lads can act the Emperors' lives all over
> And Shakespeare's chronicled histories to boot
>
> (Brome, *The Antipodes*, I.v.66–7)

Play audiences felt intimately involved, as Nashe reported quite
early. Effects would be heightened by the familiarity of great
dynastic names; Southampton might be himself in the lord's room
to hear his maternal ancestor sweep on stage with the cry 'Montague, Montague for Lancaster!' and the serving men might carry
Warwick's or Northumberland's badge on their sleeves. In *Henry
IV*, where interest is national rather than dynastic, we traverse the
streets of London, the orchards of Gloucester and the northern
moors, for Shakespeare knew these places by the mud on his boots.
There is no false smoothing of conflicts. 'Be friends, you English
fools, be friends!' cries Bates as the disguised King and his private

soldiers start an argument on the eve of Agincourt. Insistence on order and degree in Tudor England was largely theoretical; society was fluid, as Professor Hurstfield has shown ('The Historical and Social Background' in *A New Companion to Shakespeare Studies*, ed. K. Muir and S. Schoenbaum, Cambridge, 1971). Among the least of the rout, a little tailor with 'the only man-sized voice in Gloucestershire' suddenly echoes one of Prince Henry's proverbs from Shrewsbury; 'We owe God a death'. Feeble's courage, which outbuys a whole army of Pistols, serves to link more subtly the multitude and the throne. Prince Hal plays a prentice in the tavern (and the prentices were an important group in the audience). But Hal's address to the poisoned gold of the crown shows the germ of that later royal play which is set in a past wild and remote, yet in distinction to *King Lear* a Christian past. Indeed, the remorse of Henry IV also takes a Christian turn, if his longing to go on a politically useful crusade ('busy giddy minds with foreign quarrels' (*2 Henry IV*, IV.5.213–14)) is far less intense than Macbeth's vision of *le néant*, of the abyss 'To be thus is ...nothing'. King Lear faces the torment of the wheel of fire. Macbeth finds himself incapable of feeling; like a drug addict he has to increase continuously the dose which will assuage his fear. The dose is fresh atrocities. Both are plays of man *outside*; man in the cold places of outer darkness, banished from his own kind. 'Honour, love, obedience, troops of friends' – the secular rewards of good kingship – Macbeth must not look to have (even Henry V had his household traitors, and a trooper in his faithful army could wish him home in Thames up to his neck). He did not buy his followers cheaply though he would suggest it, 'We few, we happy few, we band of brothers', and play the simple soldier to a French princess. But it seems one of Macbeth's strong delusions that such a world could ever be hoped for in the desert country he inhabits, and has created for himself, a country of the mind. A positive sort of hierarchy remains only among dogs, who are distinguished according to their uses, but Macbeth would have Night 'Cancel and tear to pieces that great bond' of common humanity (III.ii.49).

How then can it be said that *Macbeth* is a play about history, if it is primarily a play about damnation? Shall we set Henry Paul against Helen Gardner?[2] This I think, is to mistake the complex interconnexions of politico-religious thought in that age, and the degree of elimination which Shakespeare practises in this most brief, most concentrated of plays. The political aspect is there – it is there most strongly in a scene which he took from his sources, the debate between Malcolm and Macduff in England, and in two spectacular scenes original to Shakespeare which offer ghastly, hellish parodies of sacred rituals – the haunted coronation banquet that follows the ceremony of hallowing and crowning, and the coronation show or masque proffered by the witches. Both are inversions of royal rites; both are heavily filled with religious overtones (as is the scene in England). I would like to stress these three scenes, as constituting one axis along which the play is constructed. The other axis, the witches' scenes, crosses it in the cauldron scene; and these, I would suggest, are not only of a lyric concentration and density, they import stage tradition of a new kind. In these scenes we meet the interplay with court theatre and city show which to my mind is a powerful aspect of Shakespeare's Jacobean, as distinct from his Elizabethan, playwriting. *Macbeth* is the sublimation of spectacle into poetry.

Some three or four years after *Macbeth*, on Candlemas Night 1609, Jonson's *Masque of Queens* was performed in Whitehall, with the Queen as the chief masquer (and representing herself, Bel-Anna, Queen of the Ocean, the leader of this troup as opposed to the Dame who had led the coven of witches in the terrifying antimasque). Another seven years, and Middleton wrote *The Witch*, a Globe 'spectacular' which did not succeed theatrically. Just about this time the most celebrated case of witchcraft occurred – the trial of Mrs Turner and Simon Forman for the murder of Sir Thomas Overbury, in which Frances Howard, Countess of Somerset, was ultimately implicated and pleaded guilty. From Middleton a couple of songs were taken to add to Shakespeare's *Macbeth*.

After a rapid survey of the present position in criticism, I shall give my own theatrically-based view of Shakespeare's play in its original setting.

It has certainly been read in ways controverting naturalism, that half a century ago raised it very high in esteem; but these ways differ from and contradict each other. Francis Ferguson describes *Macbeth* as 'The Imitation of an Action' – the action being a desperate race, and the main clue being the phrase 'to outrun the pauser, reason'.[3] On the other hand, T. B. Tomlinson postulated an absence of plot in the Aristotelian sense; after analysing the soliloquies he concluded that the play contains nothing but 'sensitive introspections' which at times become hysteria – 'a form of giggling' in the puns 'surcease/success'; these soliloquies 'just have not time in a stage play to build up a work of tragic stature'. His opening sentence 'Why is it difficult not to feel that *Macbeth* is one of the Shakespearean plays which approaches tragic status but just falls short of the mark?'[4] may be less severe than some remarks of G. B. Harrison; Mark Van Doran's extremely sensitive account of *Macbeth* places it last among the great tragedies, in spite of its 'metaphysical dimension'.[5]

The counterbalancing praises stem chiefly from the group of critics who began to work in terms of imagery and themes rather than plot or character: the Spurgeon–Wilson Knight–L. C. Knights–Roy Walker–Heilman–Cleanth Brooks' range of interpretation, gradually assumed dominance in the thirties and forties until A. P. Rossiter went so far as to assert that Macbeth, his wife and Banquo 'are parts of a pattern, a design; are images or symbols'[6] – they are not three persons but one event in a poem, and all the rest of the *human* cast are antitheses to the two protagonists. The witches, he thinks, should be masked. Others, of course, followed traditional historic patterns – Willard Farnham saw *Macbeth* as a Morality Play, Eustace Tillyard had seen it earlier as 'the culminating version of Shakespeare's concern with the man of action...the finest of all Mirrors for Magistrates'.[7]

Even those concerned with characters treat them lyrically. Freud himself saw Macbeth and Lady Macbeth as 'two disunited parts of a single psychical individuality' (note that she is given no personal name of her own).[8] Mrs Ewbank observed in more specific terms how at the end of I.vii Macbeth's will feeds upon Lady Macbeth's until he can almost speak in her voice:

I am settled, and bend up
Each corporal agent to this terrible feat.
Away, and mock the time with fairest show;
False face must hide what the false heart doth know – [9]

although later his mind swings again like a compass needle 'If 't were done when 'tis done. . . .'. Maynard Mack, however, provides the opposite and complementary viewpoint, with a comment that in the sleep-walking scene 'by a kind of poetic displacement' her slumbery agitation may be compared with Macbeth's. Although overtly he is lacking in any words of remorse such as she may utter in sleep, 'yet in some way the pity of this situation suffuses him as well as her, the more so because in every word his presence beside her is supposed'[10] and because she is reliving that scene in which her purely physical reading of events had been opposed to his deeper intuitions ('Consider it not so deeply' – 'A little water clears us of this deed', while Macbeth had cried that all great Neptune's ocean would not wash off the blood): her reading has proved so false, she is now moaning that 'all the perfumes of Arabia' will not take away the smell (her very sense is on a lower, more purely animal level).

The voice of Lady Macbeth is *not* that of something, someone, who is 'part of a pattern, a design'. Indeed, in his examination of 'Image and Symbol in *Macbeth*' (*Shakespeare Survey* 19, 1966), Kenneth Muir expressly disclaims the play as a 'pattern of imagery . . . It is a play; and in the theatre we ought to re-cover, as best we may, a state of critical innocence' (p. 53) so that these images may be 'subsumed under the total experience of the play'.

The pluralist interpretation of the plays in performance now extends to re-writing the text, improvising upon it, blending it with other texts. Whatever one thinks of Marowitz's *An Othello*, or the R.S.C.'s *King John* (tidiness and smoothness supplied by courtesy of *The Troublesome Reign of King John*), not only are we asked to consider these plays as dynamic interaction between actor and audience, but the director is allowed to present his own varia-tion as a substitute for the original. Perhaps a text is always filtered in performance; but poetic integrity is itself the source of such dynamic interaction, and the very possibility of plural meanings depends on this. The 'doctored' version *imposes* readings. Certain plays take this treatment better than others, and while at no time is playhouse custom insistent on a stable text, the total permissiveness of the modern stage makes novelty obligatory. However, the degree of novelty that is possible in *Macbeth* is more limited than in the other tragedies. *Macbeth* may be ambiguous, but it can't be 'sent up', adapted by Brecht (though it has been adapted by Zulus and West Indians with great success), turned into black comedy; it can't even very readily be played in modern dress. It is consequently the most neglected of the four great tragedies in England at present because it does not lend itself to modern theatrical fashion – to 'kitsch'.

It was the reading of the work as a 'dramatic poem' which brought it to the fore in the thirties, forties, and fifties; it has succeeded beyond most in translation to other languages and other media. The Japanese film *Throne of Blood*, the Zulu *Umabatha*, and a West Indian *Macbeth* which I saw at the Commonwealth Festival are independent variations of a more authentic kind than the adaptations of the *avant garde*. A play about witchcraft offers chances that are not offered by any other play to people who still know what it means. The Zulu Macbeth, a noble warrior, was shown resisting the forces that drew him on by every ounce of will in him that was still *man*; but a power within responded to the power without and he followed the dagger, still attempting to resist it. The chorus of warriors made this an epic production, and against this background of danced and mimed unity – the Zulu War Dance was performed with a precision like that of the Guards – Macbeth stood out as an individual, a lonely single being torn from the group by his very leadership.

In the history of performance in this century, the range of interpretation has been much wider than might be expected from the deep intensity and concentration of the writing. The story has been told by Dennis Bartholomeusz of Monash University[11] from the adaptation of Davenant, and the performance of Betterton down to the 1960s, and the last realization by Laurence Olivier, successor to Garrick, Kean, Kemble, Macready, Irving, Gielgud.

The play is remembered for these rôles and the Lady Macbeth of Mrs Siddons, Helen Faucit, Ellen Terry, Sybil Thorndike. Sybil Thorndike once told me she had felt she could never play Lady Macbeth because of the killing, but her dresser said to her 'You love your husband, don't you? It's for *him*', and this was how she worked herself into it. Edith Evans has always refused the part because she thinks it lacks the third quarter – the development between the banquet scene and the sleep-walking scene. She feels it could not be realized without some transitional scene to show Lady Macbeth's decline.

The most extreme variation was the comic treatment of the witches during the eighteenth century, when they became absurd figures, providing a sort of clowning interlude. The period in which accusations of witchcraft ceased, and the charge was taken off the Statute Book must have meant that relief of freedom from the real-life fears represented, produced a temporary inability to see witches as art.[12] We have of late found increased evidence of the magic practices that were current in Jacobean London; Dr John Dee and the infamous Simon Forman, who recorded a performance of *Macbeth* in 1611 in his diary, have become the subjects of biography; the latter, owing to A. L. Rowse's conjectures about his relations with Emilia Lanier, has been drawn into Shakespearean studies.[13]

Witches, the ghost, and the sacred magic of kingship dissolve the hard outlines of 'character'; it has often been noted how Macbeth's opening words, 'So foul and fair a day I have not seen' echo the witches' last words 'Fair is foul and foul is fair', suggesting an intimate penetration of his being akin to that which (at the first stirring of 'imaginary thoughts of murder') brings his heart to quick hammering and his scalp crawling to horripilation. There are shadowy figures like Banquo's Third Murderer – it has been suggested that he is an emanation of Macbeth's desire to see the end of Banquo, another sort of ghost – and the shadows of things to come that the witches show to Macbeth. The deep rapport, the play of mind between Macbeth and his wife has already been mentioned; to borrow a phrase from Donne's love poetry they interinanimate each other. The poetry itself is full of submerged echoes – as the image of a river of honour flowing from Duncan, when Lady Macbeth speaks of

> All our service
> In every point twice done, and then done double,
> Were poor and single business to contend
> Against those honours *deep and broad* wherewith
> Your Majesty loads our house   (I.vi.14–18)

compared with the strong current of the river of blood

> I am in blood
> Stepped in so far, that should I wade no more
> Returning were as tedious as go o'er   (III.iv.135–7)

which perhaps depends on the Ballad of True Thomas:

> For forty days and forty nights,
> He waded through red blood to the knee,
> And he saw neither sun nor moon,
> But he heard the roaring of the sea.

For the tale of *Macbeth*, compared with the chronicles of England, is legendary history; Shakespeare was well aware of this distinction[14] between Tudor and Brutan material and *Macbeth* belongs with *Lear* as 'Brutan'. They were *not* Mirrors for Magistrates so much as Mirrors for Men, although both were linked by deeper and imaginative responses with the new reign. In many obvious ways *Macbeth*, with that graceful and natural courtesy that gave Shakespeare his title of 'gentle', is designed for King James (for instance, he liked short plays). Henry Paul has noted the three main tributary currents here. First, the King's concern with witchcraft, deriving from his own *Demonologie* (1597), a book written partly against the scepticism of Reginald Scot. (The Berwick Witches of 1591, who, with their pitiful little rhymes and the grotesque comedy of their ceremonies, under excruciating tortures produced tales of an attempt to bewitch James, had probably already suggested the subject of the Oxford entertainment *Tres Sybillae*.) The royal theory of sacred kingship, with the sovereign power of Duncan's golden blood, or Edward's healing touch, are a counterpoise to the dark powers. But the most general theme and yet one most directly affecting the imaginative lives of all was the Gunpowder Plot of 5 November 1605. From this derives a folk ceremony that is still in being. The appalling realization that the entire government was to have been assassinated and the country taken over (a puppet regime under the Princess Elizabeth proclaimed) is a threat which politics of today can bring home to all. Its full explosive horror, almost as great as the sense of providential relief, was intensified by the fact that many of the conspirators were the gentry of Shakespeare's own neighbourhood; they met at Clopton Hall, whilst he lived in New Place, the old Clopton house at Stratford. The Treshams, Catesbys, Winters, Throckmortons were Warwickshire men, far more closely connected than those worthy Earls of Warwick he had written of in the old chronicles. Shakespeare's own religious views have been much debated; many of the musicians of his time were Catholics, but his child, Susannah, was as clearly a Puritan. The imaginative power of the Old Faith was far greater than that of the new, but James had not succeeded in transferring sacred images to his own person, as Elizabeth had done. The depth of understanding for *Macbeth* suggests some sympathy, mixed with horror, for Guy Fawkes and the rest.

Although James had escaped, the image of the murder of Duncan and the utter confusion of the night of storm reflect the mood of 1605. 'Confusion now hath made his masterpiece' and 'the Lord's anointed Temple' is broken – the sacred body of kingship itself. Shock, bewilderment, find their most strained expression in the porter's drunken jests about equivocation – the doctrine of the Jesuit Garnett, alias Farmer, who stood his trial for the plot and was hanged in May 1606. However, the most recent attempt to present Shakespeare as a crypto-Catholic, that of Peter Milward, S.J., has even contrived to suggest that Shakespeare was not entirely hostile to the Jesuits' doctrine of equivocation (quoting in support the Duke in *Measure for Measure*, Diana in *All's Well* and Volumnia in *Coriolanus*) and that in *Macbeth* itself there can be detected 'an attitude generally favourable to the Jesuits'.[15] Milward certainly attributes rather Jesuitical habits to the playwright, but he is more credible in finding the doctrine of Grace prevalent in *Macbeth*; yet close studies of conscience and visions of hell were equally likely to be derived from Protestant sources. The familiar association of the King's sacred person with religious sanctions, the blasphemous nature of regicide, were still to be registered in 1649 when James's son was executed by the powers of Parliament. The hysterical scene in which Cromwell and the others spattered their faces with ink after signing the death warrant (recalling the spotted faces of Ill Fame in traditional iconography)[16] the subsequent dedication of churches to Charles King and Martyr (as by Killigrew at Falmouth), prove that religio-magical aspects of monarchy were potent half a century after this play.

The shattering effect of such newly uncovered menace, which must have felt like the end of the world (the great doom's image) – a nuclear explosion being the modern equivalent – would have been further intensified following as it did hard upon all the pageantry of James's entry to London and his coronation on 15 March 1604. Here the city had exploited all the legends of unity to intensify the great national sense of relief at receiving a peaceable succession of a Protestant monarch well provided with heirs to his throne. The numbing anxiety of the later years of Elizabeth, when the image of the Virgin crowned with stars, the Rosa Mystica, had waned somewhat, was now obliterated by celebrations of Britannia Rediviva, the union of the whole island under one monarch. This was to repair the original division of the kingdom between the sons of Brute, to restore Troynovant, to fulfil many old prophecies.

The city's triumphal arches that welcomed James served as stages and were far more dramatic than in any previous royal entry.[17] They included both action and dialogue and Jonson, Dekker and Middleton were all involved in the designs. The arch at Fenchurch housed a dialogue between Genius and Thames; the Italians personified James's Tudor descent, the Dutch his religious interests. Dekker's first arch in Cheapside represented Nova Felix Arabia; it had many mechanical marvels, including a running fountain of wine, and a speech was made by a boy player from St Paul's. Dekker's second arch, the Hortus Euphoriae, was not unlike Birnam Wood and his third arch in Fleet Street, depicting the New World, contained Justice and some darker figures. The kingdoms were 'By Brute divided, but by you alone / All are again united and made one' as Zeal tells the King.

Jonson's arch at Temple Bar represented the Temple of Janus, with Peace as the dominant figure; sundry Virtues were shown trampling on sundry Vices (as in the Rubens ceiling at Whitehall, which his son later commissioned for the Apotheosis of James I) – Peace trampled on Mars, Quiet on Tumult, Liberty on Servitude, Safety on Danger, Felicity on Unhappiness. The final devices in the Strand, also by Jonson, represented a rainbow, sun, moon and Pleiades, and here Jonson set his expository speaker, who really sounds at times like Malcolm on kingship (Malcolm's little piece of Machiavellian statecraft is the only concession made to politics in this play):

> The dam of other evils, avarice,
> Shall here lock down her jaws, and that rude vice
> Of ignorant and pitied greatness, pride,
> Decline with shame; ambition now shall hide
> Her face in dust, as dedicate to sleep,
> That in great portals wont her watch to keep.
> All ills shall flie the light; thy court be free
> No less from envy than from flattery;
> All tumult, faction and harsh discord cease,
> That might perturb the music of thy peace.

Shakespeare, walking behind the King as one of the King's Men, clad in his scarlet livery, would have seen the spectacle in each arch and would have taken his place in it. The effect could not have been negligible. When, superimposed on this triumph, came the Gunpowder Plot, the fair day and the foul day rushed together in his mind. It was no faint curtain line with which Malcolm invited his faithful followers 'to see us crowned at Scone'. It was no dim memory when Macbeth held a coronation banquet, and Banquo fulfilled his vassal's oath of allegiance by appearing at the feast, according to promise. It was no irrelevant reminder of the Italians' arch when the witches presented their show of eight kings; and their prophecies offer a hideous inversion of the hopeful speeches of Dekker and Jonson. Macbeth's kingdom inverts the kingdom of James.

And yet at the same time...chaos might come again in art as in life. In *King Lear*, Brute's tragic division of the kingdoms was to be re-enacted, as James's doctrine of a Union of the Crowns failed in Parliament. At this point Shakespeare had witnessed Daniel's vision of the Twelve Goddesses descending their mountain to the Temple of Peace, and he had witnessed and perhaps, as one of the King's Men, rehearsed Queen Anne's astonishing appearance as a negress in *The Masque of Blackness*. In turn, perhaps the success of his own *Macbeth* was to influence Jonson's *Masque of Queens*, with the antimasque of witches (played by the King's Men); it is a sobering thought that Shakespeare and Burbage may have followed the chariot of Queen Anne, disguised as captive hags! This, however, was in the future. What I would suggest about *Macbeth* is that it registered the impact of two powerful and incompatible events – Shakespeare's induction into the royal service at the coronation, 15 March 1604, and his reaction to the Warwickshire-hatched plot of 5 November 1605.

The blasted heath and the flowering wood were symbols of a fading and flourishing commonwealth that were the common-places of civic pageantry from early Tudor times. Both together make up the landscape of *Macbeth*. It is the embodiment of 'visionary dreariness', a superb 'objective correlative' to a mood. It seems to me most likely therefore that the tragedy of *Macbeth* followed these events closely, and represented the effect of such outrageous stimulation upon a sensitive artist. The deep, concentrated and highly condensed form of the play reflects the immediate onset of imaginative force; therefore I would place *Macbeth* before *King Lear* – in this, adhering to a minority view (there is no conclusive evidence). *King Lear* is wider, more expansive. Its links with the later plays have often been stressed; indeed, Glynne Wickham has written on *King Lear* as prelude to the Romances (see above, Chapter 6, p. 114, and below, Chapter 8, p. 153); but still he would place its inception before the Gunpowder Plot.

In this same article Glynne Wickham demonstrates clearly how far the triumphs of the coronation entry echo ideas expressed by James in his first address to Parliament (given four days after the coronation entry but doubtless prepared beforehand, as it was in print almost at once). The union of the two princely houses of York and Lancaster, observes James, was nothing compared to the union of the two kingdoms

What God had conjoined let no man separate. I am the husband, and the whole Isle is my lawful wife; I am the Head, it is my body; I am the Shepherd, it is my Flock.

This God-like metaphor – an extension of the metaphor of the marriage of ruler and kingdom – would put the murder of a king almost in the realm of deicide. Whatever his subjects thought of James as a man – and it did not take them very long to realize how very highly they were paying for all the blessings of peace – circumstances prolonged the sense of general deliverance from great peril which had greeted his arrival. This is reflected in *The Masque of Queens*, even though as early as 1605 Jonson had been imprisoned for blasphemy and popery in *Sejanus*, and had certainly made a risky approach to James's main weakness, his homosexual dependence on his favourites. (But *Macbeth* is less a 'tragedy of state' than any of Shakespeare's earlier plays; it was written, one might say, by a man who had got *Julius Caesar* out of his system, and who left Machiavellianism to Jonson and Chapman for the time being.)

A decade later, it was the fall of the latest and most scandalous of royal favourites, Robert Carr, Earl of Somerset, which may have lain behind the unsuccessful play of *The Witch* (1616) by Thomas Middleton. This scandal, which deeply implicated James (see above, Chapter 4, p. 75, and Chapter 6, p. 119), seems to have hastened his scepticism in witchcraft. Middleton's witches are elaborated as dispellers of charms to a corrupt court, but their descent from Shakespeare is as clear as the debt to Reginald Scot's treatise.[18] The song which Hecate sings and which was afterwards incorporated in *Macbeth* – as the Folio records – suggests that the spectacular elements of the new play were added to Shakespeare's play – by now an old one. It has been suggested that the witches were given new machinery for flying through the air, and that this – contrasted with Macbeth's entry on horseback, as the Folio directs – provides a stage action embodying the poetic imagery.

Certainly *Macbeth* was a spectacular play from the beginning, but the cauldron of the witches' scene might have belonged to any Elizabethan play – it could have served Peele in the 1580s – and Shakespeare did not rely on spectacle. Costly splendours of the royal entry or (later) of the royal masques fired his imagination, and then his poetry translated their visual glories into his own medium – 'Light thickens and the crow makes wing to the rooky wood' replaces scene-setting by mood-setting. It is, in my view, the basis of his later rivalry with Ben Jonson. Jonson commanded the resources of the court, and saw his poetry as one predominant element, the 'soul' of the court masque; Shakespeare had the humbler rôle of writing for the public stages, although his plays were also designed for court. He could not invoke the magic of a royal performer as the masque writer did; but his acting company, a disciplined ensemble, was led by a star tragedian. *Macbeth* appears to me the first of the Shakespearean plays to be influenced by the new dramatic range of the Jacobean theatre and the new possibilities for joining poetry and spectacle that the steadily growing power of Shakespeare's acting troupe supplied. The simple drums and trumpets of earlier days – the substance of 'York and Lancaster's long jars' – were replaced by much more varied spectacle drawn from the different kinds of theatre that surrounded the players, the street theatre of the city and masques of the court, but it was an imagined transfer. This varied spectacle was integrated into the drama in sophisticated ways by the actor's art. In the article by Mrs Ewbank already cited, she says of Shakespeare:

He had available a verbal poetry which makes us see, in our imagination more than ever is, or could be shown on stage; but he also had a theatre which could show, to our outward eye, more than mind can find words to express.[19]

Comparing the effect of Macbeth's speech about 'Pity, like a naked new-born babe' with the apparitions of babes in the cauldron scene (one might add, with the murder of Macduff's children), she maintained that it is only by seeing the apparitions that Macbeth and we realize fully how he has been trapped by his own actions.[20]

Actual spectacle in *Macbeth* is very varied; it is partly new in kind; and it leads back to a heightening of the poetry and the series

of images which have been so often the subject of the critics' eluci-
dations. But these again feed into performance. Tomlinson's
impression that the play is a series of soliloquies does less than
justice to the interlocking of poetry and spectacle or indeed to
those ironies on which the plot structure rests and which enable
the reader or spectator to see into the future like the witches
themselves. 'There's no art/To find the mind's construction in the
face...'; 'He that's coming/Must be provided for';[21] 'If a man
were a porter of hell gate he should have old turning the key';
'What's done is done'; 'Our dear friend Banquo, whom we miss/
Would he were here!'. The shows of the witches wrought their
effect on Macbeth, and the moodiness, the inward quality of his
remorse, his development as a character – it is one of the first
studies in *developing* character – imply deep rapport and sympathy
between poet, audience and the Protean Burbage. If one line may
recall the mood of the plot, it is

> But let the frame of things disjoint, both the worlds suffer...

Feeling sinks at once to the haunted and hunted trembling of the
man:

> Ere we will eat our meal in fear, and sleep
> In the affliction of these terrible dreams
> That shake us nightly.

Then comes the image that subtly recalls and transcends the universal fear:

> Duncan is in his grave;
> After life's fitful fever he sleeps well:
> Treason has done his worst; nor steel, nor poison,
> Malice domestic, foreign levy, *nothing*
> Can touch him further. (III.ii.16–26)

At the height of his alienated despair, on the death of Lady Macbeth, Macbeth's sequence of images includes something like a
procession of players, something perhaps recalling the shadowy
kings:

> Tomorrow, and tomorrow, and tomorrow
> Creeps in this petty pace from day to day...
> And all our yesterdays have lighted fools
> The way to dusty death.

(The fool and death, familiar in Holbein's Dance of Death, meet as in the graveyard at Elsinore where Yorick's skull speaks its silent message.)

> Out, out, brief candle!

The emblematic candle of man's life, the candle carried before penitents, the votive candle and the candle we have seen in the hand of Lady Macbeth flicker and gutter.

> Life's but a walking shadow, a poor player
> That struts and frets his hour upon the stage
> And then is heard no more...

'His Majesty's Poor Players' was the official style for the King's Men in petition, and a shadow is a minor actor; but *we* may think forward to Lear 'Who is it that can tell me what I am?' and the Fool's answer 'Lear's shadow'. Although the candle is *out*, the shadow casts its darkness still, but the audacity of the player's thus recalling his *own* world serves to reinforce the image of the Player King whose robes hang loose about him like a giant's robe upon a dwarfish thief.[22]

> ...it is a tale
> Told by an idiot, full of sound and fury,
> Signifying *nothing*

challenges the art of speech still further by the new paradox of its metaphor, but it ends with the same word as the former passage; 'nothing'.

Macbeth's view of the abyss, *le néant*, is held by some to be a triumph of courage, or 'strong pessimism'.[23] The strong pessimism is Shakespeare's but it is open to the audience to decide how much belongs to Macbeth. He is given a much blacker career that Holinshed gave the original – the treacherous, secret method of the first killing, the lack of open quarrel over succession – but there is nothing of the statecraft found in Jonson's or Shakespeare's Roman plays. He is given a fighting end, instead of ignoble flight, and at the last regains the authentic courage of the fighting man, slipping his shield round on its strap, taking up the posture that he knows will not save him. It was asked in praise of young Siward, the last of Macbeth's victims, 'Had he his hurts before?' as all that pertained to a soldier's death. Though Macbeth's head is brought in on a pole – and the audience on their way home from the Bankside over London Bridge could see the rows of traitors' heads over the gatehouse – yet it was a way to death less dusty than having his head *painted* on a pole, as Macduff contemptuously promises (v.ix.26), a monster for another kind of spectacle, where he would live 'the gaze and show o' the time'.

I began by mentioning Fulke Greville, Shakespeare's very near neighbour at Alcester, and ten years his senior, who ten years earlier in 1596 comes nearest in mood to *Macbeth* in its paradoxes of life in death, surcease and success, player-king, death and folly

> When as man's life, the light of human lust
> In socket of his earthly lantern burns,
> That all this glory unto ashes must,
> And generation to corruption turns;
> Then fond desires that only fear their end
> Do vainly wish for life, but to amend.
>
> But when this life is from the body fled,
> To see itself in that eternal glass,
> Where time doth end, and thoughts accuse the dead,
> Where all to come, is one with all that was;
> Then living men ask how he left his breath,
> That while he lived never thought of death...
>
> (*Caelica* lxxxvii)
>
> O wearisome condition of humanity!
> Born under one law, to another bound:
> Vainly begot, and yet forbidden vanity:
> Created sick, commanded to be sound...
>
> (*Mustapha*, Chorus Sacerdotum)
>
> Vain superstition! Glorious style of weakness!
> Sprung from the deep disquiet of man's passion,
> To desolation and despair of Nature:
> Thy texts bring princes' titles into question:
> Thy prophets set on work the swords of tyrants...
> Let virtue's blood...
> Mankind! Trust not these superstitious dreams,
> Fear's idols, pleasure's relics, sorrow's pleasures,
> They make the wilful hearts their holy temples,
> The rebels unto government their martyrs.
>
> (Chorus Quintus Tartarorum)

This is Macbeth's world; he became 'fear's idol, pleasure's relic, sorrow's pleasure' and refused to look beyond 'time's end'.

8

KING LEAR AND THE
KINGDOM OF FOOLS AND BEGGARS

The greatest poet of this age wrote:

We think of *King Lear* less as the history of one man than as the history of a whole evil time. Lear's shadow is Gloucester... and the mind goes on imagining other shadows, shadow beyond shadow, till it has pictured a whole world [as] a shadow upon the wall, upon one's body in the firelight.

(W. B. Yeats, 'Emotion of multitude', *Essays and Introductions*, p. 215)

Shakespeare's two tragedies of ruined kingdoms also counterpoise each other. In *Macbeth* one keen incisive thrust of action achieves the rape upon the crown, in *King Lear* its dismemberment; the one issues in a mounting series of murders, the other in that stony denial of another's needs, identity, claims, which constitutes the murder in the heart.

The one deep and narrow, the other in its complex double action spreading out among a larger range of characters than any previous play of Shakespeare, they must remain closely linked. My order is one of what seems to me psychological fitness. The concentration of *Macbeth* is that of the 'night's predominance' whilst *King Lear*, in its questioning, its uncertainties, carries also in the figures of Cordelia and the Fool and Kent, its assurances.[1] Both are plays that belong to the playhouse and, as Yeats implies, to the solitary in his lonely tower.

There have been many *King Lears*; Shakespeare himself changed the old story to end it with the defeat and death of Cordelia, but for almost a hundred and fifty years, Nahum Tate's 'improvement' restored victory to her cause. Dr Johnson, feeling the end too painful to contemplate, accepted this stage version; the Japanese still regard this play as so painful that they tend to shun it. On the other hand, lately, a Brechtian production (R.S.C., 1962) succeeded

142

in darkening even the Shakespearean original by omitting Cornwall's servant, killed in Gloucester's defence, and by cutting out
Edmund's repentance. This theatre eschews 'katharsis', and would
above all avoid 'calm of mind, all passion spent', which mitigates
the alienation of the spectators.

Modern critics find the darkness of this play in its scepticism[2]
as in the most thoroughgoing study of the background of thought,
William Elton's *King Lear and the Gods* (1966); many questions
remain echoing in the mind. In a history of its stage productions,
Marvin Rosenberg showed how various are the shapings it has
undergone.[3]

King Lear deals in outrage, insult, affront; in affliction, in dereliction, in man at the extremity of his being. As many have recog-
nised, it is above all the play for our time; for this age, it occupies
the pre-eminence that in the last century was accorded to *Hamlet*,
by reason of its centrality, provoking the most bizarre responses,
inviting the most neurotic refashioning. I hold the greatest modern
version to be the Russian film of Grigori Kozintsev.

The final scene rather than the storm scene provides the modern
critic with the severest challenge; it has been compared with the
most august event conceivable by the mind of Renaissance man.
'We perhaps see a Lear that Bradley, for all his power, could never
apprehend...Lear is in part about the end of the world, and
twentieth-century critics must owe something to the fact that they
know "an image of that horror".' The apocalyptic 'turmoil' which
accompanies the collapse of human justice recalls the 'last days' of
Revelations. In the reconciliation scene between Lear and Cordelia,
with Cordelia as a 'soul in bliss' and Lear bound upon 'a wheel of
fire' (traditional punishment of the proud) there appears a reflection of the 'Doom' fresco over the Chancel arch in the Gild
Chapel adjoining Shakespeare's home.[4]

But action continues beyond this point, and the certitudes which
underlay the Christian Judgement are contradicted by it. 'The
Gods reward your kindness!' Kent had said to Gloucester when
already it is plain what reward was in store; but 'The Gods defend
her!' was to be the cue for the entry of Lear with the dead Cordelia
in his arms. In such a Pietà, or icon of grief, the state of dereliction

might ultimately present itself to the man who (it seems) wanted to lie in the chancel of his parish church. This, to him, was history

Always there has been the besetting temptation to convert deed into idea, to fail properly to do justice to what is involved in finding the very foundations of human excellence in a piece of raw history...In the endurance of the ultimate contradictions of human existence that belong to its very substance, the created Word keeps company with those...who...plumbed the very abyss of un-reason, reached that place wherein those who reach it are overcome by the contradictions between the claims of truth, the claims of calling things as they are...and the claims of compassion for an individual caught, so it seems to the eye of pity, in the toils of circumstance he has done little or nothing to make... This schism has also been allowed to work itself out in a setting of physical extremity which was also the final manifestation of the irreconcilable.[5]

The affirmation, the bare acceptance of what every nerve would avoid, every trick of repression or mitigation evade, itself con-stitutes the catharsis. After a long reign, Lear had looked for 'honour, love, obedience, troops of friends'. What he has first to meet is the storm. Insult, outrage and affront come to him through the flesh; finally, the physical death of Cordelia cannot be com-passed. The irreconcilable fact is that death has struck her rather than him: 'Why should a dog, a horse, a rat have life?' is the last of Lear's many questions.

Lear's shadow, Gloucester, denied death by Cornwall in the name of 'justice' but exposed to 'revenges', is reduced, like the bears baited in the Elizabethan arena, to a savage game that he himself has played. He is 'tied to the stake and I must stand the course'; then, like the bear, he is blinded. Lear's shadow holds before the spectator, in his flesh, the finality, beyond remedy, of physical loss,[6] which is to destroy Lear himself.

'Kind Lear' was the epithet Burbage's acting suggested to con-temporaries – a little more than kind to the daughter whom he still feels as part of his own flesh. 'Is it not as this mouth should tear this hand/For lifting food to 't?', he asks (III.iv.15–16). Kind, in the sense of being natural, human, and vulnerable, he is the only Shakespearean hero for whom part of the action might be to vomit, urinate, defecate or choke. He hits his servants; in his mad-ness he accuses Goneril, – 'she kicked the poor king, her father' – of the sort of humiliation Kent inflicts on Oswald and Cornwall on Kent. In discerning the image underlying the whole play as that of a body racked, torn and flayed, with many animal images of predator and prey, critics in the early twentieth century[7] emphasized the thematic as distinct from the psychological approach to this tragedy; the alternations of these two approaches may be seen in the range of historical interpretations.

For example, taking a psychological approach, Lear and Cordelia may each be seen in the opening scene as at fault in refusing the other the right to see the situation from a personal view. Cordelia is deaf to 'the unutterable plea for reassurance that prompts such questions as his, ridiculous or embarrassing or improper as they are';[8] and when Lear asks 'But goes thy heart with this?' her answer can be termed 'obstinate untruth'. Cordelia seems to this critic a very Shylock for her bond. In Holinshed, Lear made no such demands, had not divided his kingdom at all, but merely named his heirs, like Duncan in *Macbeth*. There Lear was subsequently deposed by the Dukes of Albany and Cornwall and fled to France. In the old play of *King Leir*, he had made the demand on Cordelia with the crafty plan of persuading her to take the suitor he would choose. Shakespeare has both foreshortened and altered the opening scene, so it is only in the light of later events that it may be read psychologically. Rather, Lear abdicates in a deeper sense, when he turns into a Dragon ('Come not between the Dragon and his wrath'). He may personify himself as the Dragon of his country; but he may be played as already mad, as Kent terms him.

If at supreme moments of this tragedy images of the Christian faith present themselves, in its setting, and in its concepts of the gods, *Lear* is a pagan play; Christendom recedes, the great goddess Nature is invoked. Historically, the accession of King Lear was supposed to have occured about a hundred years before the founding of Rome, 'at what time Joas reigned in Judah'. Imaginatively therefore, the ultimate religious questions may be asked.

In *King Lear* as in *Macbeth*, kings sacred or accursed rule over a piece of ancient earth, without cities (only castles and their peasant subjects); where ravens, choughs, dogs and wolves are as much part of the landscape as men. Malcolm fears political treachery and Edmund practises it, but these younger men belong to another world. The double time of *King Lear* is not a matter of two clocks, as in *Othello*, but of two eras; the younger generation belong to Shakespeare's own time, Cordelia, 'anima naturaliter christiana', Edmund, a sceptic of the newest cut, the product of Machiavelli and Montaigne. (The two eras had been a feature of the old biblical plays of the craft gilds.)

The opening ritual places the play at once in a world of legend. The three daughters and a hundred knights represent the pattern of Lear's power. 'Mythology is not about something; it is itself that something', as Samuel Beckett remarked. The archaic mode permits an archaic level of relationships, archaic fears and needs, to come to the surface. Without the stresses of the more socially conceived worlds of *Hamlet* and *Othello*, this play, by an absence of articulate complexity in human relationships, brings out the natural 'bond' of kin, the natural ties of bounty and hospitality. Lear's error, a natural perversion of Bounty, the primal virtue of the Loaf-ward, the Ring-giver, belongs to one who fights with the long-bow – the ancient plebeian weapon of the English yeoman. In momentary snatches, he later reassumes the rôles of soldier or of judge, but in his kingdom there are no political duties, no sense of any frame of government. From different angles, the historian and the critic may describe the conflict between the old order and the new in *King Lear*.

In *King Lear*, traditional, feudal, patriarchal loyalties are challenged by the blind individualism of Goneril, Regan and Edmund...in later Jacobean and Caroline drama the poetic tension is lost.[9]

As late as 1640, however, in *Patriarcha, or the Natural Power of Kings*, Sir Robert Filmer, a Kentish squire, assumed that Charles Stuart, as the literal heir of Adam, was entitled to exercise all the prerogatives conferred on the father of mankind,[10] and much later Marvell was to write

> But Ceres corn, and Flora is the spring,
> Bacchus is wine, the country is the king.

The map of Britain has been bisected before the play begins; the ceremony of words remains. It was in exchange for words that Lear 'threw away a pearl'; when in the storm he is rejected by his whole country, his invocation constitutes another great release of words, an assertion of *mana*. Eloquent in his cursings and imprecations, Lear cannot see himself except as a King, even after he is self-deposed. His first act is to banish Kent under supreme penalty of the law. He expects total obedience.

> The King would speak with Cornwall, the dear father
> Would with his daughter speak, commands their service
>
> (ii.iv.99–101)

'He hath ever but slenderly known himself' sums up the past and lays down lines for the future. Lear cannot in the end find the words, amid all the eloquence, for his impotence:

> No, you unnatural hags,
> I will have such revenges on you both
> That all the world shall – I will do such things –
> What they are yet, I know not, but they shall be
> The terrors of the earth... O Fool, I shall go mad![11]   (ii.iv. 277–86)

So he enters his new kingdom, the kingdom of fools, beggars and madmen, a kingdom not of this world. In terms of the story line, King Lear and his daughters, Gloucester and his sons provide the action; but Lear, the Fool and the Madman provide the thematic action, in the great symphonic scenes where, under stress, character explodes and plotting is suspended. Shakespeare invented these rôles – out of that region of the mind from which came Caliban and the witches of *Macbeth*.

By admitting Lear's Fool into the play, Shakespeare had revived an archaic rôle; Yorick had, as it were, been taken out of his grave, in an act of theatrical renunciation and disinvestment. The household jester was the prototype of all royal actors; those restraints which had been painfully evolved to control the professional acting troupe, as defined by Hamlet in his speech to the players, were withdrawn. Half pet animal, half attendant spirit, the Fool is fixed at Lear's side: he is among the elementals and, as Lear's follower, enters into his dream. His rhyming prophecies recall the old rhyming prophecies of the plays of Shakespeare's youth; by later 'improvers' he was eliminated, and was the last feature of Shakespeare's play to be restored to the stage; even then, in bowdlerized pathos, and played by a girl. The age of Charles II, which found the witches comic, had no use for the Fool.

Edgar, with his two rôles, offers the actor a bravura part which was advertised on the title page of the Quarto as 'the unfortunate life of Edgar, son and heir to the Earl of Gloucester, and his sullen and assumed humour of Tom of Bedlam'. Houseless, homeless, among the 'rogues and vagabonds' of the statute feared by all players, the terrifying energy of 'Poor Tom' becomes an explosion of personality magnified into a sort of power. Edgar's rôle, like those so popular in the choristers' theatre, allows 'two parts in one'; in terms of actor's technique, it was *avant garde*. An aura of the supernatural is created, but is more than assumed 'Edgar I nothing am'. *His* 'Fool' is introjected, incorporated.

It is now, at the play's centre, the Fool and Madman who become eloquent; they are truth tellers, but their truth continually lapses into gibberish. Traditionally, the Fool carried a mirror or a bauble, because he was intended to hold a mirror up to men; this he did by conversing with his 'double'.[12] The two aspects of Edgar cannot be reconciled, even to the same extent as the two aspects of Malevole/Altofront or of Bussy (see above, Chapter 6, p. 107); he undergoes further metamorphoses into a rough peasant, or rather several different rough peasants, and finally into an unknown knight, his identity still 'lost'. He enacts with his father the strange ritual of Dover Cliff, and then does the necessary killing; he speaks the last words

> The weight of this sad time we must obey;
> Speak what we feel, not what we ought to say

as he resumes his stability, the 'sadness' – heaviness – of mourning. His inadequate monosyllables provide the dead march that ends the tragedy.

Like Edgar, Shakespeare has taken refuge in metamorphoses among the lowest and most popular elements of speech and character. Besides everything else that it stands for, *King Lear* represents a great triumph of continuity, carrying forward into a world of social and theatrical change the image of a former time, presenting to the new Jacobean stage something of 'the world we have lost' but combining it with the *bravura* display of the new acting, although nothing else in the part or in the play – except now and then, Edmund's mockery – recalls the world of Marston and Tourneur.

The rôle of Tom of Bedlam hurls Edgar from his own identity, as the antic disposition of Hamlet did not. He is 'possessed', speaks with voices other than his own. He may be playing the old jester's game of taking many parts – an understudy for good servants, like the one who kills Cornwall, and for Albany, as challenger of Edmund. Elsewhere, he offers a stoic pattern of patience, or becomes an actor who dare not drop his rôle of blessing and cursing, of speech beyond speech.

Lear prays for the members of his new kingdom, the Fool and the Bedlam

> Poor naked wretches, whereso'er you are,
> That bide the pelting of this pitiless storm   (III.iv.28–9)

although encounter with the mirrors of his plight finally turns his wits. The choric scenes of these three represent for Shakespeare a capitulation to the grotesque, to all that civility, art, Ben Jonson, perhaps his own earlier self (the author of *Richard II*, for example) would have cast out.

The ambiguous, dangerous quality of Tom of Bedlam takes visible form in the vision of the fiend at Dover Cliff and its exorcism.[13] This gives immediate preparation for Lear's entry as the Summer King, crowned among the corn, as was the wont at harvest revelry. The deposed ruler has taken visibly the form of the king of Fools:[14] his own Fool vanishes.

The meeting of Lear and his shadow, Gloucester, has been termed 'a sustained exercise in the deployment of multiple uncertainties'.[15] Gloucester knows the voice and the King intuitively strikes at the whole horror of Gloucester's condition and its cause – his bastard – with 'Blind Cupid!'. His whirling dissonances leave him abject yet retaining an authority, priestlike or even godlike. 'None does offend, none, I say, none, I'll able 'em' (IV.vi.168). Yet Lear now sees himself as 'the natural fool of Fortune' – he himself takes up the rôle his own Fool had continually proposed him.

The old theatrical image of Fortune's Wheel has revolved throughout the play, indeed it appears everywhere in the source play of *King Leir*. Kent's lame attempt at summary is

> If Fortune brag of two she lov'd and hated,
> One of them we behold   (v.iii.280–1)

Another old theatrical image is evoked by the sight of Kent in the stocks, recalling one from the moral plays.[16] The resonance of traditional images lifts the action towards 'parable, romance or vision'.[17]

Several writers have noted the links between this tragedy and the last plays of Shakespeare; *Lear*, *Timon*, *Pericles*, not only in the extremity of their affliction, but also in the archaic mode of presentation, could appeal to an audience, part of which was sophisticated whilst another part was still enjoying such naiveties as *Mucedorus*, with 'the merry conceits of Mouse'.

Two American scholars have linked this suggestion with the idea of King Lear as inverted pastoral.[18] A tale of exile and return, of flight from the corruption of the court into the uncompromising simplicity of the country can hardly be seen here, however, because Lear's court itself is so archaic. Elizabethan and Jacobean pastoral was theoretically a sane and modest form for a beginner; only at the very end of his life, for instance, did Shakespeare's contemporary Drayton, in *The Muses' Elysium*, evolve a tragic pastoral. The unpretentiousness of *King Lear* is of another kind and does not operate within limits. Pastoral is comic; the comedy of the grotesque is by now so familiar a form in modern reworkings of *King Lear* – predictably, it attracts Jan Kott – that the Fool and Tom of Bedlam offer modern actors the greatest chance for open interpretation, of precisely the kind that they might have done in Jacobean times. In real life, 'all-licensed fooling' could be taken seriously enough to bring down penalties.[19]

If Lear passes through eloquence to the terrifying realm of the comic grotesque, his return from the kingdom of fools and mad-men is marked by a condition of utter simplicity.[20] Rage and shame are burnt out. The reunion with Cordelia, full of quietness and hesitancy, asks to be spoken slowly and weightily

> O thou good Kent, how shall I live and work
> To match thy goodness? (iv.vii.1–2)

asks the Queen of the man who has never 'gone out of dialect' of plainness except to mock Cornwall. The opening words of Lear are not only monosyllabic; with one exception, they are English in origin:

> You do me wrong to take me out o' th' grave.
> Thou art a soul in bliss, but I am bound
> Upon a wheel of fire, that mine tears
> Do scald like molten lead.[21] (iv.vii.45–8)

In recognizing her he disclaims in himself the rank that he feels in her:

> As I am a *man*, I think this *lady*
> To be my *child* Cordelia. (iv.vii.68–9)

He has restored to her the title he deprived her of, and she in turn acknowledges the 'bond'

> And so I am, I am.

The simplicity of this scene has been anticipated in earlier passages. The last dagger thrust of Regan at her father had been equally simple:

> What need one? (ii.iv.262)

Repetition marks earlier moments of tension:

> So young and so untender?
> So young, my Lord, and true. (i.i.106–7)

and Lear's own name resounds throughout the play:

> O Lear, Lear, Lear!
> Beat at this gate that let thy folly in,
> And thy dear judgement out! (i.iv.270–2)

It has been observed that

the last two acts are filled with frenzied repetitions, some of them hammered upon as many as six times in the course of a single line: 'Kill' 'Now' 'Howl' 'Never' and the monosyllabic 'No'. One comes to feel that these words are being broken on an anvil.[22]

The language of Lear's new kingdom is full of nonsense words, 'fie, foh and fum' – the sound of the wind or of hunting horns. At the end Lear calls for animal howls; no words at all are left in him. Edgar has said on seeing the meeting of Lear and Gloucester:

> I would not take this from report; it is,
> And my heart breaks at it. (IV.vi.141–2)

It is. Barely to conceive and to acknowledge the limits of human endurance, grief and stricken faith is to transform them, for a territory beyond words has been brought into the realm of the articulate. Kent echoes Edgar in the final scene:

> Break heart, I prithee, break, (v.iii.312)

but to Edgar's instinctive appeal to courage, 'Look up, my Lord' Lear, who has struggled to speak further ('Pray you, undo this button') can no longer reply, and Kent recognizes the moment of death:

> Vex not his ghost; O let him pass. (v.iii.313)

Edmund's terseness at his end shows him even in death the active ironic wit

> What you have charged me with, that have I done:
> And more, much more; the time will bring it out:
> 'Tis past and so am I. (v.iii.162–4)

He had begun this action by describing his predicament in plain terms of the event

> . . . some twelve or fourteen moonshines
> Lag of a brother (I.ii.5–6)

whilst mocking the more formal expression

> As to the legitimate. Fine word 'legitimate'!
> Well, my legitimate, if this letter speed. . . (I.ii.18–19)

Later he was reckoning up his opportunities briskly

> Which of them shall I take?
> Both? one? or neither? (v.i.57–8)

which is echoed at the close:

> I was contracted to them both; all three
> Now marry in an instant. (v.iii.228–9)

Like his brother he has assumed the actor ('Yours in the ranks of death!' he has pledged to Goneril (iv.ii.25)) but he is prepared for either of the sisters to eliminate the other. This solution he hardly stops to formulate, being at the top of Fortune's wheel. The final combat between the two sons of Gloucester belongs not to the archaic tribal society of the main action, but to an early English history play, a medieval society of knights and heraldry. It is half way out of the dream world but it is shadowed and accompanied by the secret conflict of Goneril and Regan.

As if expanding under a telescopic lens, the action of *King Lear* moves out of legend into a contemporary action, then back to a chivalrous battle, then forward to the final action which contradicts the old legend as it was known from the play of *King Leir*. Those ritual presences the three daughters, as in the opening scene, meet together again before the spectators, but the death of Cordelia comes as a hazard of blind Chance – of Fortune in her least providential, most brutally contingent modern guise. It is gratuitous.

To what extent the action, like Macbeth's, may also have extended to reflect the state of Shakespeare's England, particularly of the monarchy, must remain open. Whilst some would see the conflict of old and new conceptions of social and political structure, others would detect a closer connexion with James's own statements and even the events of his life.[23] Glynne Wickham has drawn attention to some of these, and whilst his interpretation of the play as politically a 'prelude to the tragicomedies' seems implausible, his exploration uncovers material that cannot be ignored.

Thinking men knew that James was already proclaiming in ways far more explicit than his predecessor, that kings were gods – and even by God they were called gods, he once added. In his very first parliament he ordered a conference, 'desired and commanded it' as 'an absolute King', which astounded the House of Commons.[24] James was forty, not eighty, of course, but it soon became plain that whilst in certain affairs he interfered only too much, in others he relied on his 'little beagle', Robert Cecil, and retired to the country to hunt or to pursue his intellectual and his more dubious personal pleasures.

James's plans for a political union of his kingdoms met with strong opposition from his subjects and from the House of Commons. The English had no desire to give the Scots liberty to take more than they were taking already, and the Scots feared government from the South. Whilst the coronation pageants had welcomed James as a second Brut, who had restored and redeemed the ancient unity (see above, Chapter 7, p. 134) James's demands were based on the fact that *in his person* the kingdoms *were* joined. The King's Body Politic (the Crown) imposed unity or became monstrous.

The legal background, especially as it brings in the doctrine of the King's Two Bodies, has been studied in detail by Marie Axton.[25] By 1606 there was open conflict between James and his subjects. Mrs Axton points out that an important legal decision (Calvin's Case) had dealt with the question of the dual nationality of those Scotsmen born after James's accession; that the Commons had refused his pleas for legislation, that the Bishop of Bristol had been made to alter a work on the union which he had published in 1604, to suit James's views; Mundy's *Triumphs of Reunited Britannia*, given by the Merchant Taylors as the pageant for the Lord Mayor on All Saints' Day 1606 (which stressed the 'felix culpa' of Brut so that his three sons delivered up their divided crowns) was designed to console the King for his frustration.[26]

When therefore *King Lear* was presented at court on St Stephen's Day 1606, it might indeed seem that Lear was repeating the sin of Brut, and anticipating that of Gorboduc, whose tragedy had been used half a century earlier to present the dangers of a divided kingdom. The theme was commonplace, but the time was apposite.

Lear had divided his kingdom whilst retaining the crown; he had treated the realm as his personal property, because in the sort of play Shakespeare was writing there were no public instruments of government. Lear's old retainers act in a general way as councillors, but the feudal obligations which tie the western Earl of Gloucester to Cornwall's lordship, or bring the Earl of Kent into natural authority in the region of Dover Castle, omit the very grounds of Shakespeare's contemporary conflict.

Lear reacts simply as a father so that Mrs Axton sees in his poignant words to Cordelia in captivity a terrifying echo of a denunciation of his original act

> He that parts us shall bring a brand from heaven
> And fire us hence like foxes   (v.iii.22–3)

In his amended version of his book on the unity of the three kingdoms, the Bishop of Bristol had written

An Empire of many kingdoms was thus reduced into one, not unlike the firmament of heaven which God hath adorned with two great lights, the Sun and the Moon, even the whole army and harmony of the stars in one firmament....

Whoso throweth a stone against the heavens, saith the Wise Man, it will fall upon his head. And if any one standing above the rest, speaketh and oppugneth this thing, better it were (saving my charitie) that *unus ill periret, quam Unitas*.

> (John Bristol, *A Discourse plainly proving the
> existent utility and urgent necessity of the desired happy
> Union* (Oxford, 1606), p. 11)

The heavens themselves administer the vengeance upon Lear's act of division; the thunder of the storm is followed by the destruction of his youngest child, who by the death of her sisters should have become undoubted heiress (as she appears in Nahum Tate's version). All that Lear can foresee is the vengeance upon those daughters of some equally savage and devilish monsters of the wild waste.

> The goujeres shall devour them, flesh and fell,
> Ere they shall make us weep; we'll see 'em starv'd first.[27]
>   (v.iii.24–5)

The appalling result of his original act, though in one sense gratuitous, is in another the kind of outrage which a state of disunity engenders.

Lear presents the antithesis of love and death as simply as Zenocrate had done – 'I fare, my lord, as other Empresses'. He himself, a huntsman and a soldier who has heard the cry 'Kill, kill!' has already once come out on the other side of the grave;

now he carries the limp and silent flesh of her he had seen before as 'a soul in bliss'.[28]

But there is no 'application' to the state of his kingdom here; Albany recalls his own duty to 'the gor'd state' but the note is muted.

In terms of the divided kingdom, then, *King Lear* fits in as a warning of what failure to achieve complete unity might bring. But there are other aspects of the story which might be seen to reflect a less flattering view of the court and King. Both, I think, must be entertained, although they may not have been simultaneously perceived by the original audience as a whole.

James's dislike of the business of government, his preference for living in the country and indulging in hunting, his very expensive descents upon his subjects for this purpose, whilst shunning the presence of the common people, were by him explained on the grounds of health. He was indeed cursed with a bad heredity, and did not feel at home with the common people as Elizabeth had done. His theoretical and rather grandiose plans for foreign policy did not tie in with any day to day cares of state. Yet he welcomed, in certain circumstances, a gross and undignified familiarity from his favourites, and enjoyed the semblance of good fellowship in his revels.[29]

In this play the language of court flattery, indeed the regular language of the court masque, is the language commanded so readily by Regan and Goneril. What they say to Lear was similar to what the masquers regularly said to James. The emptiness behind the pomp, the hollowness behind the ceremonies of praise is stressed by the Fool, whose devotion issues in bitterness. He calls Lear 'nuncle', a familiar term for any old man,[30] and judges his folly by vulgar analogues. His literal interpretation of the wildest actions deflates their extremity ('Tis a naughty night to swim in', he prosaically observes, as Lear begins to tear his clothes off).

Truth nevertheless resides with this humble, archaic form of royal entertainer; or truth is silent ('So young, my Lord, and true'). Shakespeare's deepest levels of imagination are released first by the Fool then by the outcast Tom of Bedlam, the 'prophet' and 'philosopher' of the storm.

'King Lear' and the kingdom of Fools and Beggars

In *King Lear* there is a choice made – a choice to stay with the popular, simple world, that must be kept part of the new scene. All time sequences are broken – the Fool, after his prophecy of confusion in 'the realm of Albion', adds 'This prophecy Merlin shall make, for I live before his time' (III.ii.95–6) – so, presumably, he is wiser than Merlin. His last word is 'I'll go to bed at noon'.

The inverted court ritual of *Macbeth* has been replaced by a turning away from all such ritual to 'a condition of complete simplicity,/Costing not less than everything.' In *King Lear*, therefore, I would see the rejection of Court rites, the decision to stay with the popular stage (or to accept that the choice had been imposed by circumstance). There is a radical split between the doctrine of the undivided kingdom and the more normal disillusion with court flattery, court lechery, court betrayals. True, this is not, except in snatches, depicted directly, in the manner of the Italianate tragedies of state (which Shakespeare avoided). It comes out in the later ravings of Lear, after the storm, and in the love intrigue of Edmund with the two sisters. But it remains rather a minor theme in the play; and therefore any Stuart 'application' seems to me subsidiary. The work comes from deeper levels than these. Like remnants of the day worked into a dream, they may be discarded.

In the humility, the sense of dispossession, the deep questionings and contradictions of *King Lear* lies the germ of works yet to be written.[31] Henceforth, the mirror held up to nature is broken. This is why, whether in strict chronology this was the order, I would see *King Lear* as spiritually and inwardly the successor to *Macbeth*, looking forward to *Pericles* and *The Winter's Tale*. Lear's death marks a release.

> Painless at last, his being escaped from the terrible
>   body of pain, Upwards, left it...
> His discharged spirit, perhaps had thought of remaining
>   inactively in the landscape
> The immeasurable act of his suffering
>   would last him awhile
>   ... breathless
> stood, surveyed his estate of Pain, was silent.[32]

It is possible, therefore, that *King Lear* is less of an anti-pastoral than a reversion to that old countrified form of drama which Shakespeare saw being superseded by the London stage (see above, Chapter 2). It brought into the modern theatre with its new techniques of acting some of the old breadth and humanity – instinctive pieties and rough jesting come as if from the humble who never look for justice. It includes elements of the antimasque, the comic grotesque, rather than of the masque itself. It has suffered so many alterations and revisions because it is the nature of the play to be 'open', to avoid intellectual judgements, the appearance of sophistication or of learning. For the intellectual feat that here is achieved involves 'thinking through the senses' and through the actions of a stage on which the shadows play till 'the mind goes on imagining other shadows, shadow beyond shadow, till it has pictured a whole world'.

9

IMAGES OF LOVE AND WAR:
OTHELLO, CORIOLANUS,
ANTONY AND CLEOPATRA

King Lear and *Macbeth*, drawing in such depth upon Shakespeare's own poetic resources and those of the Jacobean and earlier stages, stand alone in their time. They had no progeny. However far it topped them, *Hamlet* had belonged to a recognizable group of plays; and three of the remaining Jacobean tragedies are themselves concerned with the hero's conflict with his society. In *Othello, Coriolanus* and *Antony and Cleopatra*, the gods are evoked but momentarily (as when Coriolanus sees the heavens open, and Epicurean deities sitting laughing at the spectacle mortality provides). The ruling present deity of all three plays is Fortune or Opportunity. The questions of Lear, the dark mysteries of Macbeth's kingdom are replaced by questions about the nature of the man who stands at the centre of the play. The audience is left with paradoxes to ponder. In all three plays the hero, a soldier betryed by love and by his own nature, ends in suicide (Coriolanus knows well his return will be mortal). That these plays are also, more or less directly, concerned with the relation of the hero to the power on whose behalf his prowess is exercised, allows for very different proportions of that power to be invested in him. Othello, though of royal descent, is but a servant of the Venetian republic; Coriolanus is born a patrician in the Roman republic; Antony is an acknowledged ruler, one of Rome's Triumvirate.

The appeal of these plays to their contemporary audience was primarily the appeal of a great tragical history, although none is so definitely centred on a great *event* as was *Julius Caesar*.

Through this sequence – it is not, of course, a strict chronological sequence – Shakespeare moved towards a development from which social questions are excluded. This involves a continuous adjustment of relations with the actors and audience. It is from the point of view of the triple bond, and its extensions into society, that the present chapter examines *Othello*, *Coriolanus* and *Antony and Cleopatra*. In each of these plays can be discerned, in Glynne Wickham's phrase, a progress – beings who degenerate and recover, who sink to beasts or rise to gods. Here too, in distinction from the diffused but masterly exploitation of the open stage in *Macbeth* and *King Lear*, may be seen Shakespeare's response to the varied writers of Jacobean London, in their specific aims; these plays bear the sensitive impress of the work going on around Shakespeare, while in turn his own work specifically influenced the other playwrights. In other words, the social element in the tragedies finds its counterpart in the traffic and intercourse between different writers or audiences implicit in their conception.

Othello, the earliest of the Jacobean tragedies, first performed at court on 1 November 1604 – the start of the winter season – was also chosen nine years later for the wedding festivities of the Princess Elizabeth in February 1613. It had captured the popular stage, where ever since it has maintained itself; no other characters except Hamlet and Falstaff excited as much contemporary comment as the Moor and Iago. Its specific setting was important and it was referred to as 'The Moor of Venice'. The play opens in the city which Shakespeare had already depicted in tragi-comedy rather than in the special sort of 'stage Italy' common to Jacobean dramatists – a territory peopled by characters out of Guicciardini's history, the close world of plotting dukes and palace feuds (as briefly sketched in Chapter 6). Shakespeare's Venice, with its merchant princes and its great fleets ruled the waves in a wide tolerance and freedom which made her at once the first maritime empire and the chief anti-Papal power in matters political. Venice is a symbol of the exotic and the prosperous, a model for Britain. Nevertheless, the play omits from the story of Cyprus all reference to that freeing of the West from the Turks at the Battle of Lepanto, on which King James himself had written a poem.[1] This may, however, be assumed as background.

For in this history, as more obviously in the Roman histories to follow, Shakespeare achieves social relevance through a study of individuals. Othello is an original of his own creation, his Roman heroes are taken from Plutarch's *Lives*, and are not even as fully concerned as in *Julius Caesar* with the nature of the *polis*. Indeed, it has been said that for the Elizabethans the history of Rome was largely a history of its wars and turbulence[2] so that soldiers rather than statesmen might fitly stand for Rome.

Shakespeare was certainly not competing with those 'tragedies of state' produced in these years by his learned rivals, Jonson and Chapman (*Sejanus* had appeared with his own company in 1603 and had not succeeded on the boards). Neither love nor war were likely to appeal to King James, but only a few weeks after the court performance of *Othello*, Queen Anne made her remarkable appearance as the Daughter of the Niger in *The Masque of Blackness*. The shocking, the opulent, and the emancipated stranger combine in the Noble Moor, teller of travellers' tales, as in the African nymph, loaded with pearls, whose orient sheen was to be enhanced by her black paint. In both characters, the initial effect would be one of surprise and shock; Othello belongs, first of all, to the realm of wonder. The sun, where he was born, seems at first to have endowed him with a glowing security, and drawn all dark humours from him (III.iv.27–8). He bears about him the confidence that a soldier, from the nature of his profession, the respect accorded to it, may assume. With more emphasis than tact, the Doge exhorts Brabantio:

> Noble signior,
> If virtue no delighted beauty lack,
> Your son in law is far more fair than black.   (I.iii.288–90)

For the actor, the rôle would make him immediately the most conspicuous figure on stage, his movements and gestures automatically emphasized by his make-up. And here the opening song of *The Masque of Blackness* may be cited in testimony to the powerful but mixed effect – the increase in display, the impulse to self-justification – that black strangers might produce. They bring a new life, release from custom, a new kind of light-in-darkness:

> Sound, sound aloud
> The welcome of the orient flood

Into the west;
Fair Niger, son of great Oceanus,
Now honoured thus,
With all his beauteous race,
Who, though but black in face,
Yet are they bright,
And full of life and light,
To prove that beauty best
Which not the colour but the feature
Assures unto the creature.

Yet, in the act of secret marriage Othello has defied custom; Desdemona, alienating her father by an act of choice, renounces the privileges of her rank,[3] whilst Othello, because he is a stranger, because he is not young, because he is black can never enjoy that full assurance of sound matrimonial authority that a marriage between equals confers. So insecurity is built in to their adventure, their 'storm of fortune'.

Even Anne of Denmark planned a second masque to 'wash an Ethiop white'; when three years later the promise was kept in *The Masque of Beauty*, the exotic and marvellous had to undergo metamorphosis.[4]

For the traditional stage player, a black face had long been sign of a black heart. Even in folk plays the 'Turks' had proved as violent of tongue as they were malicious of spirit; they existed to be overcome by the hero.

In *Titus Andronicus*, Shakespeare had made use of Aaron the Moor's gaiety and relish of his outlaw's freedom to recall the black-visaged devils with whom he is so often compared. Ithamore in *The Jew of Malta* and many another with 'damnation dyed upon his visage' persist as stage figures until Caroline times.[5] All the expected characteristics of this figure are transferred to Iago until in that scene where the two kneel to make their compact, Othello as it were absorbs the character of Iago, learns to speak his language, the language of mistrust and violence.[6] Their pledges 'I am bound to thee for ever' and 'I am your own for ever' carry sinister, even diabolic overtones.

If Iago has been termed 'homo emancipatus a Deo', the whole play is an act of emancipation from stereotypes of every description. The fact that it does not derive from any previous dramatic treatment is itself notable in so inveterate an adaptor as Shakespeare. In its first audience it must have aroused above all the effect of suspense, of novelty. And although the vast Mediterranean is the scene, the moments of greatest power come in the scenes of intimacy, so that the new closed theatre could eventually take this play.

Affairs of state appear indeed, but marginally; metaphysical or cosmic sanctions are also indirect (as in the scene of the vow, just mentioned). To some readers, to Bradley, for instance, this limited the play's power: but the refusal to accept such traditional sanctions is in itself a sign of artistic control, of mastery, comparable with the 'pagan' assumptions of *King Lear*.[7] If the play is not wholly geared to the intimacies of private love, yet to Granville Barker it seemed 'a tragedy without a meaning and that is the ultimate horror of it'. Should Desdemona speak the right word or Othello ask the right question, the misunderstanding could be resolved, and in the brothel scene they come very close. Because they have chosen each other – and each stresses this at different times – thereby forfeiting their old freedom and status, they become utterly interdependent. 'If she be false, O then, Heaven mocks itself!' Othello sees two alternating images – 'Dian's visage' and another

> begrim'd and black
> As my own face. (III.iii.352–3)

and in the agony of an uncertainty totally new to him thinks death preferable to this horror; whilst Desdemona, whose love is wholly unconditional, refuses in spite of all the evidence to forgo her image of Othello. 'His scorn I approve'. . . . 'Commend me to my kind lord'. Her murder is not the most atrocious act of any on the Jacobean scene (Chapman in *Bussy D'Ambois*, had recently shown his heroine being put to the rack) but because of its intimate setting, it is the most harrowing; and Voltaire, in his *Lettres Philosophes* cites it first in his catalogue of Shakespeare's faults.

All this vindicates the theatrical elasticity, the challenging ambiguity of the tragedy; the amplitude of Shakespeare's original conception is attested by the possibility of relating it at once to the splendours of the royal masque and to the humble and conservative form of domestic drama. Its finely-meshed movement generates a dynamism that is foreign to the single 'revelation' of the masque; but this is joined to an opulence and splendour precluded in domestic tragedy, a form, however, notable for plot suspense.

As a mercenary soldier, Othello belongs to a new profession, which was evolving its own code in an alternative society. The clear chain of command, and its protective securities were akin to the traditional ones of a religious order or a trade gild. Othello's most assured relations are with his officers; in this society a woman has no place, and when Desdemona joins it, she finds the romance of campaigning, like the romance of exploring, to which it is akin, involves storms, night alarms, quick responses to sharply veering orders.

Indeed, Othello's generalship is of the familiar modern kind which consists in leading an expedition that is almost at once re-called by the politicians, carrying out the maintenance of discipline and civil government in a colonial outpost which is a pawn of greater forces. His exposed command means that his expedition-ary force, an organized yet mobile group (standing armies came later), like a band of colonists, carries its own structure along. It does not grow out of the soil. This is why all must trust each other, as a group always on the alert, as a team of pioneers, a ship's crew, must trust; and the utmost horror his imagination can picture is his wife copulating with every member of his own command, 'pioneers and all'.

Desdemona brings with her a certain degree of natural authority as the daughter of a Venetian senator, even though she has been cast off,[8] and this makes her interference in the appointment of officers at once natural to her and more unsettling to Othello – who in the promotion of Cassio, a Florentine mercenary, had ignored the pleas of Venetians for Iago, the native-born.

In revenge, Iago insinuates his own special knowledge of Venice, and in particular his identification of Venetian noble women with the celebrated Venetian courtesans, a great inter-national attraction to visitors. It is precisely among these that in the brothel scene Othello places her

> Cry you mercy, then!
> I took you for that cunning whore of Venice
> That married with Othello. (IV.ii.88–90)

All this, of course, is not presented as information; it is the means of evolving the action by which Othello is destroyed. The love of Desdemona had created a new world for him (he swears 'by the world' that he thinks she is honest, and thinks she is not). Like Othello, Iago too is a soldier of Fortune, an adventurer, prepared to change the settled course of things, only for a different purpose. Othello the nomad has carried about with him the shining and noble simplicity of a nature fulfilled, whilst Iago carries only an obsessive need to play the puppeteer. The military bond of comradeship can be adapted to this diseased purpose, for Iago is, as it were, the cancer-growth of this new society. Penalties, like the offence, will be secret, though Othello finds himself incapable of blemishing Desdemona's physical beauty – it overwhelms his suspicion more than once. For at every level he is susceptible, suggestible. Othello's love and praise of his first world surges up in lament as his farewell to it (III.iii.347–57). The plumed troops, the pride, pomp and circumstance, the very noise of the guns confer deep content. Strangely, an admission of weakness slips out, they make ambition virtue, they 'counterfeit' the power of heaven. His 'occupation', his daily food, the common beauty of his life, wherever it leads him – rather like a player's life – has lost its magnetism

> Far the calling bugles hollo,
>   High the screaming fife replies,
> Gay the lines of scarlet follow;
>   Woman bore me, I will rise.[9]

Iago's 'mine of sulphur' has exploded, destroying trust in his men as well as his wife – and Othello with it. 'That's he which was Othello', he answers to a question; and he looks back at both lives lost. This is what Eliot termed 'cheering himself up', as he re-creates across an immense gulf, and in the past tense, the measured gravity of his former self[10] to give another, and a final farewell.

The new world Desdemona created for him, as he for her ('each hath one and is one' as Donne had put it) had been a 'universe of two'; and to be discarded thence was for Othello to lose the whole core of his being. He falls to pieces and out of the shards of rage, violence, and grief can reassemble himself only when, having lost one sword, he finds the second. Then both worlds, though totally lost, reassemble, unattainable, resurrected, vindicated.

In depicting this universe of two Shakespeare brought within the public theatre that uniquely delicate and searching exploration of the relationship of love for which he had developed the sensitive and precise language of the Sonnets, a language which itself is full of images of state and war.[11]

Othello was written a decade later than the Sonnets; the transposition brings into dramatic form both the positive and negative aspects of that deeply personal utterance.

> Lord of my love to whom in vassalage
> Thy merit hath my duty strongly knit   (Sonnet 26)

might be the voice of Desdemona; the anguish of the double image – 'Lilies that fester smell far worse than weeds' – might be that of Othello; the nausea and disgust in the sonnets to the dark lady represent Iago.

> When my love swears that she is made of truth,
> I do believe her, though I know she lies   (Sonnet 138)

ends with the pun that maddens Othello

> Therefore I lie with her and she with me,
> And in our faults by lies we flatter'd be.

Iago, as Bradley notes, broods over his plans in the manner of an artist 'drawing at first only an outline, puzzled how to fix more than the main idea, and gradually seeing it develop'. Fortune favours him over the handkerchief – although 'his catastrophe comes out wrong and his piece was ruin'd'.

The agent of his catastrophe is Emilia who transplants into this new military society the old fidelity of the household servant and companion. Though earthy enough, in the moment of her death she echoes the song of Desdemona, and in the dying cadence of the Willow Song rises out of clamour and brawl to the special spiritual region that music invokes. Emilia gives that fidelity to her mistress that her husband simulated. All three deaths are acts of witness; Emilia's is very necessary, to seal the new society as more than a universe of two. 'No way but this', says Othello; it is a 'way', not merely an exit. The ending must be felt as triumphal; the ritual of the kiss is spousal, as it appears also at the climax of the famous and popular English domestic tragedy that had immediately preceded Shakespeare's. This had been produced by Worcester's Men at the Rose on the Bankside, neighbouring the Globe, and provides a mirror-image for Shakespeare's climax.

> With this kiss I wed thee once again

is Frankford's farewell to his repentant wife on her deathbed. The self-inflicted death of the guilty partner restores this marriage.

Thomas Heywood's *A Woman Killed with Kindness* (1603) is worth contrasting at some length with *Othello* since, whilst the attitude of the wronged husband is very far from the stage stereo-type of revenge, the social setting and assumptions are completely traditional and familiar. It is set among the country gentry. The marriage, which opens the play, had been one of sympathy; the pair had a common background, and Mistress Frankford's many accomplishments – her singing to the lute in particular – remain as tormenting memories for her husband when her adultery is estab-lished. This is a sin not only against her husband but against the corporate household of which he is the patriarchal head. His ser-vant, Nicholas, who plays the rôle that Iago merely assumes, in his indignation shows how the whole community is destroyed. As with drawn sword he is pursuing his false friend, Frankford is stayed by another servant, a maid whom he thanks for this inter-vention. The banishment of Mistress Frankford to a remote manor house is carried out by Frankford, acting as the head of his house-hold, before witnesses, after retiring to deliberate. He tempers justice with mercy. 'Hear thy sentence', he says to Mistress Frank-ford – who expects death and begs only not to be mutilated. The frame of unquestioned duty and of piety sustains Frankford, justify-ing what have been termed the 'statements' of the play, its flat enunciation of virtue and duty in the opening scenes.

At the revival at the National Theatre in 1971, the necessary codes of behaviour that social responsibility enforces were brought out in contrast with the human impulses of shame and grief that inform the main scenes of this play – the bedchamber scenes. The monstrous and inexplicable nature of the betrayal has been confessed by the man – the woman discovers the nature of the act only *after* it is done. Frankford's approach at midnight calls up something of the feeling of Faustus' last hour, for he knows the irrevocable nature of the division to be made between two who had become one flesh. The divorce will be eternal.[12] He counts over the several keys – the gate, the hall, the withdrawing chamber, and last the bedchamber 'Once my terrestrial heaven, now my earth's hell' – and after the entry he returns with the cry

> O God, O God that it were possible
> To undo things done; to call back yesterday...
> But O, I talk of things impossible
> And cast beyond the moon.   (Scene 13, 52–64)

To his wife he says 'It was thy hand cut two hearts out of one', as he sends her away with everything she possessed; for he would not have 'a bodkin or a cuff' to act as a reminder. When her lute is sent after her, she sings a lament before breaking it upon the wheel of her coach. The immense weight lent to small objects and actions is part of the mourning for a common life disrupted. When all the friends of the marriage ceremony, reassembled for the death-bed reconciliation ('My wife, the mother of my pretty babes/Both these lost names I do restore thee back'), express a wish to die with the repentant wife, Nicholas characteristically dissents:

> I'll sigh and sob, but, by my faith, not die.

This realistic touch may serve to measure the distance from the final scene of *Othello*. Within Heywood's play itself, there is a further contrast in the rigid and preposterous adherence to codes of chastity, honour and restitution in the sub-plot. This contrasts schematically with the main action, but serves only to throw into relief the warm spontaneity of Frankford's feelings, controlled as they are by the limits of his station and its duties.

Heywood's plays of adventure represent the other side of what he contributed to the Jacobean stage; some exotic scenes in Fez or the Azores – which are later than *Othello* – combine love and war with much more familiar ingredients than belong to the Red Bull. But with *Othello* Shakespeare had displaced the relatively fixed and emblematic form of social relationships, and his younger contemporaries proceeded to develop from him theatrical stereotypes of a new sort – the soldier in love, tragic jealousy in the baroque or mannerist style.[13]

The *development* of character through interaction, substitution of images, and through the sheer accidents of Fortune, in a continuous process, may be compared with the new spatial effects of perspective on the court stage, the imposition of order and proportion on the visual scene (which in this play is one of relative simplicity). The perspectives come from within the characters. John Bayley has observed of *Othello*:

It is one of the properties of the greatest dramatic poetry to suggest complexities of character which are beyond the scope of the most exacting discursive analysis, which cover the expanse of the work like ripples on the water and lose their nature if caught up in the hand...the power of creating contradictory glimpses of a personality and holding them in suspension without the smallest touch of defining control, so that they offer to the imagination...a challenge and yet... a luminous completeness.[14]

This capacity led Shakespeare eventually to develop in two directions – that of the archaic romance and that of the biographic Roman tragedies of the years 1607–9.

The first decade of the seventeenth century saw a number of Roman plays, and other tragedies of state[15] – some, as in the case of Chapman's double play on Byron, almost contemporary in subject. This play, which can be dated in the same year as Shakespeare's *Coriolanus*, depicts a heroic soldier who, as the saviour of his country, claims that he is not bound by the laws that tie other men; eventually he turns against France and plots with her enemies, for which he suffers death by law.

> O of what contraries consists a man!
> Of what impossible mixture! Vice and virtue,
> Corruption and eternesse, at one time,

And in one subject, let together loose!
We have not any strength but weakens us,
No greatness but doth crush us into air...

(*Byron's Tragedy* v.iii.189–94)

Byron is self-destroyed, yet his greatness somehow unfits him for the ordinary relationships of the world, being directed to some absolute conditions of *virtù*. A Tamburlaine trapped in a modern court, his story implies that it is ultimately a flaw in the social order, not within the individual, that concerns Chapman.[16]

Nobles in the audience might well have met the leading characters in this play, which being both contemporary and hortatory was severely censored – both in the scenes at the English court and at that of Henry of Navarre. This bold venture, as usual, came from the choristers' theatre; but Chapman was a personal servant of the Prince of Wales, and Henry of Navarre was the hero and model of the young Prince.

A play about a great soldier, to be performed by one talented youth leading a troupe of boys, needed action and speech of an emblematic kind; and the great speeches of Byron and of his enemies replace any stage activity. When Chapman's earlier play of the man larger than life, overwhelmed by nobodies, *Bussy D'Ambois*, was taken over by Shakespeare's own company, the many revisions which it underwent are to be partly attributed to Nat Field, for whom as a youth of seventeen, the part had been created,[17] who grew up with the part and trained others in the acting of it. It became a show piece for the later stage. Jonson's *Sejanus*, in which Shakespeare himself had acted (perhaps as Tiberius), had on the contrary, failed to please, whilst Jonson himself was cited before the Privy Council.[18] The close intrigue which he had taken from Tacitus, not without telescoping and re-arrangement, showed the snaring of good and evil men alike. The Rome he depicts is a small cage of Iago's, where 'the good have only to die', where Caesar, monster as he is, is already deified, and Sejanus can rise above Caesar: 'At each step, I feel my advanced head/knock out a star in heaven'. Ironic comedy intensifies the corruption of the whole society, as Livia mingles poisonings and cosmetics in the converse with her physician, whilst Tiberius, evading decisions till he has completely unsettled his senate, then delivers them obliquely, leaving ultimate vengeance to be savagely enacted by the Roman mob. Tacitus, the main source, was used politically as a means of showing that Machiavelli's theory *worked*. Between Chapman's Achillean heroes who 'wander about in a dream of greatness' and 'talk to themselves' and the ferocious world of *Realpolitik*, Shakespeare set his own Roman plays; they combine something of the best qualities of vision to be found in Chapman with the ironic exposures of Jonson, but their movement is designed for the Theatre or the great open stage of the Globe.

Their stage history, however, is remarkably different. *Coriolanus* has proved a steady success,[19] whereas *Antony and Cleopatra*, although its magnificence makes it a favourite with readers, defeated even Garrick and, after Dryden's adaptation of *All for Love*, was largely displaced by his version. It has never received the kind of acclaim, even on the modern stage, that has been many times given to *Coriolanus* – not to speak of the latter's adaptation by Brecht.

Coriolanus remains a problem play – it invites the audience to take sides for or against the hero, leaving a wide variety of interpretations open. When acted at the Comédie Française in the nineteen-thirties, the Communists rioted because they thought it a satire on the plebs, and the Fascists because they thought it a satire on dictators. Whatever the reading, the central figure dominates. The unity and simplicity bestowed by a close following of Plutarch was stronger than could be found in Renaissance biographies which were still emblematic, presenting a mirror of virtue or of vice – a Philip Sidney or a Richard III.

Coriolanus is an early Roman; he is found in the fantastic situation of confronting single-handed the whole forces of besieged Corioli, locked inside their city's gates (a thoroughly old-fashioned Elizabethan siege action). Many times he is compared with the god Mars, but his most 'Roman' act is to turn back from his native city and go to face his enemies, whom he has balked of their expected revenge. The figure of Antony seems also to expand till it seems, in the vision of Cleopatra after his death, to fill the whole universe, to become a cosmic power, like something out of mythology[20] – not merely Roman but imperial.

Yet each hero is placed in a social context – Coriolanus in his banishment suffers a kind of mutilation. Plutarch had told the story as an example of the dangers attendant on bad education; the soldier had lacked a father's hand, and so had grown up rash, choleric, haughty, a bungler who imperils the whole structure of plebs and patricians by his combination of nobility and intransigence. Volumnia, who exults in her son as a killing machine, when he has indeed turned into a kind of 'engine',[21] kneels before him in the suppliant posture more becoming to one of the mothers of Corioli, those 'mothers who lack sons'.

He is a young man, perhaps in his early twenties, and to his General represents the ultimate value of war:

> A carbuncle entire, as big as thou art,
> Were not so rich a jewel... (I.iv.55–6)

Whilst his political enemies object:

> You speak o' th' people
> As if you were a god to punish; not
> A man of their infirmity... (III.i.80–2)

Later his closest admirer excuses this same quality

> His nature is too noble for the world.
> He would not flatter Neptune for his trident
> Or Jove for's power to thunder (III.i.255–7)

whilst at other times Menenius, cool and deflationary, can mock the man he almost worships as a god. Coriolanus' speech about the necessity of taking any voice in government away from the common people lest they destroy themselves as well as the patricians – 'dangerous physic for Rome', he knows, but necessary – is deadly serious (and not so different from theories of government to be heard in England) but it is not for the market place or the Senate. This tirade against the 'rule of ignorance' alternates with tantrums that are frankly comic – Bernard Shaw was to term this play the best of Shakespeare's comedies. 'Mildly be it! Mildly!' are ejaculations in a tone that portends the very worst.

The crowd, with all its violence, displays a wit and shrewdness that can sometimes give Coriolanus his answer; there is everywhere a forthright directness of speech. 'I would they were abed', says a patrician after the uproar against Coriolanus' speech, to which Menenius retorts

> I would they were in Tiber! What the vengeance!
> Could he not speak 'em fair? (III.i.262–3)[22]

Menenius' fable of the Body Politic implies that severance, exile, is death. Coriolanus, who unlike Cordelia, is too ready to heave his heart in his mouth, departs with all the right stoic utterances as he's 'whooped' out of his city into exile.

Without further sign, he appears among the enemy (this is how the Duke of Byron relapsed). He capitulates in the end not to the Body Politic but to

> the honour'd mould
> Wherein this trunk was fram'd (v.iii.22–3)

In acknowledging the parental bond of nature he is divided again from the Volscian Body Politic where he had been celebrating a kind of marriage with their army. For in Rome he had no friends of his own age and no faithful servants. He does not seek relations with his peers; he does not admit any.

This climax of the play, where his mother successfully presents her tableau of suppliance, including the pugnacious child who is 'like him by chance', scenically achieves the archaic simplicity of *King Lear* itself; and it culminates in silence. This is the moment when Coriolanus is reborn, when his lust for dominance is killed by love. Coriolanus' strength has weakened him, his greatness is to crush him, as Aufidius observes:

> One fire drives out one fire; one nail, one nail;
> Rights by right falter, strengths by strengths do fail (IV.vi.54–5)

He does not, like Othello, carry his own world round with him; his most tragic, most ignorant boast – though splendid in itself – is '*I* banish *you*!' He needs to be the only cock in the basket, and this is the service – championship, not leadership – he can give because as Aufidius sums him up, he is proud, maladroit in seizing chances,

inflexibly given to military absolutism, to obedience and command. Coriolanus, however, knows himself at some points; he
knows that though reputation and honour are conferred by others,
yet 'I had rather be their servant in my way/Than sway with them
in theirs'. He angrily shuns acknowledgement, yet equally he
reacts angrily and quite automatically to a taunt; this is known to
the tribunes, to the Volscian Aufidius and to his mother. He will
not act a part – the 'show' in the market place offers 'a part that I
shall blush in acting' and shall never 'discharge to the life'. He
taunts his audience 'I will practice the insinuating nod' – but his
greeting to his family after exile, when he had hoped to stand 'as
if a man were author of himself and knew no other kin', is to
'melt' at one glance and one word from Virgilia.

> Like a dull actor now,
> I have forgot my part...   (v.iii.40–1)

Volumnia, however, has not forgotten hers; she can destroy his
stance or standing as 'the author of himself'. 'This fellow had a
Volscian to his mother.' Both actors have to be good at getting
inside a part.

Roman Stoicism then alternates with indulgence of passion,
oratory with silence, Coriolanus' irresistible power (when in action
he can draw even the Volscians to him quite magnetically)[23] goes
with a weakness that allows everyone to manipulate him. In this,
indeed, he resembles the crowd whom he despises. And the actor
must let this be *seen*.

The balance between Coriolanus' faults and virtues, and the
ambiguity of his opponents' case against him, is fairly held throughout the play. Jonson could only offer in a tyrant's Rome, by way
of a positive, the suicide of Silius – who before stabbing himself
speaks his own justification very rhetorically. All Jonson's parts
ask is presence and eloquence.

> Silius hath not placed
> His guards within him, against Fortune's spite,
> So weakly but he can escape your grip,
> That are but hands of Fortune   (*Sejanus*, III.i.321–4)

Coriolanus capitulates in a way that contradicts the stereotype of

Roman inflexibility, the stark inflexibility which Volumnia had cultivated and which at first he strives to present to her. It was in fact, as Plutarch implies, a woman's image of the masculine – violent, extreme, overdrawn; but the cultivation of this 'Roman' mask had been the price of maternal love.[24] (The actor therefore must bring this insight to performance.) The secret self behind the mask is the theme of T. S. Eliot's two poems on *Coriolanus*, with their application of his story to modern history.

The characteristic public preoccupation of Jacobean times was, as has already been suggested, with constitutional conflicts, and to this end the study of history became of general interest to the intelligent part of the audience. Views as absolute as those of Coriolanus could be found in the Elizabethan Sir Thomas Smith:

Day labourers, poor husbandmen, yea, merchants or retailers which have no free land, copyholders and all artificers...have no voice nor authority in the commonwealth, and no account is to be made of them but only to be ruled.[25]

The views of Sir Robert Filmer in *Patriarcha* have already been cited, and to his may be added those of his contemporary, Sir Thomas Aston:

The primates, the nobiles, with the minores nobiles, the gentry consult and dispose the rules of government; the plebeians submit to and obey them.[26]

Shakespeare and his audience would be aware that in the earliest days of Rome, soldiership was co-terminous with citizenship and the government of the state with that of the city. Life in England was more complex than this. If corn riots in the Midlands are sometimes held to be reflected in this play, the livery companies of London held stocks and sold them to citizens as the need arose.[27] England could, however, learn from earliest history. This view was held very clearly by the Prince of Wales; for him Raleigh, a prisoner in the Tower, was writing his *History of the World*, in a mood of scepticism, and Sir Clement Edmondes enlarged his *Observations* on Caesar's Commentaries. For him Chapman translated Homer; Bacon described him as 'fond of antiquity and arts, and a favourer of learning, though rather in the honour he paid to it than in the time he spent upon it', whilst a more popular authority declared 'Arms had his heart, where Love had scarce his

heel'. His reactions to marriage were ironic and decidedly negative. It has been mentioned (Chapter 6, p. 114) that it might be
possible, instead of seeking images of the Prince in the romances
(in Florizel, for example) to see some reflection of his stronger
tastes and interests in these 'tragedies of state'.

Coriolanus neither reflects contemporary events, as Chapman
did, nor studies political intrigue in the corridors of power, as did
Sejanus; but its social disposition of forces and its explanation of
conflicting systems in terms of personal relationships goes far
beyond what could at that time have been formulated politically.
Shakespeare, by sensitive response to pressures from his theatre
and audience, had produced a work of strict political relevance.[28]
But of course it was to be Chapman and Jonson who were proposed as the two literary members of King James's projected
Academy (Shakespeare, in any case, by that time was dead).

Antony and Cleopatra is not in the same way a play of political
debate. Though Antony may be placed among the flawed heroes,
no one has really preferred Octavius Caesar and his sister,[29]
although she has all the virtues of Virgilia.

C. L. Barber terms it a festive tragedy; it presents an open situation, which has many elements of comedy; it is moving towards
the romances, where the tragic aspect is swallowed up, digested,
made part of something else. On some readings, *Antony and
Cleopatra* moves 'beyond tragedy' as, in a very different way,
Timon of Athens had begun within one dimension and moved into
another.[30] The images of love and war take precedence over
matters of state, which merely supply the scale of action. Cleopatra
and, by her action, Antony, triumph over Caesar.

The sympathy of the spectator is encouraged by maximum
response and minimum didactic judgment. In the 'tragedies of
state', spectators are less concerned with the characters as individuals than with their heroic, superhuman response to intolerable
situations.[31] Chapman's heroes have always some cloudy supernatural greatness which makes mere events inadequate to express
their spirit.

In *Sejanus*, Jonson had promised a play 'high and aloof', and so it remains.³² 'Is there not something more than to be Caesar?' asks Sejanus (v.i.13) at the towering height that immediately precedes his fall, and the spectator's attitude is fixed. In *Antony and Cleopatra* the variety of points of view, the contradictions and paradoxes mean that strong identification alternates with cool detachment. All the characters vary; Enobarbus, though deflating the claims of Egypt, does not stand unambiguously for Rome; until the final scene, Cleopatra's maids reflect her laxest side. The lovers are proud, they know their supremacy – yet Antony must suffer the shame of cowardice in the face of the enemy.

Both plays, however, are ruled by the goddess Fortune. In Jonson's she is shown finally averting her face from Sejanus; in Shakespeare Antony's good and evil Fortunes, the fair and dark aspects of his Roman career are embodied in Octavia and Cleopatra, the gypsy. The fortune-telling scene (I.ii) introduces the theme lightly; but his followers turn briskly from Pompey's 'palled fortunes' at the one moment of political crisis when he laughs Fortune away. Antony may scorn her blows (III.xi.74–5) but he lives to salute Caesar as 'lord of his Fortunes' and at his final defeat cries 'Fortune and Antony part here' (IV.xii.18–19). Cleopatra whose fortunes are 'mingled with his' (IV.xiv.24) reduces her to a 'false huswife' with a wheel (IV.xv.44); at last, since 'Not being Fortune, he's but Fortune's knave' she can despise the victor; ''Tis paltry to be Caesar' (v.ii.1–4). She recreates her own greatness, knowing it is lost.

The mutable plebs do not appear; they have been replaced by the even more mutable element of Cleopatra herself, the gypsy queen, who has been transformed from the faithful and dignified princess of Daniel or the Countess of Pembroke's plays into the wild yet sophisticated dark lady of 'Alsatia'; she not only shares the drama but dominates the last act entirely. The Sonnets are again recalled but in a way very different from that in *Othello*.

Of course Rome and Egypt, bureaucracy and household loyalties are contrasted. The variety, the uncertainty, the *trompe l'oeil* of this play, including its ritual ending, seem to transmute the splendour of a courtly masque. We see satiric revels on Pompey's barge, undermined, as were court revels in other plays, by the risk of treachery; this is followed immediately by the noble Roman show of 'Ventidius as it were in triumph with Silius and other Romans, officers and soldiers, the dead body of Pacorus borne before him'. (III.i). There is the more mysterious invisible pageantry of the subterranean music with the bewildered soldiers following it (IV.iii). What is held before us also, but does not occur, is Antony with his pleached arms, bending down his corrigible neck as he follows Caesar's chariot in Rome. Before his death Antony expounds the pompous and baroque pageant of his life against the whole macrocosm:

> Sometimes we see a cloud that's dragonish;
> A vapour sometimes like a bear or lion,
> A tower'd citadel, a pendant rock,
> A forked mountain or blue promontory
> With trees upon 't that nod unto the world
> And mock our eyes with air. Thou hast seen these signs;
> They are black vesper's pageants...
> Even with a thought
> The rack dislimns and makes it indistinct,
> As water is in water...
> My good knave Eros, now thy captain is
> Even such a body; here I am Antony,
> Yet cannot hold this visible shape, my knave.   (IV.xiv.2–14)

Having explored its effects, having accepted that it was not for him, Shakespeare has here fully digested the masque, brought it into relation with his works as they were to develop over the remaining four or five years of his working life. 'Our revels now are ended' – there is almost an anticipation of Prospero's words here.

Yet, whilst appearing so easy, the play compresses and shapes the narrative of North's Plutarch; whilst close verbally, it alters balance and emphasis. However much the strength of the work may seem to lie in its negative capability – some have asked if it is tragedy, comedy or history – the total effect is governed by a shaping spirit of imagination, Coleridge's esemplastic power, although Dr Johnson could find neither 'art of connection' nor 'care of disposition'.

A systole and diastole that seem to run through Shakespeare's work, balancing for example, *Julius Caesar* and *Troilus and Cressida* against *Hamlet*, *Macbeth* against *King Lear*, balance his two late Roman plays. Antony is old; here it is Caesar who is scorned as the young Roman boy; but he is tested against the comic-ironic perceptions of Enobarbus – a character of Shakespeare's invention – as Coriolanus is against Menenius. The severest test of all is reserved for Cleopatra, who has to emerge from her tragi-comic encounter with the clown to play a queenly finale. Four times Tragedy must tell Comedy to leave the stage. (Whilst in *Coriolanus*, the player's rôle was condemned.) Even in Plutarch, Antony was noted for a masquer and reveller. The accents of North, which are also disapproving, must have touched a sensitive nerve in Shakespeare. In Rome Antony's banquets and drunken feasts 'offended the nobles', he took a player for his mistress, 'and himself passed away the time in hearing foolish plays, or marrying these players, tumblers, jesters and such sorts of people'.[33] When Antony seized Pompey's house he filled it with 'tumblers, antic dancers, juglers, players and drunkards'; in Athens he was flocked to by musicians, tumblers, minstrels and wild Bacchantes, so that they called him Bacchus; with Cleopatra his 'childish sports and idle pastimes increased' but the Alexandrians 'liked of this jollity, saying very gallantly and wisely; that Antonius showed them a comical face, to wit a merry countenance; and the Romans a tragical face, to say, a grim look'. Even at Samos, before Actium, players, tumblers, minstrels and jesters were commanded to assemble so that the streets were full of them. Later, ominous signs of his defeat were that the image of Bacchus in the theatre at Athens fell, and the temple of Hercules was burnt – these two being the gods nearest to Antony;[34] Cleopatra was already ex-perimenting with poisons and the revels became a pledge of readiness to die together. She plays her death scene as conscious drama, a repetition of the river pageant when she sailed to meet Antony; Charmian accepts her part in this triumph, adjusting the crown to remove any slight blemish from its silent pretensions: – (Cleopatra is wearing the crown of a kingdom now ruled by Rome; it belongs to the Romans as do even her robes). 'I'll mend it and then play'.

The great description of the water pageant earlier may recall the actual ceremonial pageants in which Queen Elizabeth I sailed upon the Thames.[35] Within the play what had been created by the poetry of Enobarbus in description, has finally to be recognized and outdone upon the stage itself, with 'properties' whose virtue had passed.

The element of masquing had allowed the lovers a great variety of rôles, and had been the subject of ironic comment. Each of them conceives a part for the other to play, sometimes grandiose, sometimes shameful. Antony had dressed in Cleopatra's robes, she had worn his sword. Comparing him with one of the trick perspective paintings, she says

> Though he be painted one way like a Gorgon,
> The other way's a Mars.

His followers and Caesar's vie in mockery; if Caesar is 'the Jupiter of men' then Antony is 'the god of Jupiter' (III.ii.9–11). He is also a Bacchus and Hercules; Cleopatra played both Isis and Venus. These are masquerades. The 'Eastern Star' is deified only when the body – the 'lass unparalleled' – is clay.

But in his poem *La Charité* (1572) Ronsard had described how, as Marguerite of Navarre was dancing on a hill, she drew down one of the Graces who for the space of the dance became incarnate in her; Daniel had said as much of Queen Anne (see above, Chapter 4, p. 57). And on another occasion, the Queen's black hue was praised because it was never subject to varying – no greying of the hair, no change in death. The gypsy queen still 'looked like sleep' to Caesar.

> All which are arguments to prove how far
> Their beauties conquer in great beauty's war,
> And more, how near divinity they be,
> That stand from passion and decay so free.[36]

At Antony's death, Cleopatra had assumed a heartbroken play – 'here's sport indeed!' – but by dying 'in the high Roman fashion' she fixes for ever the image of greatness and of grace, transforms the past and establishes the story as heroic; she dethrones the goddess Fortune by one act of constancy.

Something of the effect of such a death had been anticipated in Marston's *Sophonisba* (1605–6), a play which has been mentioned briefly for its sensational variety of events. Sophonisba's Carthaginian husband, deceived by a trick, vowed to hand her over to the Roman Scipio yet also to guard her honour; she drank poison, and so he presented only her dead body

> Look, Scipio, see what hard shift we make
> To keep our vows; here, take, I yield her to thee,
> And Sophonisba, I keep vow, thou still art free.

The warrior's crown, robe and triumphal wreath given by Scipio to Massinissa are then by him bestowed to adorn his dead Queen.

The Roman warrior is for Shakespeare a hand-to-hand fighter, and he is defeated by planners and politicians, men who – unlike Coriolanus – are opportunists. The young fighting man, the old sworder, belong to the class of Hotspur and Hector. *Othello* does not use the obvious heroic occasion – Lepanto – even for an image: the hero botches his attack on Iago.

In Antony and Cleopatra, war is largely a memory and a tableau. Antony can still lead his men; he does not campaign. He arms, then finally disarms for ever; 'The long day's task is done', and the 'royal occupation' in which he had toiled 'like a husbandman' is concluded by Caesar, a swift and excellent strategist, not a fighter, who aims at universal peace. As in *Othello*, the dying speeches merge the hero with cosmic nature. The same impulse can be felt in Chapman's *Tragedy of Byron*. War's instincts to resist have to be subdued in Byron, the towering figure who cannot fit into his world, whose 'perspective picture' shows him degenerating so painfully that even his valour is smirched, yet who remains a giant condemned by a 'politic' state:

> And so, farewell for ever! Never more
> Shall any hope of my revival see me;
> Such is the endless exile of dead men.
> Summer succeeds the spring, autumn the summer;
> The frosts of winter the fall'n leaves of autumn;
> All these and all fruits in them yearly fade,
> And every year return; but cursed man
> Shall never more renew his vanished face.
>
> (*Tragedy of Byron*, v.iv.245–52)

In *Antony and Cleopatra*, the immense range of setting has prepared for such cosmic enlargement at death. The forty-three different scenes, which are really continuous, exploit the old battle technique of the Elizabethan platform stage; indeed, there are even older traces of continuous staging.[37] Fittingly, the greatest mystery remains the staging of the scenes in Cleopatra's monument – for a monument built of words and deeds is essentially what is being presented in the whole last act.

No later writers could exploit this epic theatre. The regular structure of Fletcher's *The False One* (King's Men, 1619–23) – which challenges *Julius Caesar* and *Antony and Cleopatra* – is as limited as Dryden's regular *All for Love*, with its consistent and virtuous characters.[38] Both serve only to show by contrast the scale of Shakespeare's work, which remains virtually unplayable on a proscenium stage. As Coleridge observes, 'it impresses the notion of a giant strength...owing to [the] manner in which it is sustained throughout – that he *lives* in and through the play'.[39] Even Dr Johnson, who did not really like the play – he thought the 'feminine arts' of Cleopatra 'too low' – admits it 'keeps curiosity always busy and the passions always interested. The continual hurry of the action, the variety of the incidents and the quick succession of one personage to another, call the mind forward without intermission from the first act to the last.'[40] In other words, the physical activity of the old open stages has been absorbed into a poetic activity, so that language, characterization, structure, work on the *assumptions* of such a stage, to create a wholly new, flexible, intricate poetic instrument.

All three tragedies of love and war culminate in what the old theatres had so enjoyed – a prolonged, eloquent ritualistic death scene: the double ending of *Antony and Cleopatra* gives a prolonged *Liebestod* through the entire fifth act.[41]

Roman suicide as a mode of self-affirmation was among the most popular conventions of the Jacobean stage, as has already been seen; discussions on the ethics of suicide proceeded, and in 1608 Donne wrote his *Biathanatos*, whilst Chapman in *Caesar and Pompey*, with Plutarch's *Moralia* open before him as he wrote, boldly advanced in Cato's justification of suicide the most unstoical doctrine of the resurrection of the body.

Love and war: 'Othello', 'Coriolanus', 'Antony and Cleopatra'

Shakespeare's last and most ritualistic treatment of love, war and death is to be found in his very latest work, *Two Noble Kinsmen*.[42] This bears all the marks of a Blackfriars play, and dates from the time when the gradual predominance of the new form of staging was already beginning to be perceptible.[43] The two late Roman plays, which have been termed by T. S. Eliot Shakespeare's most undoubted artistic successes, rely upon the physical structure of the older stage.

10

ENTRY TO ROMANCE:
PERICLES AND *CYMBELINE*

In a lecture on the Sonnets, C. L. Barber[1] enquired what Shakespeare did with his aggression – the boundless generosity and self-immolation of the Sonnets prompting such a demand. His answer was that Shakespeare created Iago; he created Cordelia – and killed her. Perhaps in expiation he had afterwards to create Marina, Perdita, and, most distanced of all, Miranda, whose perils are shared rather than created by her father.

Like *King Lear* and *Timon*, *Pericles* lies at the verge of the articulate, where man is at the extremity of his being, and words fail. It may have been written as early as 1606, and it seems to lie between the tragedies and the romances. Shakespeare is reaching back a long way in his own literary life, to the story he had set for a 'frame' of *The Comedy of Errors*, the old Hellenistic romance of Apollonius of Tyre that had added extra wonder to his Latinate farce.

The frame for *Pericles* is provided by its 'Presenter', the ghost of John Gower, Chaucer's contemporary, who had told the tale in *Confessio Amantis*; embedded in his tale are other tales whose effects can be seen as magical. By telling her own life history, Marina revives Pericles from a state of death-in-life. By confessing his own life story at Diana's altar he then regains his lost wife. In contrast, the riddle of Antiochus by indirection confesses his incest with his daughter – but in a form which enables him to destroy her suitors. The murderer Leontine ignores Marina's story of her birth, which she recounts to him as an old tale told by her nurse.

Introducing the scene at Marina's tomb, Gower apologizes that one language only is used in 'each several climate where our scene seems to live' (IV.iv.6–7), recalling the convention of speech 'in

sundry languages' as promised – but not provided – by old Hieron-
ymo in *The Spanish Tragedy*. Gower himself speaks in Shakespeare's attempt at Middle English. In the Stratford production of
1969, speaking a mixture of Chaucerian English and modern
Welsh intonation, he recalled Owen Glendower, who may have
contributed something to Shakespeare's fancy about the narrative
spell of the old minstrels. He continually appeals to his audience to
piece out the story as he 'stands i' the gaps' to instruct them.

What cannot be told is conveyed by music, the regular accom-
paniment to manifestations of the supernatural in this theatre;
Cerimon's 'rough and woeful' music recalls the tranced queen to
life (music had been used to revive Lear). Earlier, looking on the
daughter of Antiochus with knowledge of her incestuous secret,
Pericles heard 'so harsh a chime' that Hell would dance at it – this
infernal music was known in earliest plays, but in Jacobean times
it doubtless took more sophisticated forms.[2]

Himself a musician ('music's master', Simonides called him),
Pericles is revived first by Marina's song, then by her tale. This
leads up to his hearing the heavenly music of the spheres which
heralds the appearance of the goddess Diana. This, then, is a
journey from Hell to Heaven.

Other stage 'languages' invite the audience to participate in
interpretation – shows, combats and dances herald each new stage
of the hero's wanderings or mark his supreme moments of joy or
grief (acclaimed at Tarsus, dancing with his beloved, finding his
daughter's tomb). Each art is 'displayed' by Gower. Pericles' final
dumb show of speechless grief makes him a kind of statue.

Apart from the rows of death's heads which open the play and
the vision of the goddess which heralds its close, however, these
shows are not spectacular, but depend on performance by the
actors. The simplicity of early drama which Shakespeare was
introducing went back beyond the Theatre of James Burbage
where he had practised his craft as a young man. Lydgate described
how in the ancient theatre, dumb actors came out of a tent to mime
while a poet recited from a pulpit; later, presenters carried a staff
which they used to cue in the actors or quell unruly thrusters from
the audience. On the title page of George Wilkins' narrative ver-

sion of the play,[3] Gower appears with such a staff. Heywood was
to use Homer as prologue to his spectacular quartet, *The Four
Ages* (1613) and Shakespeare's leading clown, Armin, wrote a play
in mid-Jacobean times with a presenter, *The Valiant Welshman*
(1615), but the device really belonged to pre-Shakespearean drama
– to Greene chiefly.

The naive conviction of Gower's morality, the confident and
proverbial wisdom of his commentary, speak on the same level
as the folk moralizings of the poor fishermen who rescue Pericles
at Pentapolis, or Gloucester's tenantry, or Cornwall's servants:

> Bad child! Worse father! to entice his own
> To evil should be done by none   (Prologue, 26–8)

> A better prince and benign lord...
> I'll show you those in troubles reign,
> Losing a mite, a mountain gain.   (Prologue to Act II, 3–8)

> In Antiochus and his daughter you have heard
> Of monstrous lust the due and just reward:
> In Pericles, his queen and daughter seen,
> Although assail'd with fortune fierce and keen,
> Virtue preserv'd from fell destructions blast,
> Led on by heaven and crown'd with joy at last.
>
>   (Epilogue, 1–6)

Never a man's thought in the world keeps the roadway better
than Gower's – a shrewd observation on Shakespeare the reader's
part. Yet the effect is to offer a point of view which is not authori-
tative, as it once had been, but is to be scanned from a Jacobean
perspective.

Narrative romance, as told by minstrels, had lured the hearers
into another world, where, as Philip Sidney well knew, a blind
crowder could hold children from play and old men from the
chimney corner. For the rest of the household it offered an escape
from a hard and monotonous existence into a world of endless
adventure. Pericles' adventures take the traditional form of wanderings and of a series of ordeals.

This is a revival, not a survival of Romance. Perhaps it indicates
Shakespeare's own decision to stick to the oral form – the enacted
play-world rather than the world of print, which twice as a young

narrative poet he had assayed and once (on the publication of the Sonnets) had been betrayed to. The first edition of the Sonnets came out in 1609, just as Shakespeare was turning towards Romance; and by that date the Sonnets too must have seemed to belong to another world.

Pericles was an instant success; perhaps, for the apprentices, not so different from Heywood's adventure plays at the Red Bull, but as Gower observed in his prologue, the tale was known by gentle as well as simple

> It hath been sung at festivals
> On ember-eves and holy-ales;
> And lords and ladies in their lives
> Have read it for restoratives. (Prologue, 5–8)

In 1619, *Pericles* was performed at Court for the entertainment of the French Ambassador. It fell into two parts, between which a rich banquet was served in china dishes. On such an occasion, a mere relic of antiquity would not have served, and by 1631, when Jonson termed it a 'mouldy tale', he was himself taking to an imitation of other of Shakespeare's works and soon writing his own mouldy pieces, such as *A Tale of a Tub*. The play continued to be performed in Restoration times.

The indications are that its great success was something of a puzzle to contemporaries. It was compared in popularity with Heywood's *King Edward IV*. Dryden thought its imperfections were due to its being Shakespeare's first play

> Shakespeare's own muse his *Pericles* first bore,
> The Prince of Tyre was elder than the Moor
> (Preface to Charles Davenant's *Circe*, 1677)

whilst earlier, a Caroline defender of the poet records, in order to refute it, an adverse verdict:

> 'Shakespeare, the Plebeian Driller, was
> Founder'd in's *Pericles*, and must not pass'.[4]

The image of 'foundering' in a welter of incongruous events – a child grown to womanhood, many countries and eras traversed, vulgar mirth and stately shows – is the neoclassic orthodox one; to 'drill' means not only to entice or lead aside, but to twirl, whirl or churn around.

The object of romance was to suspend the critical faculties; the audience was meant to reach a state of 'delight' or 'rapture' in which they were 'charmed', a state of being thoroughly immersed and totally overwhelmed. This is the 'delight' that the wise Cerimon discerns in the art of healing

> I hold it ever,
> Virtue and cunning were endowments greater
> Than nobleness and riches; careless heirs
> May the two latter darken and expend,
> But immortality attends the former,
> Making a man a god. (III.ii.25–30)

Cerimon within the play wields the kind of power Prospero was later to command, but of course he does not control the action

> I have...made familiar
> To me and to my aid the blest infusions
> That dwell in vegetives, in metals, stones;
> And I can speak of the disturbances that
> Nature works, and of her cures; which doth give me
> A more content in course of true delight
> Than to be thirsty after tottering honour,
> Or tie my treasure up in silken bags,
> To please the fool and death.[5] (III.ii.35–42)

Perhaps the Doctor of any folk play would claim as much, but not in these words. Gower, who stands outside the tale, had pronounced it 'restorative' too; and when the author of *King Lear* writes a play whose existence centres on and is justified by the recovery of a daughter mourned for dead, the signals seem hopeful. The work is still very largely 'poetry of the gaps'; it has the quality of a dream, of some new glimpse of a power 'more distant than the stars and nearer than the eye'.

The older romances, recited in the hall or inn, were, like drama, an art of collaborative response. By the subtle blending of many arts, Shakespeare's last plays achieved a Delphic and oracular virtue, a visionary certitude that belongs to 'the play beyond the play'. Milton was later to write of the state of 'wonder' and 'astonishment' that Shakespeare's 'Delphic lines' evoked in him, imprinting so deeply that

our fancy, of itself bereaving,
Dost make us marble with too much conceiving
(An epitaph...printed with the *Second Folio*, 1637)

The renaming of the two chief characters is not fortuitous in an age which believed that all names were bestowed on creatures by God and discerned by Adam. Marina, named, as she explains, from her tragic birth, was originally Thaise or Tarsia, whilst the name of the great Athenian who in Plutarch's *Lives* stands as a pattern of endurance, replaced the traditional Apollonius of Tyre. These two characters alone live with any depth of life, and their union supplies the climax of the play.

I have elsewhere indicated the cosmic dimension of that other remote derivative of Plutarch, *Timon of Athens*; this play of patient endurance and that of imprecation, each, by a series of emblematic images, relates Man to the cosmic order; each is divided at its mid-point. In *Pericles*, the earlier acts present evil as a dark riddle, the act of the viper. The medieval romance of wanderings culminates at the end of Act II with the marriage of Pericles and Thaisa; although only in the second half does the Shakespearean poetry emerge, the first half is justified in performance; the stage situation suggests comparison with Marlowe's *Jew of Malta*, another play badly transmitted but still, when acted, coherent.

Floating lightly in the realm of the theatrical, the play gradually focusses to the concentration of the final scene; its conventions are strong and simple, but used here tentatively and sceptically, with a due sense of their historic distance, to delineate something beyond the former usage from which their familiarity derived.

Like the medieval romances, but unlike the other last plays, this work is devoid of any sense of guilt. The shadowy figures of Antiochus, his daughter, Dionyza and the murderer, Leontine, exist only for their effect on Pericles and his daughter. Both father and daughter are sensitive, vulnerable, yet courageous, endowed with natural graces and the charming powers of Orphic music. Pericles appears as the apex of a living tree of commonwealth; he is so described by his counsellor (I.ii.55–6). He adopts this device for the tourney, presenting a branch withered except for a green top. He and his followers are likened to a circling group of planets,

moving to that harmony of the spheres which Time cannot destroy: his nobles shine round him like diamonds in his coronet.[7]
Yet his first great speech appeals to 'You gods, that made me
man', his duteous piety as 'son and servant to your will' makes
him pliant and modest to the greater kings Antiochus and
Simonides, likening himself to a blind mole, or a glow-worm that
shines only in darkness, as he recalls the departed glory of his
father's court:

> Time's the king of men.
> He's both their parent and he is their grave,
> And gives them what he will, not what they crave. (II.iii.44–6)

Among other men he is a natural king, as the eagle among birds,
yet from the first he is deeply conscious of the fragility of life and
power. 'Ready for the way of life or death', he makes his testament
before assaying the deadly riddle. The young adventurer by
divining the dark and numbing 'deed without a name' is driven to
exile and a lifetime of voyaging, coloured or shadowed with
reminiscences of other voyagers – the wanderings of Jonah and
St Paul, the afflictions of Job – as in his journey without maps, he
circles the cities of Asia Minor – Tyre, Antioch and Ephesus,
Tarsus and that African Pentapolis which later became Tunisia.[8]

Reduced to nakedness and beggary, Pericles appeals to the angry
stars – yet 'as befits my nature, do obey you' – and then, seeing
himself as the tennis ball of the elements, is driven forward to the
court of Pentapolis, where King Simonides, in his cat-and-mouse
game with his daughter and her lover, seems an embodiment of
capricious Fortune, and certainly exemplifies his own view that
kings are as gods (II.ii.60). But he too has been charmed, as his
daughter was, and rejects the idea that Pericles' 'outward poverty'
reflects the 'inward man' (II.ii.55–6). The poor stranger is chosen by
Thaisa, as black Othello by Desdemona, and his adventures had
been scarcely less incredible.

The inward man, revealed in the opening speeches, distinguishes
Pericles from the adventurers of earlier romances, and therefore he
offers a chance of identification to more thoughtful, self-conscious
types of audience. Those earlier accommodating lay figures who

move through their travels as lures for the dreams of the simple, could not reach the pitch of the melancholy that overwhelms Pericles, whose mourning becomes a form of death-in-life.

Love is 'dear as blood to life' (II.v.89); anguish and beatitude, union and dereliction are intimately known; but as the chief characters are entirely free from guilt, the wicked become mere instruments of their affliction; certain ranges of feeling, those involving conflict, are not present; as in the old romances there is a certain limitation of effect.

Not that Pericles is lacking in discernment. He detects the truth about the daughter of Antiochus, who, 'apparalled like the spring' is yet no 'fair Hesperian tree'; at Tarsus his own appearance is doubted 'Who makes the fairest show means most deceit' (I.iv. 75); later Gower comments on the false show of mourning in this very city for Marina's supposed death. In a play so full of shows, but also of violent reversals of Fortune, distrust is expressed as prudence. The poor fishermen seem to know more about the realities of political power than any at the royal courts; from the ocean itself, that mirror of the organic world, they have learnt 'all, that may men approve or men detect' (II.i.51). Pericles, though 'careful' of his people, is presented with that degree of ritual which withdraws him from a modern life that his fishermen seem to share with the bawds of Mitylene. The fishermen are charitable and merry, unembittered by the wisdom they harvest; the brothel-keeper inhabits an anti-world without malice ('She hath here spoken holy words to the Lord Lysimachus'. 'O abominable!' (IV.vi.132–4).

Marina's presence dominates the last two acts; Pericles himself, describing her, found only similitudes:

> Thou look'st
> Modest as Justice and thou seem'st a palace
> For the crown'd Truth to dwell in.   (v.i.120–1)
> Thou dost look
> Like Patience gazing on Kings' graves and smiling
> Extremity out of act.   (v.i.136–8)

Marina at the same age as Juliet embodies what lies beyond the words in the music, the storms' challenge, the ebb and flow of fortune that envelopes the action as the sea envelopes the shores. Her quickness of wit saves her in the brothel; she assures her father she is flesh and blood, 'naturally brought forth', although to his question

> What countrywoman?
> Here of these shores?

she must answer

> 'No, nor of any shores' (v.i.102–3)

The simple certainty of truth and divinity, with something indescribable, like beauty born of a changing sea, some glint of the sun in a crest of foam that has itself disappeared and yet the brightness remains...The quality she defends seems to be the initial quality of her life, its freshness – something as simple as that, and terms like innocence and chastity are too complex to express her beauty.[9]

Nevertheless, in a performance she may be presented either as the bright angel that Daphne Slater made of her at Stratford in 1947, or the sunburnt Greek girl, reacting to her trials with energy, and with hot resentment, presented by Susan Fleetwood twenty-two years later in 1969.

When her mother, Thaisa 'blows into life's flower again', her first words had been 'What world is this?'

As a mirage is the refractive image of some authentic scene too far for human eye, so here the Paradisal act of resurrection re-mains, shimmering and glimmering in the transparent artifice of archaic elements; the moral platitudes of the frame serve but to refract the difficult, all but inaudible harmonies by which an extremity of affliction is charmed and restored to life. The audience are left with unresolved contradictions since the inner feelings, the 'second life' of the spirit is separated by the interposed form of romance – what Yeats would term the 'body of Fate' and Blake, the 'Mundane Shell'. Gower may interpose his bland 'I tell you what mine authors say'; his art is restorative but like that of Ceri-mon, it is a 'secret art'. The range is such that it imposed a strain even on a unifying imagination of unexampled force. The width of random association with Shakespeare's earlier plays indicates the free-ranging nature of subliminal echo and attachment, the diversity of experience momentarily reconciled in the action. It witnesses to the esemplastic power of the play.[10]

The freshness of young life, the power of the green leaf that can force its way through crevices in the hardest stone, survives by those very qualities that make it vulnerable –

> thoughts that dodge
> Conception to the very bounds of heaven

– to be captured only by half-forgotten forms revived to new ends. To release the very pure vision of the recognition scene between Pericles and Marina, it is surrounded by a framework of archaic plays and older poetry. The story ranges over the ancient world, and includes some contemporary and realistic episodes that act as ballast.

In a sensitive linking of this play with *King Lear* and *The Winter's Tale*, C. L. Barber recognizes that 'the transformation of persons into virtually sacred persons who yet remain persons' involves something like that 'moment in a court masque where some noble couple are presented in the rôles of mythological deities'. He would stress that in the romances it is the older generation who are transformed by the recovery through the younger generation of some lost relationship with the past. With them, 'the mysterious powers which create and renew life', especially as it is found in woman,[11] transform a potentially dangerous situation. Barber has not followed up the hint of a link with the masque; given the wide social distinction between the two forms, I would think it lay in the 'delight' or 'rapture' that both aimed to arouse. The masquers and their audience entered a new world, another dimension than that of everyday; this was also the aim of the romance. With Shakespeare it is no common form but 'a strain of rareness' that combines ritual transformation with the advantages of sensitive vulnerable feelings. The 'impure art' of the romance, like that of John Webster, covers a great range of response from the archaic to the *avant garde*, and from high symbolism to such finely observed detail as the comic realism of the bawds' sales-talk. What is shown in *Pericles* is potentially the capacity to return to something analogous, in terms of the full stage, to the *effects* of the masque.

Yet, as Marina's recovery led to Thaisa's, the old Theatre was re-born too. The transformation, as compared with *King Lear*, lies in the ability to approach – although in a still rather indirect manner – what before was found irreconcilable with the inner needs and pressures of the work itself.

'CYMBELINE'

Cymbeline, the first of the romances to be acknowledged and to appear (as the last play) in the Folio, does not seem to have enjoyed the wide popularity of *Pericles* and *The Winter's Tale.* It was seen at the Globe by Simon Forman in May 1611, who recorded the plot in his diary (which suggests it was new) but it was not one of the plays called for at court, and allusions to it are comparatively few.

Whilst nominally concerned with the reign of an ancient British King (though many years after Lear, for this reign coincided with the birth of Christ, and the reign of Augustus Caesar), the play offers a great variety of artificial scenes and times, with the very different social habits and presuppositions proper to each. The misty past of 'Lud's Town' in the first days of what it would not have been tactful to think of as the Roman conquest, the proud Roman Legions, which include an 'Italian fiend', brother of the Duke of Siena, are straight out of any modern play about Italian vice; an innocent Elizabethan country gentleman lost among super-subtle Italians; Jupiter in person; the timeless world of pastoral – all combined to 'distance' the total impression. Britain has become the remote and radiant Western Island 'in a great pool, a swan's nest', although Imogen's bedchamber is furnished in High Renaissance magnificence, and she reads herself to sleep with Ovid. Ovid signifies an ancient poet, and the triumphs of Antony and Cleopatra, depicted on her mantelpiece, are ancient history, too, not a modern instance; it remains only for Imogen, disguised as Fidele, to inform the Roman Lucius that she had been the servant of the good knight Richard du Champ, to complete the apparatus for projecting the spectators into a timeless fairy tale.

The centre of the play is Imogen; if Shakespeare's comedies had depicted 'real people in unreal situations'[12] Imogen is here the one fully realized character. In terms of the King's Men, this means that a boy took the lead. There is really no part of any substance for Burbage. Pericles and Leontes dominate their plays almost as fully as does Prospero, but here it is the princess who takes the centre of the stage, it is her brothers who are lost and recovered by their father, whilst the image of the physician has turned quite black and become that of the poisoner, the Wicked Fairy who calls herself Queen and Imogen's stepmother.

This was a most unusual experiment for Shakespeare. Although the Roman plays of *Coriolanus* and *Antony and Cleopatra* have leading parts for women, these are mature and masculine rôles; and I think, like other parts for older women, they were probably taken by men. Cleopatra could speak of some 'squeaking Cleopatra' boying her 'greatness' because she was not played by any such. Imogen, however, is designed for a slighter, delicate artifice, and to put such a part at the centre lightens the whole tone of the play.

Though witty, Imogen commands a courtly eloquence and felicity of rebuke, both to Cloten and to Iachimo, that is, except for Hermione's, the most royal accent of any of Shakespeare's heroines. Like Pericles and his daughter, she is vulnerable and sensitive, but she is neither humble nor submissive. In the midst of open trials and secret betrayals she has chosen Posthumus for husband with the confidence of Desdemona or Thaisa choosing 'the mean knight'; and at the moment of recovery, it is in her sharp rebuke of a servant that her father recognizes 'the tune of Imogen'. When the identity of her brothers is revealed and Cymbeline exclaims

> O Imogen!
> Thou hast lost by this a kingdom

she can instantly reply

> No, my lord;
> I have got two worlds by 't.   (v.v.372–4)

For the worlds that these characters inhabit are in truth worlds of the imagination. Only as Fidele is Imogen timid; out of the courtly environment, putting off princely manners with her princely attire, she develops 'pretty arts' of cookery to gratify the hunters in their mountain cave. But here she meets Guiderius whose rashness and prompt avowal of his disposal of Cloten matches her rapid decisions for flight, for death at the hands of Pisanio. To some extent in Act v she hands over the lead to the 'princely boys'.

When she wakens from her trance to find 'the dream within me as without' and takes the headless body of Cloten for, Posthumus, artifice is stretched almost beyond the capacity of the modern stage. Disguised herself, she meets a 'shape' lying beside her under flowery strewings. In a subsequent comic subplot, a true lover was to win his mistress and restore her wits by taking her virginity in the clothes of a prince whom she loved.[13] This convention of disguise is in *Cymbeline* part of the self-conscious art that draws attention to itself throughout the action, culminating in the tour de force of the final discovery scene. It was the recognized end for a many-stranded romance, as Harington notes in his defence of Ariosto:

He breaks off narrations very abruptly...to draw a man with continual thirst to read out the whole work, and towards the end of the book to close up the diverse matters briefly and cleanly.[14]

Cymbeline interweaves a number of stories – the wager, the lost princes, the winning of a battle by two boys and one old man. 'The actual reign of Cymbeline is described by an editor of the play as 'so uneventful that it had defeated the inventive powers of generations of quite imaginative chroniclers'.[15] Characters disappear for long periods; Posthumus is absent for two acts, Imogen for most of Act v; Iachimo also fades out, to reappear in the finale, where he repents with a volubility and completeness equalled only by the reported death-bed confession of the wicked Queen.

The play is triple-centred; Imogen's bedchamber, Rome, the Welsh mountains represent, court, city and country, the threefold division of the modern kingdom. Imogen's story is the first established and supplies the plot line; the second part of the play is filled with dreams, fantasies, disguises, dirges, visions and gratuitous acts of repentance and restitution.

Cymbeline himself is a monarch of gratuitous decisions, who

outdoes even 'the good Simonides' in aristocratic irresponsibility. Flaring and flashing into decrees of banishment – one costs his two sons, the other his daughter – he yet abjectly follows every whim of his wicked Queen in state and domestic affairs. Though protesting deep friendship for the noble Caius Lucius, after the battle he orders a general massacre of prisoners, only at the end to throw away his victory and concede the tribute due to Rome. So Leonatus, after holding himself back with admirable self-control when challenged by Cloten, at Rome issues general challenges on behalf of his lady which even Hector might demur at. After a spontaneous repentance of his order to kill Imogen, he seeks voluntary death with such zeal that the jailer makes a jest of it – but of course the audience have had plenty of signals that the end will be happiness all round. As Granville Barker observed, no tragically potent scoundrel ever emerged from a trunk; and whatever Fletcher may have done, Shakespeare never failed to let a girl page win her lover.

In *Cymbeline* each character – or each character in a given aspect of himself, a given rôle – carries round a certain atmosphere or quality of the sort of play in which such characters occur. Imogen and her brothers belong to romance, Lucius to Roman history ('A Roman with a Roman's heart can suffer'), Iachimo at times to the satiric comedy of Jacobean city sharks. In the interlacing of their stories and the momentary disappearances, there could be some recollection of how, on the older stage, actors had displayed in turn different 'passions' for the pure pleasure of 'interchangeable variety'. On the Jacobean stage, Fletcher was reviving this habit, with his tragi-comedy in the new style.

In *Cymbeline* each actor has a chance to present a solo turn in his own style; the variety of rôles for each of the leading characters can also be made to combine, if the actor has a good 'conceit' of his part. As the identity of actual persons is built from a number of selves in more or less harmonious adjustment with each other, so the actor could combine the two or more aspects of Posthumus, or Cloten, or Iachimo. The work is left open for him to complete his skill. In *Cymbeline*, the actors are given a chance for virtuoso display of many styles within a single rôle, carrying much further that playing of two parts which the boys had developed a decade earlier (see above, Chapter 6, pp. 107–8), and which Shakespeare gave to Edgar in *King Lear*.

The audience is also asked to make quick adjustments from one mood to another; the full response demands a mixture of scepticism and susceptibility; it is a play for the connoisseur.

At one time it was fashionable to compare *Cymbeline* with Fletcher's plays, and even to suggest that Shakespeare was imitating the younger man;[16] now it is more common to involve the older romances of Shakespeare's youth and to point out the links with such early plays as *The Rare Triumphs of Love and Fortune, Orlando Furioso, Sir Clyamon and Sir Clamydes, Fidelio and Fortunio*.[17] These were popular plays of adventure, however, and the tone of *Cymbeline* is courtly, exclusive, presenting in a frame of artifice, sudden, deep and convincing but seemingly unattached passions. The connexion here is rather, as other critics have pointed out, with the courtly games of Sidney's *Arcadia*,[18] although with 'an art that displays art' it is adapted and modified to a stage distinctively Jacobean. His mood anticipates that of the Caroline stage.

The narrative courtly romance (of which the prototype was the Spanish *Diana* of Montemayor) presented in a series of complex and harrowing adventures the fine feelings of high-born lovers. The superlative qualities of royal birth are always dazzlingly evident through the pastoral disguise of shepherds or milkmaids; accents of unstinting praise are justified by unfailingly heroic and noble behaviour; nothing less than the superlative, unless it be a little contrast from clowns, is admissible. The note of admiration and astonishment is sustained by rich and sumptuous emblematic description of the scene.

Although the narrative line of development is not the same in *Arcadia* and *Cymbeline*, they use the same conventions. Basileus is an old, weak, infatuated king, whose children suffer from his arbitrary decrees. The two heroines, sequestered in a remote part of the kingdom, are persecuted by an evil queen who separates them from their lovers and subjects them to torment – even staging a mock death scene – in the hope of favouring the suit of her son.

The death-like qualities of a sleeping draught ignorantly administered, the hero's attempt at suicide when he finds his acts have defamed the heroine, disguise by exchange of garments and elopement from parental tyranny culminate in a grand judgement-cum-recognition scene, when the two young princes are arrested and condemned by the father of the younger, who has not seen his father since infancy, but of course both are united with the princesses at last.

The elegance of style aims at 'delight', 'astonishment', 'admiration'; a perfect beauty, an ideal constancy, flawless and matchless, is presented for the listeners themselves to use as a basis for compliments and for 'communing' with each other. These romances were intended for general enjoyment in reading aloud, for providing a basis of courtship among the listeners. In the Sidney circle, it is to be assumed that the fictional characters could be directly identified with members, but the element of artifice in their speech, the elaboration of the settings, heighten the level, converting life into a poem, as well as providing a script for others' courtly games, which might raise the mind to virtue.

The parts have to be played with imagination, for the listeners are well aware that it is a game, that *Arcadia* requires not so much to be read as to be cast, and projected on to the auditory. It offers a sort of fancy-dress party without costumes; this playfulness, like the playfulness of a well-turned compliment or the playfulness of a May Queen's crowning, of a tourney with blunted staves, demands perfect decorum and gravity to achieve its airy perfection. The fantasy of the game adds piquancy. Only simpletons took romance for truth and with too much playing of the game might disorder their wits.[19]

The Elizabethan attitude towards romance was highly ambivalent; on the one hand it was condemned as disordered, uncomplying with the practice of the learned or the ancients; on the other, it was very generally allowed as an aristocratic indulgence. 'I dare say honest King Arthur will never displease a soldier', observed Sidney rather patronisingly. Decked out as pastoral and with classical names, and above all, designed not as literature but as a social game, it was certainly accepted. The Arthurian story was also used by Henry, Prince of Wales, it had been earlier used by the city for the company of 'King Arthur's Knights' founded by Henry VIII. The Arthurian aspect of *Cymbeline* comes out in the Welsh scenes. This may have had something to do with the Prince of Wales, or with two brothers, the Earls of Pembroke and Montgomery, patrons of the drama and successively Lord Chamberlain to King James.

Sidney's prayer of Pamela was to be adapted, to the scandal of his enemies, as a prayer of the captive King Charles I in *Eikon Basilike*; so thoroughly had the nobility of *Arcadia* constituted a general model. The lofty speech of the Wicked Queen established a convention of deceitful eloquence for other wicked characters, upon which Shakespeare perhaps drew, for the irresistible power of his own Queen's speech seems to work only on Cymbeline, a character who is almost in the Basileus class for ineptitude and credulity.

Here is the eloquent hypocritical lament to Philoclea of Sidney's Queen:

How oft, alas, do I embrace the orphan side of my bed, which was wont to be imprinted by the body of my dear husband, and with tears acknowledge that I now enjoy such liberty as the banished man hath, who may, if he list, wander over the world but is for ever restrained from his most delightful home. That I have now such liberty as the seeled dove hath, which being first deprived of eyes, is then by the falconer cast off... My heart melts to think of the sweet comforts I in that happy time received, when I had never cause to care but the care was doubled, when I never rejoiced but that I saw my joy shine in another's eyes.

Such is the tribute vice pays to virtue. Cloten's tribute to Imogen raises his power of speech beyond its clownish level to fancy:

> I love and hate her, for she's fair and royal,
> And that she hath all courtly parts more exquisite
> Than lady, ladies, women – from every one
> The best she hath, and she, of all compounded,
> Outsells them all – I love her therefore; but... (III.v.71-5)

Imogen implies some artifice even in the grief of parting from her husband:

> I did not take my leave of him, but had
> Most pretty things to say. Ere I could tell him

How I would think on him at certain hours...
            or ere I could
Give him that parting kiss which I had set
Betwixt two charming words, comes in my father... (I.iii.24ff.)

The riches of her chamber are borrowed from an early Elizabethan romance, there 'fashion'd to affections' of chastity (with a Diana bathing, two modest cupids and a lamenting Orpheus).

The two pillars of the door were beautified with the two Cupids of Anacreon, which well shaped modesty seem'd often to whip lest they grow over wanton.
            (Lodge, *The Marguerite of America* ed. Harrison, 1927, p. 122)

In *Cymbeline*, in place of Orpheus there is inset for the tapestry, like the air from *Figaro* inset into Mozart's *Don Giovanni*, a reminiscence of Shakespeare's most opulent celebration of the flesh

Proud Cleopatra when she met her Roman
And Cydnus swell'd above the banks... (II.iv.70–1)

This is like a mirror reflection from Shakespeare's own play upon the married chastity of Imogen. The effect of slander is also like a mirror reflection or dream. Posthumus' speech of rage in which he finds the whole world darkened and doubts the chastity of his mother – 'Is there no way for men to be, but women must be half workers?' – ends in absurdity and bathos, and his very acts prove that beneath the rage there is an underlying trust, for if Imogen had really proved false and given away 'the manacle of love' she would not have been conjured by love to make the journey to Milford. Eventually Posthumus spontaneously rejects the image Iachimo had implanted, her 'dear idea' returns; she once more becomes the gift of the gods. Instinctive union exists below the level of conscious sympathies, as it also links Imogen with her brothers.

Symbolic death lies at the centre of the play but the only two real deaths occur off-stage; nowhere is there any true fear aroused lest Imogen should be killed or ravished, the battle lost, or wickedness triumph. Illusions may be frightful and there is one moment when even the divine Imogen puts on an aspect of betrayal as she refuses to beg the life of the noble Roman who has just begged hers

> Your life, good master,
> Must shuffle for itself   (v.v.104–5)

but this is only the prelude to the recognition scene to end all
recognitions. After which, 'Pardon's the word to all'.

Dramatic ironies and control are best sustained in the wager
story, which belongs to the tradition of contemporary ironic
comedy, transforming the temptation of Othello by Iago into a
much lighter mode. All this takes place in what is really an Elizabethan 'Romeville' with the sharking cozener preying on some
credulous Master Easy.[20] The unwary victim is cautioned by his
friends but insists on being deceived as, with circumstantial relish,
Iachimo indulges his natural taste for drama.

The response of the audience might be defined by some words
prefixed to Shakespeare's Second Folio by a 'friendly admirer':

> our fears
> Take pleasure in their pain; and eyes in tears
> Both weep and smile; fearful at plots so sad,
> Then laughing at our fears; abus'd and glad
> To be abus'd; affected with that truth
> Which we perceive is false...
> Stolen from ourselves...

– that is, they must perceive the artifice, as Posthumus does not.
Dr Johnson condemned the 'unresisting imbecility' of the plot,
but ironic control is evident enough; as in Imogen's fancy when
she misses the bracelet (a variation of Desdemona's handkerchief):

> Last night 'twas on mine arm; I kissed it.
> I hope it be not gone to tell my lord
> That I kiss aught but he.   (ii.iii.146–8)

Or, in the implications of her jubilance as she prepares for Milford,
crying out against Pisanio's estimation of their speed:

> Why, one that rode to's execution, man
> Could never go so slow.   (iii.ii.70–1)

After disclosing from Posthumus' letter that this was indeed the
purpose of the journey, Pisanio says

> What shall I need to draw my sword? the paper
> Hath cut her throat already   (iii.iv.32–4)

But Posthumus' jailer, jesting with his prisoner, in a manner suggesting contemporary London, meets cool replies in spite of the fact that the prisoner has been visited by Jupiter who, in response to the appeal of his family ghosts that a happy issue should ensue, has expounded intentions of satisfying everybody. Here everything depends on the staging; the special device of the god descending on an eagle would be as familiar to the courtly audience (who might have acted in such a masque) as to the strayed revellers from the Red Bull. It was the latest theatrical fashion and as such prepared the way for the last scene. The murders are not real murders; in the very act of striking Imogen, Posthumus invokes the artifice of the whole performance:

> Shall's have a play of this? Thou scornful page,
> There lie thy part   (v.v.228–9)

Pisanio, rushing forward to revive the princess, removes her 'part' of Fidele from her, whilst Cymbeline and Posthumus recognize the total metamorphosis of their world:

> Cymbeline: Does the world go round?
> Posthumus: How come these staggers on me?   (v.v.231–2)

The remorse of Posthumus and the fears of Bellarius dissolve; Cymbeline shows no more repentance for having been misled by his wicked Queen than does his nonchalant young heir for having disposed of her son. The reunited lovers in their embrace bring together the spiritual and the organic worlds of the play. Imogen has become the governing principle of her lord's being:

> Hang there like fruit, my soul,
> Till the tree die.   (v.v.263–4)

The royal children, not their father, carry the true sovereignty of this play. The princely boys, associated with the pristine virtues of the earth, are prepared for the legendary battle by a life of hunting; and more penetrating than the words of Jupiter is the dirge they give equally to the princess and to the clownish villain

> Though mean and mighty rotting
> Together have one dust, yet reverence,
> That angel of the world, doth make distinction   (iv.ii.246–8)

Who would suspect that these lines refer to Cloten? Or were written by a player who had received the condescending compliment that if no gentleman he behaved like one?[21]

As the play unfolds, the audience too might begin to feel 'How come these staggers on me?' This was the effect of old romance 'full of interchangeable variety, beyond expectation' 'interlaced with many diverse and strange adventures' 'as full of delight as profit'. Also of the future Caroline masque with many scene changes.

While it is possible to argue that a number of associated features – the use of Milford Haven, the fact that the family of Cymbeline consisted of two boys and a girl – might chime in with the royal legend, it is equally possible to link this play with the theatrical fashions, to see it as an attempt to work out a new form, accomplished rather than profound, consistently inconsistent. Tennyson's most cherished play, Ellen Terry's triumph, the subject of Granville Barker's penetrating consideration, *Cymbeline* belongs to a craftsman's theatre, and marks a kind of resting place between the half-apprehended vision of *Pericles* and the further experiments of the two later Romances.

The selective lens of this form brought out depth, delicacy and intensity of sentiment whilst blurring time and place; the idyllic pastoral scenes in the Welsh hills might represent something devised for a court, as Michael Drayton's *Polyolbion* also represented an England without cities, trade or trafficking.

Compared with the Elizabethans, whose work lay in a realm of publicly accepted emblems, the Jacobeans worked and thought in a world that was historically and psychologically more firmly based in the great literature that the Elizabethans had provided. The mirror of history was used in a different fashion. Here it might be suggested at court are three beautiful young people, your ancestors; their adventures are not yours but their virtues could be. What would then be presented is not the reflection of a story, but the lineaments of a face.

Those beautiful young people, Elizabeth, Henry and Charles, were as yet untried. Imogen differs from other Shakespearean heroines in being a wife; her relation with Posthumus is not that of the lovers' wooing game that Rosalind or Viola plays, but – in spite of circumstances – a complete union, of some standing; in situation, therefore, she belongs rather with Desdemona and the Duchess of Malfi – except that this is a romance and not a tragedy, and therefore the whole work is designed as a game for any number of spectators to become participants. The aristocratic mirror would work as well – or almost as well – for any young Herberts or if, later, the two brothers and their sister, the young Egertons for whom Milton wrote *Comus*, were to take up the fancies, they would be found apt. Such was the orthodox theory of 'application' – that it should be general and not exclusive; and exclusive application in a public show might be considered indecorous, apart from the obvious risk of libelling James and his Queen, socially degrading the Elector Palatine, justifying such behaviour as the Ruthven Raid and the Gowry Plot with regard to princelings and suggesting the possibility of an alliance with Rome![22] Nothing can please many and please long, observed Dr Johnson, but just representations of general nature; the specific identities of Shakespeare's characters are given by his art, and they remain open to a wide variety of interpretations by the actors, and a wide range of collaboration from the audience. That poignant anticipation of future hazards which Gerard Manley Hopkins felt on seeing the portrait of two beautiful young people[23] is a sentiment of such a general nature.

11

OPEN FORM IN *THE WINTER'S TALE*

> A sad tale's best for winter.

The childish words of Mamillius to the Queen, his mother, are cut short by the entry of his father, to arrest her for treason and adultery. His tale of sprites and hobgoblins has become an imaginary garden with real toads. *The Winter's Tale* marks an obvious development from *Cymbeline*; the jealousy of the hero is self-generated and harder to dislodge; the slandered lady takes the solution of Hero in *Much Ado About Nothing*, rather than disguise, which is the involuntary fate of her infant daughter, raised among country folk; above all, the perspective of the final half of the play allows a very different treatment of the recognition scene, which has made this play in the present century the chief pillar of anthropological interpretation of the final Romances. In the thirties, a pattern of death and rebirth, of winter followed by spring, the death and revival of the Corn Queen acquired a sort of independent existence. Later F. R. Leavis was to point out the danger of incapacity for 'seeing what actually is' and missing the significance of these plays 'by assuming the organization is of a given kind', whilst G. E. Bentley traced the new form to the influence of the roofed Blackfriars Theatre.[1] Since then, growing understanding of the complexity of entertainment in Jacobean London, and a sense of the adaptability of these plays, fully tested in the modern theatre, has confirmed their open form, and their individuality.

The spectacular and non-verbal elements of this play are much more closely defined by the poetry which surrounds them, because they are part of the story; the goddess who appears is not Diana but Hermione, the intervention of Apollo is not by means of a riddle, but of a judgement followed by the sharp administration of the penalty for its disregard. Even when he followed a pattern, Shakespeare never repeated himself, and close attention to the local effects is demanded by the complex yet precise interlacing of his poetry and action. The silence of Hermione in the final scene has been built up for five acts and is defined by its context. An open form is not an indeterminate one.

The coherence of its seeming incongruities is effected by a very delicate balance between surrender to and mockery of the old winter's tale, which in this case was taken from the work of that Robert Greene, long dead, who at the beginning of Shakespeare's dramatic career, had attacked him as an 'upstart crow'. The tragic part of the story itself comes from Greene's tragic romance, *Pandosto or the Triumph of Time*, whilst the chief comic figure, Autolycus – who in performance is capable of stealing the show – owes much of his nature and habits to Greene's coneycatching pamphlets. The wronged queen had also been a central figure in many of Greene's plays in which Shakespeare may have acted when young.

Here, then, the wider debt to the earlier age which had already been notable in *Cymbeline* (see above, Chapter 10, p. 198) has narrowed itself to much more specific adaptations. It incurred good natured new banter from Ben Jonson, delivered at the most most popular of all the public theatres, the dual-purpose bear-baiting house where an induction shows the scrivener drawing up articles of agreement to defend the present performance.

If there be never a servant monster in the Fair who can help it he [i.e. the author] says, nor a nest of antics? He is loath to make nature afraid in his plays, like those that beget Tales, Tempests and such drolleries, to mix his head with another man's heels. (Induction to *Bartholomew Fair*, 1614).

If the chief target here is *The Tempest*, and Trinculo's proposal (II.ii.) to bring Caliban to a fair in England and exhibit him, what brought in *The Winter's Tale* may well have been not only the celebrated bear but that 'nest of antics', the dance of the twelve satyrs in four threes 'one three of them by their own report sir, hath danced before the king' (IV.iv.337–8). For this 'gallimaufrey of gambols', a wild antic dance, had indeed formed part of the antimasque for Ben Jonson's own *Masque of Oberon*, presented to the King by the Prince of Wales on New Year's Day 1611.[2] It was in the spring of that year that Simon Forman recorded seeing the play at the Globe, when the company would be opening in their new summer quarters. Here they would be able to present, out of doors to the larger audience, what might well prove a star attraction to certain playgoers who would be eager to enjoy a Court spectacle, advertised as such.

The Winter's Tale was later given as part of the wedding festivities of the Princess Elizabeth, celebrated on St Valentine's Day 1613; it was perhaps staged as a simple 'offering' from the poor players. Shakespeare may well have felt confident enough by then to accept and make use of Greene's suggestion that he was an unlettered countryman, much as Chaucer depreciated his own poetry as 'lewd' and unlearned. 'With all its absurdities, very entertaining', Dr Johnson was to say of *The Winter's Tale*; for he responded to a structure he did not recognize – a compliment indeed, compared with his castigation of the 'unresisting imbecility' of *Cymbeline*.

The Winter's Tale is a diptych: Time, as Chorus, divides the play, and Part II provides a matching series of reversals and recognitions to Part I, as in the old bi-part plays; Part I moves from court to country and from kings to shepherds; Part II from country back to court and from shepherds to kings.[3] The suspicion of disguise in Polixenes and Hermione is balanced by the real disguises of Florizel and Perdita. In each part an accusation is followed by a flight, then by a confrontation; in Part I banishment follows, leading to a death; in Part II recognition of Perdita leads to a resurrection of Hermione. Yet the audience is never brought up against the dynamics of the real world; jealousy is the most subjective of emotions; everyone recognizes that Leontes moves in a waking dream. In Part II the chief acts are wooings, ordeals, friendship, yet Burbage as Leontes would dominate Part I and Armin as Autolycus, Part II.

This play provides material both for royal rituals and for popular theatres. Ben Jonson imposed a rigid division between the Platonic idealism of his masques and the satiric comedy of his public 'works'; neither is an 'open' form, for response in the comedies is guided by the figures of the Induction; Jonson schooled his audience like a dominie. In *The Winter's Tale* Shakespeare intermingles hornpipes and funerals triumphantly. Ben Jonson's joke against Shakespeare and his clowns (given in the bear-baiting house) implies 'I could bring on a live bear if I chose – but of course I don't'. There is no doubt that the bear that is summoned by the hunting horns in fulfilment of Apollo the Hunter's decree is a human bear. How, otherwise, could the play be repeated anywhere but on Bankside? Jupiter on an eagle might be transported from the Bankside to Blackfriars but a live bear would prove intractable. Jonson himself put three dancing bears into a masque; Shakespeare's bear effects the difficult transition to comedy. It recalls Bottom's lion. The only live animal on the Shakespearean stage is Crab, the dog, and a man-and-dog act was traditional for the clown.

However, the double structure of Jonson's masques provides an analogue to the double structure which Shakespeare used in several of the Romances – one half dark, the other bright. Clearly, he could not compete with Jonson. But under the guise of pastoral humility and simplicity, indeed of the revival of archaic forms, he could evolve a complex type of play, satisfying with an 'open' invitation the virtuosity of his company and the stratification of his audience. Simon Forman was clearly taken with the story-line of *The Winter's Tale*, which he summarized; others might go to see the dance that had been performed at Whitehall, others to watch Burbage or Armin, others to see the bear and the living statue, those two emblematic objects that end Part I and Part II respectively.

The statue scene may serve as an example of the way in which Shakespeare transformed the old drama into the new. In Lyly and Peele women might be turned into trees. In 1607, in *The Lord Hayes' Masque*, Campion had shown a group of lovers imprisoned in trees restored to their right form by Phoebus; two years after *The Winter's Tale*, in *The Lord's Masque*, he showed statues turned into living women.[4] In this final scene the balance and reconciliation of both parts is at once ritualistic and intimate. Hermione reappears as what Time and Leontes have made her; her funeral effigy (these were highly realistic and often dressed in the clothes of the dead) perpetuates what he had inflicted on the living woman.

O, thus she stood,
Even with such life of majesty, warm life,
As now it coldly stands, when first I woo'd her.   (v.iii.34–6)

Contrary to *all* precedents in Shakespeare, the audience are not here
in the secret. This in itself is in the tradition of the masque rather
than the theatre, for in masques an element of shock and wonder
was integral to the effect.

The marvels of the play are constantly underlined by comment
from the courtiers, whose accents of courtly compliment in the
opening scene have established the level of sophistication appropriate to a noble drama – to a player addressing royalty (memory
of Autolycus, peddling, peeps out, however):

Such a deal of wonder is broken out within this hour, that ballad makers cannot
be able to express it...This news, sir, which is called true, is so like an old tale
that the verity of it is in strong suspicion   (v.ii.21–9)

while the last scene passes beyond the arts of speech:

That she is living
Were it but told you, should be hooted at
Like an old tale; but it appears she lives.   (v.iii.115–7)

The recovery of Perdita, as described, not witnessed, caused
swoons, tears, near hysteria in Leontes and Paulina; the recovery
of Hermione passes in reticence and almost in silence. Of the first,
it is said, in spite of its uninhibited demonstrations, 'The dignity
of this act was worthy the audience of kings and princes, for by
such it was acted' (v.ii.79–80). This dignity is finally shown in the
last sequence.

In reaction from the apologies for these Romances, they have
been held by some to provide courtly rituals quite closely akin to
Jonson's masques. Glynne Wickham has put forward the theory
that *The Winter's Tale* was designed for a Garter Feast (see above,
Chapter 6, p. 115). Although the two latest Romances were certainly given at court as part of the wedding festivities for Princess
Elizabeth, they retained the pastoral mixed form which authorized
a blend of noble and simple.[5] It was within a delicate and fastidious
convention that Perdita distributed her flowers, and made her
choice between art and nature; it was in the language of the farm-

yard that her royal father had attacked her mother. Paulina, whose language is equally frank, assumes at the end the new rôle of mourner, and the language of constancy.

> I, an old turtle,
> Will wing me to some wither'd bough, and there,
> My mate, that's never to be found again,
> Lament till I am lost. (v.iii.131-4)

We have seen Antigonus' 'exit, pursued by a bear', which brings on the two clowns and results in a grotesque traditional scene which has been justified by Neville Coghill: 'The terrible and the grotesque come near to each other in a *frisson* of horror instantly succeeded by a shout of laughter'; the only on-stage death is thus presented as 'a dazzling piece of *avant garde* work',[6] in contrast with the tragic reported death of the little prince.

At the same time as they put on *The Winter's Tale*, Shakespeare's company revived *Mucedorus*, a truly naive old romance which bounces along through inconsequent adventures, including the encounter of the heroine both with a bear and a cannibal Wild Man. The Induction conjures up an envious Poet, whom the unfriendly might think bore a certain likeness to Ben Jonson (who was himself to revert to these models in A *Tale of a Tub*).

The transposition of the kingdoms of Sicilia and Bohemia (the former, pastoral's natural home) is a gratuitous absurdity in *The Winter's Tale*, which was commented on by such a simple soul as Taylor, the Water Poet. The clowning, the disguises, and the insouciance of Florizel are really a matter of skill and confidence. 'Be advised', Camillo warns Florizel, who replies

> I am – and by my fancy; if my reason
> Will thereto be obedient, I have reason;
> If not, my senses, better pleased with madness,
> Do bid it welcome. (iv.iv.474-8)

Equally, with the 'dangerous lunes' of Leontes, this is a surrender to madness

> My life stands in the level of your dreams
> Which I'll lay down

the Queen tells the King. The sense of unreality, of dream-life, only intensifies the anguish for each. So Imogen had felt her dreams 'around me, as within me', and all the characters of *The Tempest*, except Prospero, live in a waking dream.

One earlier critic, S. L. Bethell, based his study of *The Winter's Tale* (1942) on a comparison with *King Lear*; the tragic intensity of the Romance, found within the parts of Leontes and Hermione, is particularly susceptible to modern handling. Edward Armstrong had traced in the speeches where the onset of Leontes' jealousy occurs, the subliminal image of a cannon exploding.[7] In each of the Romances a powerful element of disgust and outrage intrudes but is finally dissolved; the feelings here involved are dramatically realized in the verse and action; especially the trial scene, which is the gravest moment, a dream that ends with God Apollo striking, through the death of Mamillius.

The court masque had depended on an overwhelming effect.[8] But its effect, like that of *Arcadia*, depended also on the 'casting' of the noble actors and their audience, who at the end intermingled. In his plays, Shakespeare could command neither the immense resources of the court where thousands of pounds were spent on costume and setting, nor the particular magic of its once-for-all performance. His share in such scenes must have profoundly affected his dramatic imagination, but his own writing had to be open and adaptable to an audience that ranged from royalty to ragamuffins. Certainly the advantages of spectacle were not ignored, but in *The Winter's Tale* these depend more on the human actors than on machines, and on an increasing power to vary the range of the actor's part without losing the depth that distinguished the men's from the boys' troupes. In the first part of *The Winter's Tale*, Burbage could draw on his performance in *Othello*; in the second, Armin could draw on his performance in *King Lear*. For Shakespeare too, perhaps, the play offered an acceptance, a resolution of these tragedies, which are now gradually transformed – 'like far off mountains turned into clouds' – into new stage material. The revival of Hermione is the validation of this new art, which does not, of course, lack its spectacular aspect. Cymbeline, a royal statue who fails signally to come to life, speaks the last words of his play in accents of religious awe:

> Laud we the gods,
> And let our crooked smokes climb to their nostrils
> From our blest altars. (v.v.476–8)

Would the felicitous adjective 'crooked' have sprung to mind if the descent and ascent of Jupiter earlier in the play had not been by the zig-zag process of a descending eagle worked on a 'degrading drum' (a model may be seen at the theatrical collection of the Victoria and Albert Museum)? Shakespeare, as a man of the theatre, used what machines he could; but his real resource was the transforming power of his words, and the 'Protean' variety of his leading actors, who seem to have enjoyed the opportunity of playing tragic-comic parts, taking the centre of the stage in turn.[9] This could never have been a variation upon the older pattern of 'doubling' parts and of the quick-change artist, or sometimes, in the case of professional Fools, giving a one-man show, acting all parts in turn. Shakespeare makes use of this in his 'Seven Ages of Man' speech. The rapid changes of mood in Romance belong to the men and contrast with woman's constancy. Disguise offers other opportunities for contrast in acting styles.

This particular process culminates in *The Winter's Tale*. Louis MacNeice has identified the author with Autolycus, littered under Mercury, god of lies and learning:

> O master pedlar with your confidence tricks,
> Brooches, pomanders, broad-sheets and what-have-you
> Who hawk such entertainment but rook your clients,
> And leave them brooding, why should we forgive you
> Did we not know that, though more self reliant
> Than we, you too were born and grew up in a fix?
>
> (*Autolycus*, 1946)

L. G. Salingar suggests that he is 'an autobiographical joke' in which the author assumed and betters the rôle of strolling vagabond originally thrust on him by Greene.[10]

In 1973 the MS of an unknown play from Gray's Inn appeared from the library of the Marquis of Lothian, descendant of one of King James's masquing favourites.[11] Its story of Tom-a-Lincoln, the Red Rose Knight, is taken from a romance by Richard

Johnson, but its form contains some parody of *The Winter's Tale*, including Time as Chorus

> I that have been here since the world began
> I that was since this orbed ball's creation
> I that have seen huge kingdom's devastations,
>> Do here present myself to your still view –
>> Old, ancient, changing, ever running Time...

Time presents a babe, Tom (the hero) who after being abandoned, is found by an old shepherd and in this interval attains sixteen years of age. Tom combines aspects of Shakespeare's lost prince-lings with the instincts of a Cloten, the predatory power of an Autolycus and the unsinkable resources of a Stephano. His adventures make *Pyramus and Thisbe* seem like an exercise in classic restraint. In my view, this play parodies both Shakespeare and Heywood, and is not the work of the latter (as has been suggested) but of some young lawyer at Gray's Inn to provide the Christmas Revels with a jest at the expense of the latest theatrical success. It was transcribed and signed by a law student named Morgan Evans. Whilst once again identifying Shakespeare with the popular idea of romantic tradition, it implies that the play parodied would be familiar and was sufficiently connected with the court to serve at the ceremonies of a Christmas Prince at Gray's Inn. These were always modelled upon the monarchy of the day.[12] This frivolous little entertainment is further witness to the open nature of Shakespeare's romance, which actors and critics have found so pliant to their several needs. It may have been in *riposte* to such jests that Shakespeare in his final romance, *The Tempest*, chose paradoxically to present new wonders under the strict form of the Three Unities, thus turning Romance into its opposite.

12

THE TEMPEST

Characters whose life is in their action; adventures full of variety and always interweaving; such was the old romance. In *The Tempest*, encounter supplies all the action given to anyone; simply to meet suffices. The quest to find one's fellows is to regain society out of loneliness. For character exists without need for action. Miranda has no need to do anything, she has simply to appear 'the goddess on whom these airs attend'[1] to gratify Ferdinand at his labours. The sublimation of romantic escape lies in the musician, Ariel, who finally escapes from man, as his songs escape, in perpetual holiday from 'poor little talkative humanity', its conflicts and loss, to somewhere on the other side of despair. 'Full fathom five thy father lies; / Of his bones are coral made; / Those were pearls that were his eyes' (1.ii.396–8). Grief is transmuted – as the medieval author of *Pearl* discovered after he had a vision of his lost daughter by the riverside.

But if Ariel is free, his author is bound by the strictest rules: the Unities. Prospero's charm also depends on an exact moment and much calculation, if to others it seems a blind maze and the action 'more than nature was ever conduct of'.[2]

The effect is paradoxical – a fantasy obeys strict canons of art, at the end of the play to become itself the matter of wondering words suspended between actors and audience. Prospero's first epilogue, 'Our revels now are ended', with his second, the epilogue proper, unwinds the charm and yet leaves his mystery more mysterious.

The play, both a masterpiece and an enigma, where severity of control is balanced by freedom to use the language of show and of music, and by the luminous depth of the character as idea, might stand as illustration of Puttenham's distinction between true and false fantasy. When it is misused, 'then doth it breed chimeras and monsters in man's imaginations, and not only in his imaginations, but also in all his ordinary actions and life which ensues'; but when it is not confused, it represents to the soul 'all manner of beautiful visions, whereby the inventive part of the mind is so much holpen, as without it no man could devise any new or rare thing....'[3] The unusual severity of composition released the fantasy into a new world beyond nature.

Without offering the interlacing variety of *Cymbeline* or the depth of character in action of *The Winter's Tale*, after we have 'founder'd' in scene 1 the poet leaves the exploration of his brave new world to unfold in successive layers of illusion and revelation. He holds up a mirror in which each may see the image he himself casts, with exceptional clarity, so that at the end the treasures that each seeks are found, but also 'all of us ourselves, / When no man was his own' (v.i.212–13). As in romances the story is distanced, the response unqualified, but it is an individual response, not a group response. The island setting provides the superlatives that romance exacts. Purity and isolation so great lie beyond any pastoral dream; this is Eden, an unfallen world where the air is full of music, the virgin sand bears no footprint as the spirits dance over it. Prospero's absolute dominion, however is ruled by working through natural sympathies, by shock and hypnotic power over human sinew. Ferdinand thinks that Miranda (like her father) would have power to reanimate the dead; her charm is tested by setting the Prince of Naples to bearing logs like Hob or Dick. Caliban is no monster of brown paper to be subdued by the hero in combat; he curses and plots, and though subdued is not destroyed, but rather acknowledged in a deeper sense than the literal one: 'This thing of darkness I acknowledge mine' (v.i.275). To the servants he is something to show at a fair, like the strange fish about which Autolycus hawked ballads.

The transformed elements of the old romances, though so numerous, do not seem to belong to communal tradition any more. The magician or conjuror, with his magic wand and book, seeming in some fashion related to the author of the play, is to be found in early drama.[4] Prospero begins with a long narrative of old adventures that sound like one of the romances of ordeal – indeed it has not a little resemblance to *Pericles*. Besides the new kind of monster and spirit, the Ship, the Cave, the Enchanted Banquet, the Masque of Goddesses, the coat to go invisible remain; there is a hunting with hounds upon the stage that recalls the hunt in the hall of early revels at the Inns of Court and the Universities (IV.i. 254), and Ariel's former imprisonment in the Hollow Tree looks back to a favourite device of Lyly's stage.[5] Echoes of old plays survive because an individual dramatist chooses to recall them, harmonized into the Jacobean play – these are not ghosts of a vanished stage, but the discoveries of a new one. *Pericles* erupted from a deep centre and bore marks of the conflict that preceded; *The Tempest* builds up to an abdication of the play world, and also of the transient realm of magic, returning to a city that is as transient, though in another sense and dimension.

The childish magic of *John a Kent and John a Cumber* lies behind both *A Midsummer Night's Dream* and *The Tempest*, as Professor Coghill made plain in *Shakespeare's Professional Skills*.[6] Here two rival magicians impersonate each other in turn, and everyone else changes shape, or becomes transformed in a magic mist. The action is gratuitously complicated by the magicians and treated as if it were a play. 'Must the first Scene make absolute a play? / no crosse? no change? what? no varietie?'[7] The magician's apprentice, who can fly through a keyhole, reveals a conspiracy in a song which he puts into the mouth of clowns, who are blamed for it. He leads astray travellers by playing on an instrument, charms them asleep, leads them in a circle round a magic tree. Princes appear in antic form, darting in from all sides and from beneath the stage; the music and dancing present the state of enchantment in which no one is quite sure who is 'shadow' and who is 'substance' – 'shadow' being a term used equally of actors and of apparitions. For in addition to the magic transformations, this play includes a troupe of rustic actors, led by a serving man named Turnop, who offers welcome to the bridegrooms and a scene of ritual abuse against one of the conjurors; him they dress in a fool's coat as part of their Morris dance. These substantial and lively characters are sharply contrasted with the chameleon magicians and the sextet of lovers, rivals, ladies.

The play is set firmly in particular places – Chester and the country around – and may therefore have been commissioned for some great marriage in those parts. The manuscript was preserved in the library of a local magnate, Lord Mostyn. It is a characteristic of the most fantastic romance to be given a particular setting – and though the precise locality of Prospero's isle is 'somewhere in the Mediterranean', the basis of its adventures is quite definite and situated in very different waters.

The story of the *Sea Venture*'s wreck on the islands of Bermuda in July 1609 impressed itself on contemporaries, and is still the most important event that has ever happened there – a creation *ab initio*, the beginning of history. In an uninhabited island, such as this (or Iceland before the Norsemen) the first settlement acquires a mythic grandeur and scale; no half-obliterated story of the conquered blurs its pristine clarity. The image of the shipwreck forms the arms of the islands, for it was from the first a happy wreck. A rich coast had been shunned by all seamen as 'the dangerous and dreaded island, or rather islands of the Bermuda...[since] they be so terrible to all that ever touched on them, and such tempests, thunders and other fearful objects are seen and heard about them that they be called commonly, The Devils' Islands'.[8] Another writer speaks of them as by common belief 'a most prodigious and enchanted place'; they turned out to be 'the richest, health-fullest and pleasing land'.[9] For nine months the party from the *Sea Venture* wintered there happily, before sailing on to Virginia, whither they had been bound.

No legend, but the latest exploit of the Virginia Company, furnished the groundwork of the plot – a venture in which Shakespeare's friends and his former patron, Southampton, were engaged. The colonists had exorcised the devils and disproved the marvels. The play's Neapolitans at first thought themselves on such a deadly coast – Ferdinand threw himself overboard as St Elmo's fire burst from the ship's rigging, crying, 'Hell is empty, and all the devils are here' (I.ii.214–15).

The Tempest does not seek to rouse the comic response of 'delight' but the graver tragic one of 'admiration'. Through Ariel's shows, or the beauty of admired Miranda, or the wonder of the strange fish, astonishment strikes the characters of the play so that they are petrified or 'made marble with too much conceiving.'[10] Statues are magically brought to life in two of the great masques for Princess Elizabeth's wedding in February 1613 – by Campion and by Beaumont (see above, Chapter 11, p. 209).

Caliban thinks the revellers must have dropped from the moon – in the third of Princess Elizabeth's wedding masques Chapman's *Masque of the Middle Temple and Lincoln's Inn*, a band of Virginian knights arrives, but they are really Caribbean Islanders.[11] However much an entertainment of that kind has been planned, it was expected to look spontaneous. The surprises in this play are of a more theatrical kind. The opening presents a scene of genuine horror – cries of "All lost, to prayers, to prayers!' and 'Farewell, my wife and children!' The mariners look to be as cold under water as those of *The Winter's Tale* – only Gonzalo's humour hints ironically at survival.

The first words of Miranda dissolve this tragic moment: 'If by your Art, my dearest father, you have / Put the wild waters in this roar, allay them' (I.ii.1–2). The distancing of feeling was probably accompanied by a scene change. A bare stage would be an unsuitable prelude to the marvels following – at least the wave-machine and thunder-box, or some interesting variant of the medieval Ship Pageant Waggon, is needed.

The Mock Banquet appears as a kind of show, introduced by the sort of pageant that excited more wonder, for even the cool Sebastian says:

> Now I will believe
> That there are unicorns; that in Arabia
> Ther⁻ is one tree, the phoenix' throne; one phoenix
> At this hour reigning there. (III.iii.21–4)

The banquet vanished by a special trick, which actors termed a 'secret',[12] but the table was left behind. The wonders of the Neapolitans grow steadily, Prospero offering more rare sights as they tread the 'maze'. Prospero breaks off the second interlude, the Marriage Masque, with a single word – as a host indeed might do if displeased – and all vanish to a 'strange, hollow, and confused noise.' Designed to cover the exit, this is the very opposite of music, something like 'the chimes of hell' muffled perhaps; there are other points where alarming noise is called for.[13] The Hunting Masque follows.

The illusions of this play belong in their conception to the lighted indoor theatre of the court and of Blackfriars with many others. It was given as part of the marriage celebrations of Princess Elizabeth, and though it need not have been specially composed for that occasion, its singleness of vision, with a kind of authority or security in the tone of utterance, suggests that it could be offered to the public as a special attraction. It is rather short for a full bill, but placed in the position of honour at the front of the Folio. Insofar as the island itself is one of the chief characters of the play, it is an enchanted ground with a good firm basis in theatrical machinery; *The Tempest* can even today be put on expensively as a showpiece. The play is both curious and costly and in a firm way assumes the compliance of the spectators until the very end.

Yet when Prospero, in his plumed hat and rapier, comes forward as Duke of Milan for his second epilogue – 'Our revels now are ended' being epilogue to all shape-changing except the hunt, which follows it – he resumes the octosyllabics of Ancient Gower in *Pericles*. These Milton was also to use in a masque much indebted to *The Tempest*. The 'beautiful vision' presented by a composed imagination as the device of 'a new and rare thing' has vanished. Yet if the magician has abandoned his art, the player has not fully abandoned his rôle and finally addresses, perhaps, his royal master, whose badge he wore, in a mixture of playful fancy and deep entreaty. Even a prayer for the King would not follow well on 'As you from crimes would pardon'd be, / Let your indulgence set me free'. It is Christian charity that is begged, not a contribution to the players' box.

Not only as actor of the main part but as director of the 'shows' (and one who had begun with a long narrative like a minstrel's), the part of Prospero combines a multiplicity of older roles. In its complexity, it is set off by the flatness of other characters and by the 'gaps' in the story. He himself breaks off the Masque of Ceres with all the curtness of royalty dismissing poor players. Even if their senses are not being charmed, characters do not communicate with each other; Miranda does not understand her father's story, since she has no experience of the kind of world inhabited by Sebastian and Antonio, whose sophistication enables them to communicate by cool hints and Machiavellian jests the project of a murder. They belong to a modern world – the world that Iachimo had also known.

Miranda answers Prospero therefore with the prim phrases of morality she has been taught; but when she meets Ferdinand, their communication, even more perfect than that of the conspiracy of evil, needs almost no words at all: 'They have changed eyes'. In the betrothal scene she offers herself to Ferdinand with a sweetness like that of the island, where Providence 'hangs in shades the Orange bright, / Like golden Lamps in a green Night'.[14] She looks out on the brave new world with a happy unguarded radiance which the poet Auden has caught perfectly in the Song he gives her: 'He kissed me awake and no one was sorry; / The sun shone on sails, eyes, pebbles, anything, / And the high green hill sits always by the sea'.[15] In its condensed poetry, *The Tempest* constantly invites such extensions of its own hints and guesses. The complex feelings of Prospero are themselves enigmatic; the whole play is like a great chamber, full of echoes. Many writers have been caught up to develop it. Dryden, absurdly, by doubling all the rôles out of admiration for its mechanical beauties, loaded it with the mathematical symmetry of *John a Kent* and dubious innuendo of his own. Auden played with extending it beyond the conclusion, putting his ironic commentary, as Browning did, into the mouth of Caliban.

The offering carries almost the power of a rite; to foster openness of interpretation, it permits an immense number of mythical, personal, and social extrapolations, and is accommodating to them all. Sidney knew 'the poet never affirmeth and therefore never lieth'; but by this very neutrality he drives others to passionate affirmations and denials. The play is among Shakespeare's shortest but it is his most elastic, most mutable composition.

Within the primary level of the action, Prospero as a white magician relies on invoking the cooperating powers of nature (although the scene where he hunts his enemies recalls Faustus' revenge on Benvolio).[16] The natural sympathy and unity between all parts of the world, whereby the more powerful controlled the less (as the sea is governed by the moon), enabled the man of art to put himself in sympathy and in tune with the whole natural process. Even the ranges of power beyond the moon, and therefore beyond the mutability of sublunary objects, were accessible. By talismans, on which the appropriate signs were inscribed, the magician could, as it were, harness the power behind the sun; he could get 'on the beam' of the supreme powers. Sycorax manipulated her black art to exert a physical compulsion on these heavenly spheres – for so I read the crux that she 'could control the moon... | And deal in her command, without her power' (v.i.270–1). 'Her command' is Sycorax's; 'without her power' means 'beyond the moon's range'. The guilty Alonso hears the whole universe speak with one voice as Prospero works on him:

> O, it is monstrous, monstrous!
> Methought the billows spoke, and told me of it;
> The winds did sing it to me; and the thunder,
> That deep and dreadful organ-pipe, pronounc'd
> The name of Prosper. (III.iii.95–9)

This power Prospero sums up in the torrential evocation that proclaims and abjures power at once (v.i.33–57). Ariel, half demon and half fairy, is tricksy and not wholly under Prospero's will – he, too, had his forerunners in old plays. His malleable shape-changing is the demonstration of Prospero's power. In this play Prospero is supreme. The Neapolitans say their prayers, and what Ariel in rebuking the 'men of sin' terms 'Destiny' or 'Fate' – which uses the lower world as an instrument – Prospero and Ferdinand term 'Providence'.[17] But if Prospero has to work when the stars are auspicious, he is left to play the god in a world where the spirits obey him; he claims to have raised the dead, but begins to feel death working within himself where he cannot command it. The humility of the final epilogue seems a necessary retraction after the extraordinary arrogance of the claims within the part itself, which leave him almost beyond mortality.

An overruling Providence was strongly present in the original story of the discovery of the Bermudas, as it is in Marvell's later poem:

> What should we do but sing his Praise
> That led us through the watry Maze
> Unto an Isle so long unknown,
> And yet far kinder that our own?...
> He gave us this eternal Spring,
> Which here enamells everything...
> He makes the Figs our mouths to meet;
> And throws the Melons at our feet.
>> But Apples plants of such a price,
>> No Tree could ever bear them twice.[18]

Prospero, too, discovers a new self; it would seem – the story is not clear – that though he has planned the wedding of Ferdinand and Miranda, yet the arrival of his betrayers stirs up other thoughts that would not fit in with such plans. Only by attaining the self-mastery that knows 'the rarer action is in virtue than in vengeance' (v.i.27–8) does Prospero, by this final ironical 'rarity', become strong enough not only to accept his enemies, but to abjure the magic by which he had wielded Jove's thunder. The great transformation increases his power over others by increasing his power over himself.

His relation with Ariel (and with Caliban) is what really needs solving, even more than his relation with other mortals. The ship-wrecked characters at first relate to Prospero only through their relation to his creatures. The King and his party encounter not the man, but Ariel; the servants meet not the master, but his deformed and savage slave. The play moves towards a final meeting; once this is achieved, the enchantments are dissolved.

When the trance of the King and the company is lifted, whole groups of statues come to life and return from the interior journey on which they have been sent by art; the wonder they feel grows greater and Alonso thinks only an oracle could resolve it. But Prospero, the director of shows, winds up with his last and best – the discovery of the lovers at chess.

This high and lofty game, used as the climax for more than one play,[19] casts, over the dispositions of followers and subjects, the cool and civilized grace of a mind that 'knows now what magic is; – the power to enchant / That comes from disillusion'.[20] The interweaving of different groups at last brought together, Prospero finishes his game. The theme of usurpation dissolves in a lovers' jest:

> *Miranda:* Sweet lord, you play me false.
> *Ferdinand:*   No, my dearest love.
>   I would not for the world.
> *Miranda:* Yes, for a score of kingdoms you should wrangle,
>   And I would call it fair play.   (v.i.171–5)

If allegory be an interaction between the play and its audience, stage audience and greater audience watch a game with more than one level here. Alonso, after passing through a series of ordeals, finds that they lead to the doorway of a fellow man, where he meets his son, his servants, the familiarity of the common world. The same boatswain and sailors, who had bid the world goodbye, make their landfall to return with the rest to the world of men.

The abdication of the magician's power could be an impoverishing choice, yet the moment of abdication itself confers an increased power; the hero shows a knowledge of the world coupled with detachment, which is also the effect of the play. It is upon the final self-conscious reflection of art looking on itself that the last of the romances comes to rest: 'We are such stuff / As dreams are made on' (iv.i.156–7). Auden spins the mood out in Prospero's speech to Ariel:

> Stay with me, Ariel, while I pack....
> Now our partnership is dissolved, I feel so peculiar:
> As if I had been on a drunk since I was born
> And suddenly now, and for the first time, am cold sober...
> I never suspected the way of truth
> Was a way of silence...even good music
> In shocking bad taste; and you of course never told me.[21]

The illusion that romance had so beguilingly indulged is carefully, layer on layer, penetrated, not simply as it would have been done in mimed narrative, but with the added depth and complexity of the developed stage arts. Romance, the least inherently dramatic of the forms that contributed to the Elizabethan stage, was the most powerful in terms of group response and group affirmation.

Shakespeare's series of romances began with *Pericles*, directly invoking an archaic narrative form; he ended with a play where not only the narrative and its narrator, its leading figure, were identified at the opening, but the complex relations of life and the poor player, of magic and death and change, were articulated.

Perhaps a formal structure was necessary, the artifice of the Unities serving as a launching platform for this extremely difficult ascent to a unified speech, in Prospero's three great moments – the first epilogue, to Ferdinand, 'Our revels now are ended'; the speech to Ariel, in which he renounces fury, leading into the evocation and renunciation of his magic power; and the final epilogue. There was surely also one climactic Occasion, one Rite, to elicit these words. The play may have been performed many times; it must have been performed once on some great ceremonial occasion when these great set pieces were authenticated, for the author and director at least.

The first epilogue ('Our revels now are ended') closes the last beautiful show and recalls in its imagery the dissolution of the body in death. From the heroic last speech of Antony's 'Sometimes we see a cloud that's dragonish', the dissolving rack, the dissolving 'shape' of a mortal, has become also the dissolving dream of a masque and the dissolving, finally, of the 'great globe' in cosmic mutability, that includes all organic nature. The union of the life of the stage and the life of the world in a royal masque – where at court, royalty itself took part, sometimes – and the uncertainty of both, supplies Prospero's instruction in statecraft – by means of these toys – to his new son, his new heir, Prince Ferdinand. It precedes the Ovidian summary of Prospero's darker 'shows', of which the opening scene had given a powerful impression. The darkening of the sun, the stirring up of winds and seas, and the tearing up of forests and shuddering of rocks cram more imagined action into a dozen lines than we are given in the rest of the play. The awesome and ominous power flashes a current back through the storms of *King Lear*, through Glendower to Oberon. It is, of course, a straight translation from Ovid, and it is written as an abdication of the power now invoked for the last time – the power to wield Jove's thunderbolt. The actor, the author and director, is absolved – at least he asks absolution – in the final epilogue, in the flat archaic language of Gower in *Pericles*, and something in the posture of Alonso appealing to Prospero.

The devil's chapel of the theatre (so its early opponents had termed it)[22] had been replaced by a scene at the court of a double new-joined kingdom, where royalty itself would enact the shows, as well as receiving the offerings, where the actors were royal servants. Ariel is out of his apprenticeship;[23] Prospero, though with a large area left unspoken in spectacle and song, in this last play closed his series. But it led forward to others, by other men. This epilogue raises the curtain on the drama – and the poetry – of modern times.

13

SHAKESPEARE AS COLLABORATOR

All drama, being an art of performance, is by nature collaborative.[1] As full member of the most famous Elizabethan gild of players, Shakespeare gained his privilege by never being merely a writer. That perhaps may have made him the kind of writer he was; participation is deeply invited by his dramatic style, whereas the lyric poet of *Venus and Adonis*, if splendid, is not incomparable.

After a brief survey of the history of this theme, I shall concentrate on one early and one late play – these being the two periods in which Shakespeare is assumed to have collaborated with other poets.

Among scholars deep wishes for some new epiphany of the Divine Shakespeare conflict with deep impulses to separate his pure essence from base accretion. The First Folio of 1623 'gathered' and 'collected' such plays as had been before unworthily printed, with 'all the rest, absolute in their numbers as he conceived them'. Seven plays, including *Pericles*, were added in the Third Folio of 1663 from the store that booksellers had found profitable to attribute to Shakespeare. The eighteenth century's growing idolatry swelled the hope for new plays, till in 1796 William Ireland gratified it with an entire tragedy, *Vortigern and Rowena*, staged at Drury Lane by Sheridan and exposed as forgery by Malone.

A counter-move from the Romantics showed Coleridge prepared to disencumber Shakespeare of every word unworthy of his genius. 'I think I could point out to half a line what is really Shakespeare's in *Love's Labour's Lost* and other not entirely genuine plays,' he modestly averred in *Table Talk*; in the Porter's speech of *Macbeth* he distinguished that Shakespeare 'with the remaining ink of a pen otherwise employed, just interpolated the words':

I'll devil-porter it no further; I had thought to let in some of all professions that go the primrose way to th'everlasting bonfire.

the main speech having been 'written by some other hand, perhaps with Shakespeare's consent'.[2]

In 1841, Charles Knight cautiously added a volume of Doubtful Plays to his *Illustrated Shakespeare*. With ecclesiastical overtones, as of a General Council of the Church promulgating Holy Writ, the contents of the Folio became 'the Shakespeare Canon', and, by analogy, any appendages 'the Apocrypha'.

The last quarter of the nineteenth century and the first quarter of the twentieth was the fashionable era of Shakespearian disintegrators – an age when Homer, too, was parcelled out among many poets. Greene's jibe at the 'upstart crow', and the habits of Henslowe's literary bondslaves, seemed to warrant an author who continually cobbled other men's works or his own. The age that opened with Fleay's *Metrical Tests applied to Dramatic Poetry* (1874) culminated in the work of J. M. Robertson, who finally left to the master only one play uncontaminated and unrevised – *A Midsummer Night's Dream* (he is now remembered merely as prompting T. S. Eliot's iconoclastic essay on *Hamlet*). In 1924 E. K. Chambers disposed magisterially of *The Disintegration of Shakespeare* in a British Academy Lecture; although traces of a revisionary Shakespeare, who blotted many a line and revised yet more, may be found in the first volumes of the Cambridge New Shakespeare, where all rhymed passages tend to be read as verse fossils – generally the fossilized remains of those once described as the University Half-Wits.

Bridge's notorious essay of 1907 blames the audience for 'preventing the greatest poet and dramatist in the world from being the best artist'.[3] The disintegrators created, largely in their own image, a purist tinkerer, who would have given the maximum inconvenience to the players studying their parts while offering the minimum novelty to the audience.

Meanwhile, the new school of bibliographers and paleographers added a collaborative work to the canon. First proposed as partly Shakespearean by Spedding in 1871, *The Book of Sir Thomas More* was so well established by the series of essays which Pollard collected in 1923, *Shakespeare's Hand in Sir Thomas More*, that the relevant sections have since been reprinted in several editions of the complete Works. Younger scholars carried out the vindication of Heming's and Condell's choice; yet difficulties revealed about the First Folio printing of one or two plays suggested that beyond the fringe lay other works, ephemera that yet may float among interstellar spaces with *Love's Labour's Won* and *Cardenio*. It is as hard to limit the possibility of Shakespearean collaboration as to crystallize a definitive text.[4] Within 'the Shakespeare area' all kinds of compositions may lie at greater or lesser approximation to the centre. It was sheer common sense that prompted E. K. Chambers to hazard 'I am prepared to think that Shakespeare wrote some very poor work', and Hardin Craig in 1948 to defend 'Shakespeare's Bad Poetry'.[5] Within a decade, however, Jan Kott was writing (in 1957) '*Titus Andronicus* is already Shakespearian theatre; but a truly Shakespearian text is yet to come.' In the new theatre of the fifties, the sovereignty of the text had been replaced by the sovereignty of the sub-text: performance claimed to have supplied a check on authenticity.

The doubtful plays remained editorially very much a side-issue. Alfred Hart's vocabulary tests and Edward Armstrong's image clusters improved on the discredited verse tests of Fleay;[6] soon the computer may yield new and more objective methods of determining Canon and Apocrypha, since it has already been applied significantly (I believe) to an even more august collection, the Epistles of St Paul.

Without reaching further than a modest probability, however, evidence of a sort other than the purely stylistic or verbal might be brought to bear. It may be that, if not asking the wrong questions about the doubtful plays, we have at least ignored another set of questions that might also be asked.

In the last twenty-five years, no area has been more intensively studied than the social and physical aspects of Elizabethan performance. Indeed, in popular interest it ranks so high that the sensation of the age has been not the 'discovery' of a new play but the 'discovery' of what is claimed as a picture of the Globe interior. This news made the headlines.

The development of the modern open stage, of workshop techniques, of audience participation, has led to reinterpretation of many Elizabethan plays; minor works of Shakespeare have succeeded on the boards where till recently some of them were never seen. Unfortunately, the doubtful plays outside the Folio are not good box office.

Yet the work of Harbage, Nagler, Wickham, Jacquot, Hosley, and others suggests the question: for what kind of theatre and for what kind of audience do these doubtful plays appear to have been written? Do they appear to fit in with what is known of Shakespeare's working life? Assuming the general acceptance of *Pericles* in part and *Sir Thomas More* in part, I shall look at two which remain doubtful, *The Raigne of King Edward III* and *Two Noble Kinsmen*. My conclusions, which I will give in advance, are that the first is probably not by Shakespeare but comes from his circle; the second, as stated on the title page, is by Fletcher and Shakespeare in collaboration; that both were written for the private stage, the first perhaps for a noble household.[7]

'A Book entitled Edward III and the Blacke Prince their Warres with John of France' was entered in the Stationers' Register on 1 December 1595, and in the nineties printed twice as 'The Raigne of King Edward III, as it hath been sundry times plaid about the Citie of London'.[8] Neither author nor company is given, so it could hardly have been a notable public success. The first two acts – attributed to Shakespeare[9] – present Edward's wooing of the Countess of Salisbury, and remain entirely detachable; they could have been an addition, since the original title omits this theme. A prologue scene sets out the English rights to France – the King has rather surprisingly to be informed that his mother was the French King's daughter and heiress – and both parts are thematically joined by the 'argument' of the whole play, which turns on feudal loyalty, the nature of allegiance, and the sanctity of an oath; being rhetorically based on pleas and counterpleas. The lady repulses the King's siege of love by reminding him that the marriage oath is more venerable than the oath of allegiance, and that he is guilty of High Treason against Heaven's King if he commits adultery. Unwillingly enlisted as devil's advocate under his own oath of allegiance, her father ingeniously turns his plea into a dissuasion. The Countess, exacting a promise from the king to perform her commands if she submits, demands the murder of both their spouses. When to her horror the King agrees, she whips out her wedding knives and prepares to kill her husband, whose image is 'lodged within her heart', unless the King swear an oath to desist. He suffers an instant conversion and departs for France, where, however, the Black Prince rather than his father holds the stage.

Although the play celebrates Creçy and Poitiers, it in no way resembles a civic show; the battles are not presented by drum and trumpet fighting but in long descriptive orations, and one or two heraldic entries. The common soldiers are not shown or given speaking parts; not so much as a pair of single combatants appears! Such treatment of great victories would have been totally un- acceptable to the common stages, and strongly suggests the play was written for private production by non-professional players or by boys.

In the second part the sanctity of an oath is upheld by the Dauphin against the King, his natural lord and father; the English Queen pleads with her lord the King against his unkingly decree to hang the burghers of Calais: both pleas succeed.

This noble theme would appeal to readers of Malory or courtly romance, but lacks the direct popular appeal of battle plays. The concept of imperial rule and the nature of sovereignty was made use of by Henry VIII to free himself from papal authority; it was a live issue still in late Tudor times,[10] especially in relation to the north country, where feudal ties still held.

The first part has been compared with Edward IV's wooing of Lady Grey (*3 Henry VI*, III.ii) but, by comparison with that lively scene, it is more like a set debate, rhetorically poised. Even in the Earl of Warwick's speech to his daughter, retracting his first plea, which has been singled out as 'the best poetry in the play'[11] we have a 'field of reasons' or a catena of proverbs, among which is incongruously set one of the most powerful lines from Shake- speare's sonnets:

> The freshest summer's day doth soonest taint
> The loathed carrion that it seems to kiss;
> Deep are the blows made with a mighty axe:
> That sin doth ten times aggravate itself
> That is committed in an holy place:
> An evil deed, done by authority,
> Is sin and subordination; Deck an Ape
> In tissue and the beauty of the robe
> Adds but the greater scorn unto the beast.
> A spacious field of reasons could I urge
> Between his glory, daughter, and thy shame:
> That poison shews worst in a golden cup:
> Dark night seems darker by the lightening flash;
> Lilies that fester smell far worse than weeds:
> And every glory that inclines to sin,
> The shame is treble by the opposite.   (II.i.437–53)[12]

Shakespeare does not literally repeat himself like this and in Sonnet 94 the ebb and flow of feeling – what Empson called its 'interpenetrating and fluid unity'[13] – dramatically culminates in the spurt of love and loathing that associates the floral emblem of purity with corrupted flesh by the power of the concentrated metaphor 'fester':

> So shall I live, supposing thou art true,
> Like a deceived husband; so love's face
> May still seem love to me, though alter'd new…   (Sonnet 93)
> For sweetest things turn sourest by their deeds.
> Lilies that fester smell far worse than weeds.   (Sonnet 94)

A totally different set of Shakespearean connections is provided in both parts by thematic likenesses to two plays which Shakespeare had not yet written – *Henry V* and *Measure for Measure*, both of which are subsequent to the publication of *Edward III*. Again, however, rhetorical persuasion of a non-dramatic kind distinguishes this work from Shakespeare's, even in the set speech of consolation to a young man facing death. The Duke's consolation to Claudio in *Measure for Measure* does not hammer at the topic as does the speech of old Audley which is intended to strengthen the Black Prince against the odds at Poitiers:

> To die is all as common as to live:
> The one inch wise, the other holds in chase;

For, from the instant we begin to live,
We do pursue and hunt the time to die:
First bud we, then we blow, and after seed,
Then presently we fall; and as a shade
Follows the bodie, so we follow death.
If then, we hunt for death, why do we fear it?
If we feare it, why do we follow it?
If we do follow, how can we shun it? (IV.iv.133–42)[14]

If the play was written for private performance, appealing to chivalric ideals rather than civic sentiment, and if it may be regarded as belonging to earlier forms of the private stage (as later, for instance, Chapman's rhetorical history plays), it could have been used at feasts within the city – for instance those of 'Prince Arthur's Knights', the city archers; or it could have been used at a great house in compliment to a great lady. The literary references tie it close to the date of publication, i.e., in the period 1594–5. The boys' theatres shut down in 1590 (see p. 14) and during 1592–4 the public theatres were also closed for plague. It is possible that Shakespeare, like Marlowe, took refuge with a noble patron. *Love's Labour's Lost* and *A Midsummer Night's Dream* were very possibly written for private performance. The first was regarded with especial interest by the Southampton family;[15] it has been suggested that *A Midsummer Night's Dream* was composed for the remarriage of the Dowager Countess of Southampton. If she presided over her son's fortunes during his minority, she might well be the further object of compliment in a play written for his circle, which glorified her ancestress, the Countess of Salisbury (both were Montagues, and it was through his mother that young Southampton was linked with the old nobility).

Could this play have been written by a friend during the period when all theatres were closed, but enacted by Shakespeare as part of a private group? If so he could well have had it in mind with the rest of the early repertory which has occasionally echoed even in his latest work.[16] The author would thus have quoted Shakespeare's private unpublished sonnets, and glanced at the poem addressed to Southampton, while Shakespeare in turn refashioned the material into something far more powerful when later he composed *Henry V* and *Measure for Measure* – the first as Southampton was leaving for Ireland with Essex, the second as he was released from the Tower by King James, where he had lain for three years under sentence of death for the Essex conspiracy.

The briefest comparison between *Edward III* and *Sir Thomas More* – now datable after 1590[17] – reveals that they belong to quite different types of performance. This is the jest-book style of history; a great man but one with the common people, More jests with his friends, his servants, even on the way to the scaffold, where his courageous mockery has been foreshadowed in that of the common rebel, John Lincoln, and Doll Williamson. Not only does the play depict the rioters of Ill May Day sympathetically, it hints at state matters that under the present 'fifty years' rule' would be only just released. The play appeals to the solidarity and sense of humanity among the Londoners, in the same manner as Peele's *Edward I*; but the aliens depicted in More's Shakespearean speech – his appeal to the rioters – are quite inconsistent with the swaggering thieving scoundrels of the opening scene, who try to abduct the redoubtable Doll.

Five hands collaborated in *Sir Thomas More*, mainly the work of Mundy, a city pageanter, who was used to work with a group; in the Shakespearean plea of More, the living accents of persuasion, urgent and passionate, are heard. To compare it with *Edward III* is like comparing Brutus' oration with Antony's; the one is correct according to the books, the other flows out in an appeal to imagination, sympathy, and participation:

> Grant them removed, and grant that this your noise
> Hath chid down all the majesty of England:
> Imagine that you see the wretched strangers,
> Their babies at their backs and their poor luggage,
> Plodding to th' ports and coasts for transportation,
> And that you sit as kings in your desires,
> Authority quite silenct by your brawl,
> And you in ruff of your opinions cloth'd,
> What had you got? I'll tell you: you had taught
> How insolence and strong hand should prevail,
> How order should be quell'd; and by this pattern,
> Not one of you should live an aged man,
> For other ruffians, as their fancies wrought,

With selfsame hand, self reasons and self right
Would shark on you, and men, like ravenous fishes,
Would feed on one another.   (II.iv.92–107)

These two early histories have in common only a certain elasticity. Each could have been expanded or contracted; More plays a jest which is attributed to Thomas Cromwell. The story of Edward III and the Countess of Salisbury was not told as historically established, even by such a liberal embroiderer of fact as William Painter in his *Palace of Pleasure*; in relying on social assumptions, in one case chivalric and in the other civic, the plays celebrate the societies to which they were addressed.

In our own day, the need to interpret Shakespeare's histories has led to adaptations in the home of classic Shakespearean performance, the Royal Shakespeare Theatre at Stratford. In his introduction to *The Wars of the Roses*, Peter Hall observed that stage adaptation is not like 'improving' a painting, when the damage is irrevocable. Moreover, any performance involves some adaptation and selection – as does any other act of interpretation. 'But a production cannot help creating as well as criticizing, and so turning the original text into something it is not by itself.' The aim, he concluded, was to fill out what was taken to be Shakespearean thematic design. 'It is a piece of directorial interference certainly but it is not a piece of Shakespearean pastiche';[18] this text should not be used as a basis for other productions, for it was designed for one time and place, one set of actors. The emphasis on order and degree reinforced for the modern audience assumptions which would have been implicit in Shakespeare's own day.

The play which a French critic recently termed 'le chante de cygne de Shakespeare'[19] can safely be assigned to the King's Men, the Blackfriars, and the year 1613; it is difficult to resist also the claims of the title page of 1634 that it was 'written by the memorable Worthies of their time: Mr John Fletcher and Mr William Shakespeare, Gentm.' The Jacobean audience would have hastened to see what most readers look on as its chief weakness – the Jailer's mad daughter, a parody of Ophelia, in her unrequited love for Palamon. In a wood near Athens, this She-Fool entertains the bridals of Theseus and Hippolita with a Morris Dance of Country People, which had been presented at court in the Masque of the Inner Temple and Gray's Inn to celebrate the nuptials of Princess Elizabeth and the Elector Palatine, married on St Valentine's Day 1613. The Masque, by Francis Beaumont, was introduced by its antimasque, in which all characters, instead of being of the same species, and dressed alike, were 'a confusion or commixture of all such persons as are proper for country sports' to signify the love of the common people. 'All these persons apparell'd to the life', the twelve 'Dancers, or rather actors, expressed every one their part so naturally and aptly' that the audience were deeply stirred and diverted, and raised 'the laughter and applause above the music'. The King himself called for an encore.[20]

A repeat performance before a select audience at Blackfriars by the King's Men would be highly profitable; but the antimasque was brief, as the professional act had been only a curtain-raiser to the main masque of young lawyers. The play was perhaps only commissioned to provide a setting for the antimasque. It is said that in performance the Jailer's daughter turns out to be the star part.[21]

Two years before, the dance of satyrs from Jonson's *Masque of Oberon* (given 1 January 1611) had been seen in *The Winter's Tale*, but mention of Oberon is sufficient to recall the conflict of national feelings which later lay behind the façade of gaiety – the 'mirth in funeral and dole in marriage'. On 6 November 1612, Henry, Prince of Wales, the Oberon of the Court, gallant, popular, and only eighteen years of age, died of typhoid fever at the beginning of his sister's wedding festivities. His funeral was celebrated in December, the postponed wedding following in February. Many of the marriage odes were bound up with elegies for the Prince; brother and sister had been devoted to each other.[22]

The hymeneal opening scene of *The Two Noble Kinsmen* keeps decorum, therefore, in being crossed by the dark pageant of three mourning queens, whose plea for their dead husbands brings funeral rites to the wedding, postponing the festivities. When Theseus has avenged them and conquered Thebes, the two young kinsmen are carried on for dead – though with hopes of revival.

The ritual of the three kings' funerals follows, with the ceremonial parting of the queens (a mimetic rendering of the Virgilian 'Mille viae mortis'):

> This world's a city full of straying streets,
> And Death's the market place, where each one meets.
>
> (I.v.15–16)

This concludes the first act, generally thought to be Shakespearean. The story of the kinsmen follows to its conclusion, which again combines the wedding of the widowed bride Emily, to Palamon, with the funeral of his rival Arcite, follower of Mars (Henry, too, had been martial).

A chivalric tale, which had been staged with great success early in Elizabeth's reign, is here presented in ritualized fashion; the comparison is with the tradition of *Edward III* rather than with that of *Sir Thomas More*. War and love are still the argument, which, however, is given by spectacle rather than debate. A most percipient critic has observed that the Shakespearean scenes

are static and, though with splendour, stiff. They are slow and dense, compared with Fletcher's easy liquescense. They have a deliberate yet vague grandeur, a remote and half exhausted exaltation; they are expressed through a clotted rhetoric that is the poetry of a man that has finished with action.[23]

As Theodore Spencer goes on to say, 'Slow lines move, like figures in heavy garments' to 'an adagio rhythm, haunting, evocatory, spoken as it were behind a veil.' The lovers never exchange anything but formal words in public with the princess, the final combat occurs offstage (and of course Palamon never meets the Jailer's daughter). Theseus dismisses the shattered wreck of the victor as if his whole life had been artifice:

> His part is played, and though it were too short,
> He did it well. (v.iv.118–19)

The three altars of Venus, Diana, and Mars could have come from Lyly's stage; neither crowd scenes nor elaborate stage effects were used; the play requires none of the extravagant setting that distinguished *King Henry VIII*, staged the same year. In the Shakespearean scenes, images of rivers and fishing, of pastoral and

237

woodlands suggest a scene 'far in a Western brookland', culminating in the May Queen's invocation by Arcite:[24]

> O Queen Emilia,
> Fresher than May, sweeter
> Than her gold buttons on the boughs, or all
> Th'enamelled knacks o' the mead and garden...   (III.i.4–7)

This is in 'Diana's wood'; by contrast, Auden has well noted the
'humiliating and horrid' imagery of Palamon's invocation to
Venus, and 'the disgust expressed at sexual vanity'. 'To make a
cripple flourish with his crutch' and bring an octogenarian to wed
a girl of eighteen leads a monster into Venus' pageant, almost
a death's head, to the bridal:[25]

> The aged cramp
> Had screwed his square foot round,
> The gout had knit his fingers into knots,
> Torturing convulsions from his globy eyes
> Had almost drawn their spheres, that what was life
> In him seemed torture.   (V.i.116–21)[26]

The widowed queens use a beautiful but terrifying image of a be-
headed dove (Venus' bird), Hippolyta can talk unmoved of
cannibalism among the vanquished (I.iii.15–19), but Emily is no
Amazon and responds directly to the tears of the widows:

> Pray you, say nothing, pray you.
> Who cannot feel nor see the rain, being in't,
> Knows neither wet nor dry.   (I.i.130–2)

Her nullity is part of the pattern; when invited to preside over the
combat for her hand ('you the only star to shine') she refuses and
would rather die herself:

> I am extinct.
> There is but envy in the light which shows
> The one the other.   (V.iii.26–8)

For Theodore Spencer, 'the whole thing is two dimensional and
unreal, a piece of tapestry, not like the story of Troilus and
Cressida, an active conflict'. But since it is meant to replace a
masque and to throw into relief the rapid gaiety of the antimasque, this effect is not inappropriate. Moreover, the peculiar

flatness of the characters – what Spencer terms their 'albinism' – allows the handling of a situation with both heterosexual and homosexual elements.

Palamon and Arcite, like the older pair, Theseus and Pirithous, are symbols of masculine devotion; in prison they claim that each replaces for the other wife and offspring, indeed the whole social world. Their quarrel over Emily simply replaces love by hate without weakening the bond; they fight for her as an object, a 'jewel', and as she says, 'The misadventure of their own eyes kill 'em' (III.vi.191). In Fletcher, fighting and insults as a form of erotic play are common enough. The two sisters discourse on the rivalry of sexual love and male friendship, and Emily describes her childhood love for a girl who died at eleven years, with whom she shared all actions and preferences.

This formality of structure, the masque-like concern with rôles rather than characters, allows the topic of homosexuality to become pervasive without being acknowledged. The relation of the kinsmen to each other lies at the centre of the action, and their theme reflects what everyone knew to be the habits of the monarch himself.

In condemning both lovers to death for fighting without the ceremony of the lists, the chivalrous Theseus may be reflecting James's Edict against Private Combats (October 1613); but he, too, in the end submits to Fortune, the sovereign deity of the play, whose influence overrules Diana, Mars, and Venus.[27]

In the cosmic order which Stuart masques celebrated, the highest and most godlike states are embodied in the chief masquers, as when in Daniel's *Vision of the Twelve Goddesses*, Pallas descended in the form of Queen Anne, 'being otherwise no object for mortal eyes'.

The stately grief of the main story is contrasted with the antimasque for which it was a setting, out of which grows the story of the subplot. The Jailer's daughter, chief figure of the antimasque, falls in love with Palamon, and sets him free at peril of her father's life; following him to the greenwood on May Eve, she hopes that the rites of the time will be celebrated with rustic freedom. Like the Morris Dance itself the exchange of rush rings and a night in the greenwood belonged to that old 'Merry England' which had already passed away.[28] This is *not* Diana's wood:

> Let him do
> What he will with me, so he use me kindly,
> For use me so he shall, or I'll proclaim him,
> And to his face, no man. (II.vi.28–31)

Missing her tryst she grows melancholy, plaits rush rings by the waterside in a parody of the forsaken Ophelia, whilst imagining Palamon to enjoy the favours of innumerable country girls; she is cured by her humble lover, who puts on Palamon's garments and takes her virginity. At their meeting, the Jailer's daughter, now imagining herself at sea, begins to imitate another famous scene from the elder collaborator's repertory:

> *Daughter:* You are Master of a ship?
> *Jailor:* Yes.
> *Daughter:* . . . For the tackling, let me alone.
> Come, weigh, my hearts, cheerily all! O, O, O, 'tis up!
> The wind's fair, top the bowline! Out with the mainsail!
> Where's your whistle, mariner? (IV.i.181–91)

This bold piece of parody, a scene of intimate jesting, puts a new antimasque into the players' own domestic repertory. If 'an art which plays over the whole gamut between firm convention and complete realism'[29] is stronger than one which ranges from the sublime to the ridiculous without ever touching the realistic, this show reveals limitations in spite of great variety. The Jailer's daughter, in her tragic-grotesque vision of Hell, castigates her own early hopes, and displays that kind of 'dislocation' which Clifford Leech has distinguished as the main feature of Fletcher's art.[30] In the same way, the two Kinsmen at one point condemn the licentiousness of Thebes, at another gleefully recall their own amorous exploits, and yet again, Palamon, at the end, primly repudiates such conduct. This is possible only in an 'olla podrida' which included parodies of theatrical art. If acted with the 'variety' that distinguished the quick-moving antimasque, the two halves of the show might cohere as theatrical collage, designed to reflect the confusion which had so pleased in the original entertainment at court. The work was perhaps too topical to be revived in the public theatres, but to condemn the whole play as 'nothing more than frivolous'[31] is to ignore its dual character – an old, native heroic setting for an *avant-garde* hit.

In the following year Ben Jonson parodied *Two Noble Kinsmen* in *Bartholomew Fair*. Rival suitors, whose fate is to be determined by drawing lots, chose the names of Argalus, out of *Arcadia*, and Palamon 'out of the play'; 'Palamon' wins the lady (IV.iii.67–8). The puppeteer shows two faithful friends Damon and Pythias falling out for love of Hero, and abusing each other till the puppet master intervenes and is himself abused – whereat he retorts 'I say, between you, you have but one drab'.[32] *Bartholomew Fair*, with its puppets leaning out of the booth, must visually have evoked the two prisoners leaning out of their prison window; it testifies to the earlier show's success; for Jonson would not waste his satire on a failure.

The case for Shakespeare's part-authorship is so strong that, as Kenneth Muir says, the onus of proof really rests on the sceptics; yet few would follow Paul Bertram[33] in assigning to Shakespeare the whole play. The reasons for collaboration may have been, first, speed; secondly, to emphasize variety by engaging the two best authors of the King's Company. If the whole town were talking of the antimasque, it would be profitable to put it on quickly, and Shakespeare had rushed out a play on at least one previous occasion. He wrote the slow stately opening and closing acts, Fletcher added to the piquancy of the jests and jibes by recalling his new partner's successes, while shaping the work of his former partner, Beaumont, who had composed the original antimasque, the speediest, merriest part of the show.

Jacobeans loved variety; two famous names on the playbill would be an asset. Yet, since the main design was Fletcher's and hardly amounted to a drama, it remained outside the collection made a decade later in Shakespeare's memory. Piety and curiosity will always search for fragments of his work which may throw light on his greater achievement; but the First Folio may well represent what the writer himself would have wished to be remembered by.

Part III

CAROLINE CURTAIN ACT

14

MASQUE AND PASTORAL

The year is the eighth of Charles I's reign – 1632. Shakespeare had retired and the First Globe had burnt nearly twenty years before. Richard Burbage had died in 1619. Not only the first but a second edition of Shakespeare's plays had appeared in Folio – this with an invocation to him as 'Dear Son of Memory, great heir of Fame', by a young Londoner, John Milton. November, traditional start of the Revels season, saw a squat heavy book, the product of seven years' compilation, with an average of perhaps thirty citations on each of its thousand pages, but sustained throughout by a steady blaze of rage – William Prynne's *Histriomastix*. The direct attack on players and playhouses had begun.

Though Prynne roars at Papists and Quakers with equal fury, he is ready to cite any Pope or Jesuit Father who disapproves of plays; certain damnation does not destroy the validity of witness; behaviour rather than belief is impugned; it is the *acting* of plays not their composition that puts 'player-poets' on the bad eminence of being 'first movers' of an 'infernal cosmos'. Prynne is as physically outraged by what he finds in the playhouse as he is by those who bow at the name of Christ or wear 'profane Lovelocks'. His book (a parody of play design) is set out in acts and scenes, each scene beginning with a syllogism that combines diatribe and mimicry. Some of his arguments go back to Wycliffe, but the dread of public disorder is largely replaced by hatred of courtly extravagance and wantonness. He scolds the universities for allowing acting, and praises his own society of Lincoln's Inn as the least theatrically minded of the Inns of Court.

Prynne's punishment was savage. What gave offence was the assertion that all Kings or Emperors who acted were degenerate as Antony or Caligula, whilst all women who acted were 'notorious whores' (like Cleopatra?). Prynne's insults might be held to apply to Charles and Henrietta Maria, who in 1631 had appeared in two masques composed by Ben Jonson, and the next year as Heroic Virtue and Divine Beauty in two further masques by Aurelian Townshend. Deprived of his Oxford degree and disbarred, expelled from Oriel and Lincoln's Inn, after a year in the Tower, on 17 February 1634, Prynne was sentenced to be fined £5,000, to stand in the pillory, to lose both his ears, and to be imprisoned for life. Later, as in prison he continued to write against bishops, he was branded on both cheeks, fined again and resentenced under more stringent conditions. He lived to be received back in the City of London with triumph, and to quarrel over divorce with John Milton, who indulged in several savage jests against 'margineared' Prynne.

With such ferocity was the vision of the golden age, the apocalyptic beauty of the court masque, attacked and defended. The attack on it was equally an attack on all social functions of playing – on actor–audience relationships as such, and on writers as they completed the 'triple bond'. For Charles I, an ideal image of himself was a necessity. His behaviour was a model of dignity – a rather theatrical model.

Caroline masquing differed radically from Jacobean in being 'the donatives of great princes to their people' as Jonson termed it (see above, Chapter 4, p. 82). That is, it was no offering *to* royalty but an offering *by* royalty; Charles and his Queen took the leading parts. Only after the assassination of Buckingham in August 1628 did Charles I, to the amusement of his courtiers, begin to fall in love with Henrietta Maria; only after the birth of their first living child, the future Charles II, at St James's Palace on 29 May 1630, did their joint masquing really begin. Charles had already embarked on his 'eleven years' tyranny', rule without a Parliament, which completed the severance that his own temperament had begun between himself and his people. The devotion of the royal pair was based on their shared limitations: Henrietta Maria has been characterized as possessing.

A gaiety which was conscious and innocent and a rather careful and regal virtue ...The scene through which she moved was lavish and mannered and pastoral.

All her portraits combine to indicate a desire for stateliness and a sense of carriage. She was capable of a driving and fragile energy. It was only the coming storm that would reveal her lucid understanding, and her hard and brittle mind. One is left principally with three impressions – the directness; the ignorance; the diamond quality.[1]

The King gave the Queen a Twelfth Night masque in which he offered her homage. She returned the compliment at Shrovetide. When in 1632 Gustavus Adolphus, the Protestant champion, was killed, one writer of masques wrote a verse epistle to another:

> Tourneys, masques, theatres better become
> Our halcyon days; what though the German drum
> Bellow for freedom and revenge, the noise
> Concerns us not, nor should divert our joys;
> Nor ought the thunder of their carabines
> Drown the sweet airs of our tuned violins;
> Believe me, friend, if their prevailing powers
> Gain them a calm security like ours,
> They'll hang their arms upon the olive bough
> And dance and revel then as we do now.[2]

The climax of the first of Townshend's masques had been the figure of Peace, descending from the clouds till 'lions and lambs together live'. Indeed the figure of Peace begins to appear with ominous frequency in the masques; she might look very like the Peace who had greeted King James a quarter of a century before, but the same image could be used by different parties. A year before the arrival of the infant Charles II caused the Whitehall rejoicings, the young Londoner, destined ultimately to justify Charles I's execution, had celebrated the silencing of pagan gods by the miracle of a more august birth, diffusing over the whole earth and sea a 'halcyon' calm.

> But he, her fears to cease,
> Sent down the meek ey'd Peace;
>   She crown'd with olive green, came softly sliding
> Down through the turning sphere,
> His ready Harbinger,
>   With Turtle wing the amorous clouds dividing,
> And waving her wide myrtle wand,
> She strikes a universal Peace through Sea and Land.
>
>   (*On the Morning of Christ's Nativity*, stanza III)

The chiming of the 'chrystal spheres' the bass of heaven's organ, herald the descent of all four Daughters of God, as Truth, Justice and Mercy also appear in the clouds, and heaven 'as at some festival/Will open wide the gates of her high Palace Hall'. Milton did not denounce masquing language; he appropriated it.

Other traditional emblems were being used by both parties, but the courtly mythology steadily set out the royal pair as reformers of pagan licence. In *Albion's Triumph*, which moves from a Roman Forum to a sacred grove and thence to a 'Landscape in which was a prospect of the King's Palace at Whitehall and the City of London seen afar off', the royal pair convert the gods from evil habits, reform Circe and infuse marital temperance into Jove. The golden age had been achieved in Whitehall in 1631. Three years later, the brutish signs of the zodiac were drawn down from heaven and banished (the worst to the plantations in America) whilst the King, Queen and Court were stellified, as being much better fitted than the old gods to give examples to mankind at large.[3] The performance of this masque coincided with the sentencing of Prynne.

Earlier the same month, February 1634, by presenting a most sumptuous masque, *The Triumph of Peace*,[4] the four Inns of Court had dissociated themselves from him (his book had been dedicated to the students of the Inns, particularly his own). It cost over £21,000 and was given both at court and in the city; a better title for it would be *The Triumph of Ostentation*. There were dazzling parades through the streets of London, with 200 halberdiers in attendance, first to Whitehall then to the Merchant Taylors' Hall for the city performance, where the Lord Mayor was host. It celebrated the birth of a second son, the Duke of York – destined as James II to end the Stuart Monarchy. The author, James Shirley was educated, like Milton, in London and at Cambridge; he had been a parson and schoolmaster but had lately turned Papist and playwright.

The masquers are the Sons of Peace, Law and Justice, powers who act as presenters, though including social criticism of 'projectors' (i.e. patentees). The twelve antimasques are presented by such characters as Opinion, Fancy, Jollity, Confidence, Novelty,

Laughter and Admiration whilst the last of all, heralded by 'noise and confusion within', was of the workmen who had produced the costumes and staging. The Revels were closed by Amphiluce, the dawn twilight, 'a young maid with a dim torch in her hand' who sings a curious and rather sinister little song.

Shirley had also written a comedy containing a masque, which he had ironically dedicated to Prynne, incarcerated in the Tower (its title, *The Bird in the Cage*). He was now made a member of Gray's Inn and Valet of the Chamber to the Queen.

In his play *Love's Cruelty* (1631), Shirley had previously paid a graceful tribute to Jonson, whose two final masques belonged to that same year, and set out the power of a masque to charm away melancholy. This, however, seems to depend more on Inigo Jones's share of the 'wonders': it reveals how a very competent playwright thought of the audience reaction; they must project themselves into a series of changes:

A Masque prepared and music to charm Orpheus himself into a stone, numbers presented to your ears that shall speak the soul of the immortal English Jonson, a scene to take your eye with wonder, now to see a forest move, and the pride of summer brought into a walking wood; in the instant, as if the sea had swallowed up the earth, to see the waves capering above tall ships, Arion upon a rock playing to the dolphins, the Tritons calling up the sea nymphs to dance before you; in the height of this rapture a tempest so sudden and artificial in the clouds, with a general darkness and thunder, so seeming made to threaten, that you would cry out with the Mariners in the work, you cannot scape drowning; in the turning an eye, these waters vanish into a heaven, glorious and angelical shapes presented, the stars distinctly with their motion and music so enchanting you, that you would wish to be drowned indeed in such a happiness.[5]

Theatrically, this is a totally new world. It was not Ben Jonson's. His latest farce, *A Tale of a Tub* (1633) is full of preposterous 'changes' for a Valentine's Day 'cross-wooing' but in old Elizabethan style alternates horse-play and 'humours'. Appearing as it did shortly after Prynne's attack on masques, it celebrates humble and rustic pleasures, but additionally the whole 'frame' is drawn from the popular stages of Jonson's youth. It is still a matter of dispute whether Jonson revised an early work of his own, or wrote a new one in the old style. Considering the Shakespearean form of more than one of his so-called 'dotages' I would take the latter view.[6] This is Jonson's entry to the old Kingdom of Fools – and by now he was himself a Beggar, asking old friends for money with the admission that he could never hope to repay. Assuming here a pastoral lowliness, he was taking aim at someone now much higher than himself – he, the half-paralysed and half forgotten, out-of-favour poet, put on a mechanicals' play to lampoon the King's surveyor, who had built the Banqueting Hall and the Queen's House at Greenwich, as well as producing the masques over which they had quarrelled. Inigo Jones was important as a creator of ideal images for both King and Queen.

In the same month when the farce was licensed, Jonson also wrote a country entertainment of a mock-wedding, to be given before the King at the Earl of Newcastle's country seat, Welbeck. Both show and play derive directly from the mock-marriage written for the Princely Pleasures of Kenilworth. Pastoral was the last refuge of one who was falling behind the times. His Platonism (see above, Chapter 4, pp. 62–4) had been garbled by Jones in a commentary on *Tempe Restored*, a stale rehash of the *Ballet Comique de la Reyne* (1582).

The country sport of tilting at the Quintain is introduced at Welbeck by six figures (like those from an antimasque) to celebrate the marriage of Stub of Stub Hall. In *A Tale of a Tub* it is Sir Tripoli Tub of Tub Hall, a young boy, unsuccessful suitor for Awdrey Turfe, who leads the sports of St Valentine's Day. The play is built on a recognizable old pattern which might be called 'Hunting the Bride'; the hunt extends throughout Finsbury Hundred, led by the bride's father, its 'wise High Constable'; it gallops through the villages of Hampstead, Highgate, Belsize, Chadcote (Chalk Farm), Kentish Town, Marylebone, St Pancras, Islington and Kilburn, from which his 'Wise Council' of fools is drawn. The company, producing at a 'private' house, was *avant garde*.[7]

Toby Turfe, the constable, is about to marry his daughter Awdrey to John Clay the tileman (an occupation traditional for the hen-pecked). Awdrey is only too ready to marry anyone, but by plot of a rival suitor the wretched Clay has been accused of robbery with violence. Concealing himself from the hue and cry, he emerges grotesquely from the straw where he has been hiding and is taken for the devil himself. The whole play being written, as Jonson declares,

> to show what different things
> The cotes of clowns are, from the courts of kings

ends with the marriage of Awdrey to a cunning servant man, Pol-Martin (his name suggests the old beast fable), whilst Sir Tripoli Tub writes a 'motion' to celebrate these adventures. This 'motion' is produced by In-and-In Medlay,[8] a joiner (like James Burbage) of Islington; who transparently conceals the personage of Inigo Jones; and displayed at Tub's renamed 'Totnam Court'. The last act has evidently been heavily revised in response to complaints received by the Master of the Revels. Originally Medlay was named 'Vitruvius Hoop' – and indeed another character with that name appeared in the very latest work of Jonson written for a last country show in 1634, *Love's Welcome*. The attack on the masque here seems reduced to a very harmless parody; but the whole action of the day is rehearsed by 'lantern-leery' (a sort of shadow-puppet work) at break-neck pace in a way that would certainly allow a good deal of gagging and by-play to be slipped in by the actors. This is obviously a scenario that performance could modify in all sorts of ways. The helter-skelter gaiety of the bride hunt (Awdrey has three rival suitors, besides her lawful bridegroom, who brings in representatives of the church and the law) means that she is carried off, recovered, another riotous chase is begun, and the whole band gets up a pursuit which can only be faintly adumbrated in the final shadow motion of the Tub.[9] Sir Tripoli's Court could burlesque the one and only Court; his lady mother whose husband made money out of saltpetre (what is usually called 'the powdering tub of infamy', the cure of venereal disease, comes to mind) is more than likely to have granted her favours to the clever Pol-Martin, her usher. Minor characters with pre-posterous names make up the sort of folk game which had more than once been used as a cover for attacks on the unpopular.[10] The mock pedigrees for instance, allow In-and-In a chance to boast 'I am truly Architectonicus professor' though the boyish Tripoli can correct his Latin. Apparently the device did not escape general remark, for the Master of the Revels, besides ordering various deletions, charged twice his usual fee. The play was put on at the Phoenix by the Queen's Men; when presented at court in the Christmas season it was tersely noted by the Master of the Revels as 'not liked'. Jonson could still succeed with a set speech and a little horseplay and high spirits to follow, when in rural surroundings; but there was no response at the court, a few months later to the revival there of old festivity.[11] Jonson, who must have enjoyed his success at Welbeck, bravely reshaped part of it for the next summer's rural welcome. Every sequence is thoroughly traditional; if no 'medley' it yet could find its original in Elizabethan plays; the play itself is set vaguely in the 'Queen's time'. Its nostalgia for the good old days and bucolic joys skilfully sets the author's claims low and his opponents' still lower. One or two of Inigo Jones's favourite expressions are kept – 'feasible' and 'conduce' – but it is the attack of a man who feels himself at a disadvantage and yet (this is the touching and heroic feature of this latest comedy) it is genuinely festive, as are the two pastoral welcomes. In performance it succeeds as farce.

Jonson may be recalling those farces based on theatrical successes that the Inns of Court had put on at Christmas, and attempting to apply this method – a sort of self-depreciatory mockery – to the court masque from which by this date he had been quite plainly dropped. He puts in some literary–historic colouring, with references to Skelton's *Eleanor Running* or the boys' play *Tom Tyler* (1560). Medlay disclaims any learning – 'that's reading and writing and records' – he says but he also rejects the suggested help of a poet 'old John Heywood' – Jonson is writing a sort of popular 'costume play'. At a moment when masquing had become not so much a form of entertainment as a way of asserting the ideal, his 'revenges' on Inigo Jones could not hope to succeed. Tripoli Tub is compared favourably, for wit, with 'any of the Inns of Court or Chancery', but they themselves were just preparing the first show that they had ever presented to King Charles, and Jonson could indeed have been suspected of mocking *their* efforts.

It is now 1634 and in September of that year Henry Lawes, whose brother had composed part of the music for *The Triumph of Peace*, composed for and acted in a masque presented on Michaelmas Night at Ludlow Castle to the Earl of Bridgewater. It was Lawes who in 1637 published *Comus* to which Milton had not appended his name. He had already written for this family the rustic welcome of *Arcades*, a ritual with three movements (song, speech, finale) that led masquers along an avenue, where many years before, the aged Queen Elizabeth had received the last of all Summer shows in her honour. *Comus*, too, is pastoral and celebrates, by adapting courtly forms, a noble family in exile from court.[12]

Even William Prynne had conceded that the beauties of nature might afford recreation or refreshment – indeed, in his prison on the Isle of Wight, he was waxing eloquent on this subject. Yet for a man of Milton's principles, given the strength of public feeling, the situation in 1634 must have presented a challenge.

Comus was a children's performance; the Earl of Bridgewater, as Lord President, had been sent to govern Wales; indeed, he had resided there for over a year. His two sons, who had appeared as torchbearers in *Coelum Britannicum*, at eleven and nine years of age, were experienced performers. Their sister, Lady Alice, aged about fifteen, who had danced in *Tempe Restored*, took the more demanding part of the Lady (incidentally, the married chastity of the Earl and Countess had resulted in no less than fifteen children).

Three scenes are presented; a wild wood, the palace of Comus, and lastly 'the scene changes, presenting Ludlow Town and the President's Castle' – where the performance was being held. Only the antimasque of Comus and his rout, and the last sequence, are truly masque-like; after a country dance, the children are presented to their parents

> To triumph in victorious dance
> O'er sensuous folly and intemperance.

This was a harvest festivity; the use of such a season and of such a courtly form to celebrate the Virtues of temperance and restraint is highly paradoxical, though Prospero's *Masque of Ceres* is recalled.

'No doubt you have often practised turning yourself into an angel of light as a parade ground exercise', wrote Screwtape to his nephew, the junior devil; 'Now is the time to practise doing it in the face of the enemy.'

Milton often practised turning himself into a tempter; not a few would conclude that he did it once too often, and that the speeches of Comus are 'richer, subtler and more sensitive' – and more Shakespearean – than anything in his later works.[13]

Comus was an antimasque, not in the Jonsonian sense, but rather as we would speak of an anti-play, from a poet who could accept neither the virulent denunciations of Prynne nor the *paradis artificiel* of the court. It is full of echoes of Shakespeare, especially *The Tempest*, of Jonson, especially of *Pleasure Reconciled to Virtue*, which opens with Comus, and of innumerable figures released from imprisonment in enchanted chains, or trees, of Browne's *Inner Temple Masque*, where Circe joins the Sirens, of Townshend's Circe from *Tempe Restored*, and Hedone from Carew's *Coelum Britannicum* – those other masques in which the Earl's children had appeared.

> Bewitching siren, gilded rottenness,
> Thou has with cunning artifice displayed
> The enammelled outside and the honeyed verge
> Of a Fair cup where deadly poison lurks.   (ll. 809–12)

But it reverses the intentions of the court. In Comus's celebration of the cosmic dance, the celebration of Nature's bounty, we feel

> The sounds and seas with all their finny drove
> Now to the moon in wavering morris move   (ll. 115–16)

This is the lowest level of the great chain of being.

In act of homage to man, the silk-worms in their 'green shops' are weaving 'the smooth-haired silk' for a masquerade.[14] As in any pastoral, the particular place is hallowed, and against Comus' hellish 'morris', celestial powers provide, poetically, the ordered traction of the masque's most inevitable 'machines' – the heavenly spirit descending, and the rising river goddess staying her 'sliding chariot'

> thick set with agate and the azure sheen

Of turkis blue and emerald green
That in the channel strays.

In abjuring 'Nature's waste fertility', as offered by Comus, the
Lady is also abjuring the excess of the usual court masque. This
austere little 'corrective' is not a matter of insufficiency but of
choice.

The fusion or pressure of such spectacle as could be contrived is
often paradoxical; Comus's followers dance a ring-dance bearing
torches; their rites are dark, consecrated to Hecate. When he is
banished, Sabrina, tutelary goddess of the Severn, princess of the
ancient British house, by a combination of rural virtues, royal
power and chastity, rises from the river to rebaptize the Lady.
Whether or not as had been suggested, she typifies the Reformed
Church,[15] her new world is felt to be as sensuously rich as that of
Comus:

> Sabrina fair,
> Listen where thou art sitting
> Under the glassy, cool, translucent wave,
> In twisted braids of lilies knitting
> The loose train of thine amber-dropping hair...
> Listen and save.

(Perhaps all the final sequence was sung.)

In the second edition of *Comus*, published after the outbreak of
the Civil War, the Lady's rejection makes plain, by an addition,
the social grounds for her repudiation of the orthodox masque:

> If every just man that now pines with want
> Had but a moderate and beseeming share
> Of that which lewdly pamper'd luxury
> Now heaps up for some few with vast excess,
> Nature's full blessings would be well dispens'd
> In unsuperfluous even proportion,
> And she no whit encumber'd with her store,
> And then the giver would be better thank'd,
> His praise due paid; for swinish gluttony
> Ne'er looks to heaven amid his gorgeous feast,
> But with besotted base ingratitude
> Crams and blasphemes his feeder. Shall I go on?
> Or have I said enough?   (ll. 767–79)

255

She does 'go on' to some straight abuse, adding that the cause she pleads is itself powerful enough to make 'dumb things to sympathize/And the brute earth would lend her nerves and shake'. Finally the Spirit invites the audience to rise with him 'higher than the spherey chime'; but without any cloud machine to supply illusion.

As tension grew, the courtly masque itself became argumentative; in *Britannia Triumphans* (1638) Davenant expressed some strongly anti-Puritan sentiments and, under claims for naval sovereignty, disguised the case for the hated Ship Money, aiming to convert

> such as impute
> A tyrannous intent to heavenly powers.

Those 'sullen clerks that love/To injure and to scant themselves' and to 'feed on salads' are also denounced. *Comus* had appeared the previous year.

In the last masque of Charles's court, *Salmacida Spolia*,[16] given 21 January 1640, the King and Queen both danced. It was a rite aimed at reclaiming the beloved but ungrateful People, who provided the chorus. Charles, who had already faced the Scots in arms, presents his forced pacification as an act of patience and clemency, whilst Henrietta Maria descends as a *dea ex machina*, with her 'Martial ladies', 'in Amazonian habits of carnation embroidered with silver, with plumed helms and baldrics with antique swords hanging by their sides (see above, Chapter 4, p. 83).

The masque ended with perspective view of 'a bridge over a river' and beyond 'the suburbs of a great city', whilst from above descended a cloud with eight persons representing the heavenly spheres. These thus joined themselves to Charles's kingdom. The City of London was distanced and out of sight – it had been directly represented in the masque of 1638, *Britannia Triumphans*. Perhaps it was already realized, even at court, that the City of London was to provide the sinews of war for the Parliament. It withheld money from the King. It protected the five members of Parliament whom in 1641 Charles tried to arrest. Its trained bands gave Parliament the nucleus of an army. Charles's visions of harmony remained a dream, whilst in the coming conflict the cause of Prynne was to triumph.

Those city theatres where Shakespeare had played were soon to disappear. Though closed in September 1642, many of the London playhouses remained standing in surreptitious use; but the lease of the Second Globe, successor to the Theatre, expired, and by the ground landlord it was pulled down to the ground on Monday 15 April 1644, 'to make tenements in the rooms of it'.[17]

So ended more than sixty glorious years, and the first age of London's theatrical history.

NOTES

1. The 'game place' owned by the town, was usually a fenced enclosure, used for sports, seasonal merrymakings, visiting bearwards, tumblers, etc. See Glynne Wickham, *Early English Stages, 1300–1660* (London, 1963).

2. Cf. Chapter 2, p. 16, and, Chapter 6, p. 106 for the freedom of these types from classic restraint, and for their own self-regulated modification at a later date, see Chapter 3, pp. 41–2.

3. As an example of the risks inherent in present study, the *Revels History of Drama in English* for the period (Vol. 3, London, 1975) shows a complete dichotomy between the part dealing with theatre structures (which might have housed nothing but tumblers and tenth-rate players) and the study of the plays themselves (designed for a reader who need never have been to any kind of theatre). On the other hand, some solid work has been done in France at the Centre National de la Recherche Scientifique under Jean Jacquot, some at the bi-annual conferences on the Elizabethan Theatre held in Canada, more perhaps at Stratford-upon-Avon, to marry academic and theatrical studies.

4. Cf. Chapter 6, pp. 110–11, and Chapter 8, p. 158.

5. Compare the much broader burlesque treatment of *The Winter's Tale* at Gray's Inn some years later (Chapter 11, p. 214).

6. See my British Academy Annual Shakespeare Lecture, 1965, *Shakespeare's Primitive Art* for the recall of stage images, or icons. For the general argument, see below, Chapters 10–12.

7. I have discussed this in *Shakespeare and Elizabethan Poetry* (London, 1951).

8. This is the period covered in *Shakespeare the Craftsman* (London, 1969).

9. See below, Chapter 6, p. 109 for the consequences.

10. See below, Chapter 6, pp. 103–4 for the Second Paul's and Blackfriars theatres.

11. See Chapter 6, p. 109 for the further history of the Children now cut off from their chapel connexion, operating as common players.

12. See G. E. Bentley, *The Jacobean and Caroline Stage* (Oxford, 1968), VI, 14–16; 193–4, for the inferior status and inferior financial returns of the (Second) Globe.

13. Jonson used bears to draw the chariot of Oberon and to dance in an anti-masque (see Chapter 11, pp. 209, 211, and Chapter 4, p. 70).

CHAPTER 2. THE TRIPLE BOND: ACTORS, AUDIENCE, PLAYWRIGHTS

1. Dates are taken from Alfred Harbage and Samuel Schoenbaum, *Annals of English Drama, 975–1700* (London, 1964). Cambises asks the audience to 'accept this simple deed'.

2. Charles T. Prouty, 'An Early Elizabethan Playhouse', *Shakespeare Survey 6* (Cambridge, 1953), pp. 64–8.

3. O. L. Brownstein, 'A Record of London Inn-Playhouses, 1565–1580', *Shakespeare Quarterly*, 22 (1971), 17–24.

4. Charles T. Prouty (ed.), *Studies in the Elizabethan Theatre* (Hamden, Conn., 1961), p. 44.

5. William Ingram, 'The Playhouse at Newington Butts: A New Proposal', *Shakespeare Quarterly*, 21 (1970), 385–98.

6. Marie Axton, 'Robert Dudley and the Inner Temple Revels', *Historical Journal*, 13 (1970), 365–75.

7. W. R. Gair, 'La Compagnie des Enfants de St. Paul Londres (1599–1606)', *Dramaturgie et Société*, ed. J. Jacquot (Paris, 1968), II, 655–74. Cf. below, Chapter 6, p. 103.

8. Cf. Gabriel Harvey, *Letter Book*, ed. Edward J. L. Scott (Westminster, 1884), pp. 67–8; and *The Works of Thomas Nashe*, ed. R. B. McKerrow and F. P. Wilson (Oxford, 1958), III, 46.

9. See Roy Strong, *Portraits of Queen Elizabeth I* (Oxford, 1963). Plate VI.

10. Norman Rabkin, 'The Double Plot', *Renaissance Drama*, ed. Samuel Schoenbaum (Evanston, 1964), VII, 55. For tragedy and comedy see Chapter 3, pp. 41–2.

11. F. P. Wilson, *Marlowe and the Early Shakespeare* (Oxford, 1953), pp. 105–8; for prefiguration, cf. V. A. Kolve, *The Play Called Corpus Christi* (Palo Alto, 1966), Chapter IV.

12. 'And so they said, these matters be king's games, as it were stage plays, and for the most part played upon scaffolds, in which poor men be but lookers on, and they that wise be, will meddle no further, for they that step up with them when they cannot play their parts, they disorder the play and do themselves no good.' Quoted by Philip Brockbank in *English Drama to 1710*, ed. Christopher Ricks (London, 1971, *History of Literature in the English Language*, Vol. 3), p. 174.

13. C. L. Barber, *Shakespeare's Festive Comedy* (Princeton, 1959), p. 83. This is the best commentary on Nashe.

14. Gabriel Harvey, *Fovre Letters, and certaine sonnets...* (London, 1592), letter 3.

15. Anne Righter [Barton], *Shakespeare and the Idea of the Play* (London, 1962), a work which deals with the audience on a much wider scale than the title would suggest.

16. I. A. Shapiro, 'The Significance of a Date', *Shakespeare Survey, 8* (Cambridge, 1955), p. 101. For the relation of this play to *The Tempest* see Chapter 12, pp. 217–18.

17. L. G. Salingar, Gerald Harrison, and Bruce Cochrane, 'Les comédiens et leur public en Angleterre de 1520 à 1640', *Dramaturgie et Société*, p. 531. The article provides a graph of known visits to the provinces which shows a spectacular rise about the year 1560 and a spectacular drop in the year 1600. Thereafter for a variety of reasons players were increasingly refused permission to act. Cf. below, Chapter 3, p. 42.

18. Philip J. Finkelpearl, *John Marston of the Middle Temple* (Cambridge, Mass., 1969), pp. 119–24.

19. Prologue, *Jack Drum's Entertainment* (1601). Cf. Gair, 'La Compagnie des Enfants...', and below Chapter 6, p. 107.

20. Jarold W. Ramsey, 'The Provenance of *Troilus and Cressida*', *Shakespeare Quarterly*, 21 (1970), 223–40. I do not find this case very plausible.

21. M. C. Bradbrook, *Shakespeare, the Craftsman* (London, 1969), Chapter 5.

22. G. K. Hunter, 'The Heroism of Hamlet', *Hamlet*, ed. John Russell Brown and Bernard Harris (Stratford-upon-Avon Studies, vol. 5, 1963), p. 108. Cf. below Chapter 3, p. 44.

23. Brian Gibbons. *The Jacobean City Comedy* (Cambridge, 1968), Chapter 1 and Appendix A. See below, Chapter 5.

24. The point is taken from H. S. Bennett, *Shakespeare's Audience*, British Academy Annual Shakespeare Lecture (London, 1944), to whom I am also indebted for the passage from Middleton.

25. Inga-Stina Ekeblad [Ewbank], 'The "Impure Art" of John Webster', *Review of English Studies*, n.s., 9 (1958), 253, 267. Cf. below, Chapter 6, pp. 116–17, for further development of Webster's poetic art in the play.

26. Ibid., pp. 253–67.

CHAPTER 3. SHAKESPEARE'S HISTORIES AND THE STRUCTURE
OF TUDOR SOCIETY

1. Jean Piaget, *Le Structuralisme* (Paris, 1968), p. 124. My translation.

2. For examples, see my *Rise of the Common Player* (London, 1962), Chapter 11, and cf. below, Peele's *The Arraignment of Paris* (1583/4).

3. A. L. Rowse, *The England of Elizabeth* (London, 1951), p. 17.

4. Sydney Anglo, *Spectacle, Pageantry and Early Tudor Politics* (London, 1969); David Bergeron, *English Civic Pageantry 1558–1642* (London, 1971). Cf. John Phillips, *The Reformation of Images* (Los Angeles, 1973).

5. William Dunbar, 'To Aberdeen', in *Poems*, ed. W. Muir Mackenzie (Edinburgh, 1932), p. 137.

6. Greene's well known passage from his *Groatsworth of Wit* (1592) appeared in the same year as Nashe's tribute in *Pierce Penniless* (*Works*, ed. R. B. McKerrow [Oxford, 1958], I, 212).

7. F. P. Wilson, *Marlowe and the Early Shakespeare* (Oxford, 1953), p. 108.

8. David M. Bergeron, *English Civic Pageantry 1558–1642* (London, 1971), pp. 208, 269.

9. Wolfgang Clemen, *English Tragedy before Shakespeare* (London, 1961), Chapters 13–15.

10. C. L. Barber, *Shakespeare's Festive Comedy* (Princeton, 1959).

11. Cf above Chapter 2, pp. 15–17.

12. *Early English Stages 1300–1660*, Vol. II, Part II (London, 1972).

13. See the article cited above, Chapter 2, note 17.

14. See Irving Ribner, *The English History Play in the Age of Shakespeare* (New York, 1965), Chapter 9; however, cf. note 15.

15. Andrew Gurr, *The Shakespearean Stage, 1574–1642* (Cambridge, 1970), p. 74. In his *Apology for Actors* (1612), Thomas Heywood varies Nashe's praise of the effects of acting in English histories 'as if the personator were the man personated; so bewitching a thing is lively and spirited action that it hath power to new mould the hearts of the spectators and fashion them to the shape of any noble and notable attempt'. Quoted in David Klein, *The Elizabethan Dramatists as Critics* (New York, 1963), p. 217.

16. Klein, *Elizabethan Dramatists as Critics*, p. 57.

17. See *Shakespeare the Craftsman* (London, 1969), Chapter 7.

18. The fullest account of this will be found in R. F. Jones, *The Triumph of the English Language* (Oxford, 1953). A good popular account is in Patrick Cruttwell, *The Shakespearean Moment* (London, 1954), Chapters 1–3.

19. F. P. Wilson, *Elizabethan and Jacobean* (Oxford, 1945), p. 112.

20. Although his life continued a scandalously gay one, Lope took priest's orders in 1614 and in 1620 became a Familiar of the Holy Office, i.e., the Inquisition. He died in 1635.

21. R. D. F. Pring-Mill, in his preface to Lope de Vega, *Five Plays*, tr. Jill Booty (New York, 1971), pp. xxi–xxii.

22. 'Images et Structure dans *Peribañez*', *Bulletin Hispanique*, LI (1949), 125–59.

23. See Joel Hurstfield, 'The Historical and Social Background', *A New Companion to Shakespeare Studies*, ed. K. Muir and S. Schoenbaum (Cambridge, 1971).

CHAPTER 4. SOCIAL CHANGE AND THE EVOLUTION OF
BEN JONSON'S COURT MASQUES

1. 'The Induction', *Bartholomew Fair*, in the articles of agreement with the audience (VI, 16), dismisses the 'sword and buckler age' (ll. 116–17), rejects provision of 'a servant monster' (l. 127), 'a nest of antics' (l. 128), 'Tales, Tempests and such like Drolleries' (l. 130) because the author is 'loath to make Nature afraid' (l. 129). In *Discoveries* he condemns 'the Tamburlaines and Tamerchams' (l. 777) of the last age as flying away from Nature (VIII, 587, ll. 772–3): and in the 'Ode to himself' the 'mouldy tale, / Like *Pericles*' (VI, 492, ll. 21–2) and all romantic plays in *The Magnetic Lady* (VI, 527–8).

All references to Jonson's works are taken from the Oxford Jonson, edited by C. H. Herford and Percy and Evelyn Simpson, 11 vols. (Oxford, 1925–52) and hereafter abbreviated as H & S. Spelling and punctuation have been modernized throughout.

2. *The Arte of Rhetorique* (London, 1553), sigs. biiʳ–biiᵛ.

3. In the fourteenth-century romance, *Sir Gawain and the Green Knight*, ed. J. R. R. Tolkien and E. V. Gordon (Oxford, 1930), the grotesque and terrifying figure of the Green Knight breaks into King Arthur's Christmas feast, where he is accepted as a jest by the king: 'Wel bycommes such craft vpon Cristmasse, / Laykyng of enterludeȝ, to laȝe and to syng' (ll. 471–2).

4. See Anne Righter [Barton], *Shakespeare and the Idea of the Play* (London, 1962), Chapters I–III. For contrast, see my *Rise of the Common Player: A Study of Actor and Society in Shakespeare's England* (London, 1962), Chs. XI–XII.

5. For the riotous masque at Henry VIII's court, see Enid Welsford, *The Court Masque: A Study in the Relationship between Poetry and the Revels* (Cambridge, 1927), p. 124 and for Edward VI, see p. 147. For Ferrars see my *Rise of the Common Player*, p. 124; and pp. 256–7 for the survival of such sports in the early years of Elizabeth. One of the most curious works to describe the eerie quality of these entertainments is W. Baldwin's *Beware the Cat* (1570).

6. John Stevens, *Music and Poetry in the Early Tudor Court* (London, 1961).

7. *The Defense of Poesie*, in *Prose Works*, ed. Albert Feuillerat, 4 vols. (1912–26; rpt. Cambridge, 1968), III, 11. The citations which follow are to pp. 20, 32, 24. For Jonson's views on Sidney and the *Arcadia*, see H & S, I, 132, 136.

8. *The Defense of Poesie*, III, 24 and, below, III, 40.

9. C. S. Lewis, *English Literature in the Sixteenth Century Excluding Drama* (Oxford, 1954), p. 230.

10. *The Complete Poems of Sir John Davies*, ed. Alexander Grosart, 2 vols. (London, 1876), I, 209.

11. See *The Poems of James VI, of Scotland*, Scottish Text Society, ed. James Craigie, 2 vols. (London, 1955, 1958), I. For the masque, see II, 134–44. For an account of the Scottish poets, the 'young Castalians' see Helena Mennie Shire,

Song, Dance and Poetry of the Court of Scotland under King James VI: Musical Illustrations of Court-song, ed. Kenneth Elliott (Cambridge, 1969). Jonson himself celebrated the powers of King James in an epigram 'How, best of kings, dost thou a sceptre bear! / How, best of poets, dost thou laurel wear!' (VIII, 28, ll. 1–2).

12. See David M. Bergeron, *English Civic Pageantry 1558–1642* (London, 1971), p. 87. He gives a full discussion of this royal entry, with illustrations, pp. 71–88.

13. Samuel Daniel, 'The Vision of the Twelve Goddesses' in *A Book of Masques in Honour of Allardyce Nicoll*, ed. T. J. B. Spencer and Stanley W. Wells (Cambridge, 1967), pp. 36–7.

14. On New Year's Day, preceding, in a masque of Indian and Chinese knights, the King had been presented with a jewel worth £40,000; this 'made a fair show' to the French ambassador, who did not know, as some did, that James was buying it for himself from a merchant. See E. K. Chambers, *The Elizabethan Stage*, 4 vols. (Oxford, 1924), III, 279–80.

15. Chambers, *Elizabethan Stage*, III, 280; Carleton's account.

16. *The Masque of the Inner Temple and Gray's Inn*, intended for the marriage of the Princess Elizabeth and the Elector Palatine, had to be postponed because after two nights' revelry the King was too weary to face it – and the hall had become overcrowded with spectators. Cf. also Chambers, *Elizabethan Stage*, I, 203.

17. *Basilikon Doron*, Scottish Text Society, ed. James Craigie (London, 1944), I, 181.

18. *Defense of Poesie, ed. cit* p. 38.

19. H & S, x, 448; Carleton's account.

20. On the first Shrove Tuesday of Henry VIII's reign, the King had appeared in a masque followed by six ladies whose faces and arms were covered with 'fine pleasance black' so that 'they seemed to be negroes or black Moors' (Hall's *Life of Henry VIII* quoted by Welsford, *Court Masque*, p. 127). Queen Anne evidently wore paint; her torch-bearers, the Oceanides, were painted blue.

21. H & S, x, 448; Carleton's account. The quotations which follow are from x, 448, 449, 448.

22. The best account remains that of D. J. Gordon, 'Hymenaei, Ben Jonson's Masque of Union', *JWCI*, 8 (1945), 107–46; see also his 'Imagery of Ben Jonson's *The Masque of Blacknesse* and *The Masque of Beautie*', *JWCI*, 6 (1943), 122–42; and 'Poet and Architect: The Intellectual Setting of the Quarrel between Ben Jonson and Inigo Jones', *JWCI*, 12 (1949), 152–78.

23. H & S, x, 466; John Pory writing to Sir Robert Cotton. Cf. Jonson's epigram on the union, 'The world the temple was, the priest a king, / The spoused pair two realms, the sea the ring' (VIII, 28, ll. 3–4).

24. David Harris Willson, *King James VI and I* (London, 1956), p. 192; Dudley Carleton's account of the previous great wedding – that of Sir Philip Herbert – which came just before the *Masque of Blackness*, in 1604.

25. H &S, x, 466; the Venetian ambassador's account.

26. H &S, x, 486.

27. *The Plays of John Marston*, 3 vols., ed. H. Harvey Wood (London, 1939), III, 266.

28. H &S, x, 449. Cf. also Chambers, *Elizabethan Stage*, I, 207 for a further list of disorders.

29. *Nugae Antiquae*, I, 348–54; Chambers, *Elizabethan Stage*, I, 172n.

30. Twelfth Night, 1515, at Greenwich; see Welsford, *Court Masque*, p. 126. Cf. the projected masque to be enacted before Elizabeth and Mary, Queen of Scots in 1562, pp. 153–4.

31. H &S, I, 151. He told Drummond that he had spent an entire night looking at his great toe, around which he saw Tartars, Turks, and Carthaginians fight in his imagination (H &S, I, 141).

32. H &S, x, 499.

33. H &S, x, 513.

34. H &S, x, 522; a contemporary account from the Downshire MSS. Inigo Jones paid a great deal of attention to coloured lighting, effected by placing lights behind coloured glass. The House of Fame was most strikingly decorated in this way. He used wheeling lights to distract attention during scene changes.

35. For the lions see Allardyce Nicoll, *Stuart Masques and the Renaissance Stage* (London, 1937), pp. 127, 205. The white bears may have been a romantic indication of the Northern origin of the Stuarts, but they often appear in early romances, from whom, of course, Huon of Bordeaux (Oberon) as a magic figure also came. There was, for instance, an enchanted prince as a white bear in the fourteenth-century romance, *William of Palerne*; see also Erestus the enchanted knight in Peele's *Old Wives' Tale*, who is termed 'the white bear of England's wood'.

36. James's anagram (Charles James Stuart / Claims Arthur's Seate) was paralleled by his son's Henricus Fridericus Steuartus / Arthuri in Sede Futurus Crescis. See Elkin C. Wilson, *Prince Henry in English Literature* (New York, 1946), p. 9.

37. See Stephen Orgel, *The Jonsonian Masque* (Cambridge, Mass., 1965), p. 90, and the following discussion of what he regards as 'the complex failure of this masque as poetry'

38. Anthony Mundy, 'Londons Love to the Royal Prince Henrie' in John Nichols, *The Progresses, Processions, and Magnificent Festivities of King James the First, His Royal Consort, Family, and Court*, 4 vols. (London, 1828), II, 322. The following quotation is from Wilson, *Prince Henry in English Literature*, p. 83.

39. H &S, x, 531.

40. See Chapter 13 below.

41. Quoted by Willson, *King James VI and I*, p. 386.

42. Willson, *King James VI and I*, p. 192; see also the whole chapter entitled 'A Sylvan Prince'.

43. Willson, *King James VI and I*, p. 356, quoting Anthony Weldon.

44. *Poems of King James VI*, p. 177. Buckingham became a Duke two years later. The second performance of the masque was at the home of his father-in-law, the Earl of Rutland.

45. 'Satires and Epigrams', The Muses Library (London, 1905), II, 185–8.

46. Glynne Wickham, *Early English Stages 1300–1660* (London, 1963), II, Part 1, 237–8.

47. H &S, x, 576. For the King's reaction, see x, 583.

48. *Poems of King James VI*, II, 192. James may have evolved private rituals, for in 1624 he hopes 'to make at the Christenmas a new marriage' with Villiers (Willson, *King James VI and I*, p. 445).

49. *Poems of King James VI*, p. 179.

50. H &S, VII, 782. For Captain Cox, see my *Rise of the Common Player*, Chapter VI. Captain Cox's library of romances, an impressive list of popular books, consisted of just the sort of things that Jonson in his *Execration upon Vulcan* declared had been excluded from his own library – 'the learned library of Don Quixote, Arthur, Palmerin, and Amadis de Gaulle'.

51. H &S, VIII, 403–4. Poetry is pedlar's ware – penny broadsheets.

52. 'The masque was performed last Tuesday night, myself being so wise as not to see it. They say it was very good, but I believe the disorder was never so great at any', Robert Read, quoted by C. V. Wedgwood, 'The Last Masque' in *Truth and Opinion: Historical Essays* (London, 1960), p. 154. The masque, Davenant's *Salmacida Spolia*, is reprinted in *A Book of Masques in Honour of Allardyce Nicoll*. It was given on 21 January 1640. For further consideration of the Caroline Masque, see Chapter 14 below pp. 256–7.

CHAPTER 5. JONSON AND THE IMAGE OF JACOBEAN LONDON

1. Brian Gibbons, *The Jacobean City Comedy* (St. Albans, 1968). See also my *Growth and Structure of Elizabethan Comedy* (London, 1955), Chapter 9.

2. See F. P. Wilson, *The Plague in Shakespeare's London* (Oxford, 1927).

3. See Jill Mann, *Chaucer and Medieval Estates Satire* (Cambridge, 1973).

4. See T. W. Craik, *The Tudor Interlude* (Leicester, 1958). In the sixties appeared plays with such titles as *All for Money, The Trial of Treasure* and *Liberality and Prodigality*.

5. John Awdelay, *The Fraternity of Vagabonds*, 1561 and Thomas Harman *A Caveat for Common Cursetors* are reprinted in A. V. Judges, *The Elizabethan Underworld* (London, 1930).

6. For Peele, see Chapter 2, pp. 16–18.

7. In 1626 in Jonson's *The Staple of News*, still the centres of newsmongering (with St Paul's as fourth).

8. See Nicholas Harmer, *The Black Dog of Newgate* (1596) and later works by Dekker and Middleton.

9. Thomas Wilson *A Discourse upon Usury*, 1572, sets out orthodox views; cf. Francis Bacon's essay *Of Usury* (1625), a grudging acceptance of regulated interest rates.

10. She palms off her baby on a pair of 'promoters' on the watch for the sale of meat in Lent. They impound her basket, only to find the child hidden under a leg of mutton (*A Chaste Maid in Cheapside*, 1611).

11. For an excellent discussion of the levels of this play, see D. F. McKenzie in *A celebration of Ben Jonson*, ed. W. Blissett (Toronto, 1973), pp. 83–127.

12. See below, Chapter 6, p. 110. The Hope, which replaced the old bearbaiting house, belonged to Henslowe. A play by Jonson would constitute a grand event.

13. The scene of the Fair was to be depicted by many artists, and in its latest days, even by the countryman Wordsworth, who termed it 'a parliament of monsters' (*The Prelude*, Book VII, lines 609ff.).

14. See Chapter 4 above, for a discussion of this 'show' as the Folger MS. terms it (pp. 78–9).

15. This was *The Masque of Augurs* (1622). For Jonson's final use of rustic scenes from London's environs, see Chapter 14, pp. 249–50, on *A Tale of a Tub*.

16. See R. H. Ball, *The Amazing Career of Sir Giles Overreach* (1939). Dates given for the play range from 1621 to 1629. It was printed in 1633, as having been acted by the Queen's Men at the Phoenix.

17. See Clayton Roberts, *The Growth of Responsible Government in Stuart England* (Cambridge, 1966) pp. 27ff. Cf. Joel Hurstfield, 'The Politics of corruption in Shakespeare's England', *Shakespeare Survey 28* (Cambridge, 1975).

18. Francis Bacon, who had declared the extortions to be legal, was himself shortly after impeached and ruined as a result of the Mompessen scandal.

19. See Margot Heinnemann, *English Literary Renaissance*, v, 2 (Spring 1975) who identifies the play as part of Pembroke's struggle against James's Spanish policy.

20. For this play which dealt with a London scandal involving the marriage of a wealthy but weak-minded old woman, as well as depicting the latest London murder, see C. J. Sisson, *Lost Plays of Shakespeare's Age* (Cambridge, 1936).

21. This is also Jonson's aim in *A Tale of A Tub*. See below, Chapter 14, pp. 249–50.

CHAPTER 6. THE MANIFOLD THEATRES OF JACOBEAN LONDON AND THEIR POETS

1. The names of Kyd and Marlowe did not appear on the title pages of some of their plays. See Chapter 2 above, p. 17.

2. Read to the Sixth International Conference on the Elizabethan Theatre at Waterloo, Ontario, in July 1975.

3. In the seventeenth century, two shops stood at the west end of Great St Mary's, Cambridge.

4. See Herbert Berry, articles in *Elizabethan Theatre*, ed. Galloway (London, 1973), I, III; and in *Shakespeare 1971*, ed. Margeson and Leech; C. J. Sisson, *The Boar's Head Theatre*, ed. Stanley Wells (London, 1972).

5. The latest summary of information about this theatre is given by Richard Hosley, in *The Revels History of Drama in English*, ed. Leech and Craik, (London, 1975), I, 197–226.

6. See G. E. Bentley, *Jacobean and Caroline Stage* (Oxford, 1968), VI, pp. 34–5, for special evening performances at Blackfriars attended by the Queen. Others might have occurred without being recorded. Was the house simply left empty in summer? It seems unlikely.

7. Induction to *Antonio and Mellida*, line 74; cf. above, Chapter 2, p. 27.

8. There is a parody of 'What a piece of work is man', the falconers' call 'Illo ho' is used, and of course the revenge action is on the usual lines, with a surprise ending.

9. G. K. Hunter, Introduction to the *Revels* edition (London, 1975), pp. lxvii–lxviii. This distinguished it from the old jester's trick of giving all parts to himself, as Armin recounts of Jack Miller (*Works*, ed. Grosart, p. 28).

10. 'The clamorous fry of Inns of Court' had been accused earlier by Sir John Davies of crowding the private rooms (*Epigram* 3; before 1596).

11. In *Poetaster* II.i. the boys cry alternately 'Vindicta!' 'Timoria!' 'Vindicta!' 'Timoria!' 'Veni!' 'Veni!' for the ghosts; also imitating a lover's soliloquy.

12. As, for instance, in the anonymous *Comedy of Timon* or *Tom-a-Lincoln* (see pp. 213–14).

13. The ironic phrase in the Prologue to *King Henry V*, 'Can this cockpit hold the vasty fields of France?' implies a real difference in scale, as everything at the theatre was being cut down to size in comparison with the real-life history (cf the naval and aeronautic use of the term).

14. *King Henry VIII*, v.v.57–8.

15. Edmund Gayton, writing in 1654 (see G. E. Bentley, *Jacobean and Caroline Stage*, Oxford, 1941, II, 690–1).

16. See above, Chapter 2, p. 28. 'Of old, the art of making plays was to content the people....'

17. See below, Chapter 11, p. 213, for the newly discovered play *Tom a Lincoln* from Gray's Inn, and for the banter of Shakespeare, p. 207.

18. 'To the Reader', prefixed to *The White Devil*.

19. Glynne Wickham and following him, Frances Yates, are the chief exponents of this view, and their suggestions are dealt with below.

20. This is the view of Alfred Harbage, recently challenged by Ann Jennalie Cook (*Shakespeare Studies*, VII, 1974.)

21. G. E. Bentley, *The Profession of Dramatist in Shakespeare's Time* (Princeton, 1971), p. 37.

22. The plays listed in *Annals of English Drama* include *A Warning for Fair Women, The Merry Devil of Edmonton, The London Prodigal, The Miseries of Enforced Marriage, Sejanus, Volpone, The Malcontent, The Revenger's Tragedy, A Yorkshire Tragedy, Philaster, The Alchemist, The Maid's Tragedy, A King and No King, Catiline, The Second Maid's Tragedy, Bonduca.*

23. David M. Bergeron, *English Civic Pageantry 1558–1642* (London, 1971), p. 91, on a visit to Bristol.

24. Glynne Wickham, 'From Tragedy to Tragicomedy; *King Lear* as Prologue', *Shakespeare Survey 26* (Cambridge, 1973), p. 43. Cf. below, Chapter 8, p. 153.

25. The last was suggested by Glynne Wickham, in '*The Winter's Tale*, a Comedy with Deaths' in *Shakespeare's Dramatic Heritage* (London, 1969); 'Shakespeare's Investiture Play', an article in *T.L.S.* 18.12.1969; and *The Elizabethan Theatre* III, ed. D. Galloway (London, 1973). The other study is Frances Yates, *Shakespeare's Last Plays* (London, 1975).

26. See below, Chapter 8, pp. 154ff. The chief exponent of this view is Mrs Axton.

27. Frances Yates, *Shakespeare's Last Plays* offers as evidence parallels from Donne's *Epithalamion*, which however does not present one Phoenix bride, but two Phoenixes. The parallel with Elizabeth as Phoenix can hardly mean anything, for Phoenixes were as common as sparrows, as Rosemary Freeman demonstrated long ago. Miss Yates's suggestion that *The Alchemist* (1610) is an attack on Shakespeare's alleged Rosicrucian sympathies would present a difficulty of dating.

28. See above, Chapter 3.

29. *Richard II*, II.ii.18–20. I owe this point to Inga-Stina Ewbank, 'Webster's Realism' in *John Webster*, ed. Brian Morris, Mermaid Critical Commentaries (Tonbridge, 1970). Her articles on 'The Impure Art of John Webster' and 'Masques and

Plays' are also relevant to any consideration of this topic. George Wither wrote an Echo scene between Britain and Prince Henry's spirit, which may have given the idea of the Echo scene between the Duchess and Antonio (*Britain*: Canst thou our safe deliverance assure? *Spirit*: Sure. *Britain*: Then not withstanding the late loss befell/And we fear'd much, I trust 'tis well? *Spirit*: 'Tis well). For this and other matters on Prince Henry I am indebted to Elkin Calhoun Wilson, *Prince Henry in English Literature* (New York, 1946).

30. See above, Chapter 4, on Tourneur's plays, p. 65, and on *The Maid's Tragedy*, p. 66.

31. At the Fair of St Germains in 1607 William Drummond of Hawthornden saw a picture of Venus lying on a bed, receiving a young man who was adoring her, and at whom Cupid directed a dart, 'but on the other side, which should have been the hinder part of the head, was the image of Death'. Inga-Stina Ewbank quotes this in 'Webster's Realism' in *John Webster*, ed. Brian Morris. It goes back to the old heraldry game of 'Two faces in a hood', the Janus-faced Fortune of the early stage and Erasmus, *Praise of Folly* (see Leo Salingar, *Shakespeare and the Tradition of Comedy* (Cambridge, 1974), p. 284).

32. Clifford Leech, 'Elizabethan and Jacobean' in *The Dramatist's Experience* (London, 1970) p. 157. Compare G. K. Hunter on Hamlet, suggested above, Chapter 2, p. 29.

33. Jonson's play world on the contrary grew increasingly self contained, even repetitive; it was his own world of 'art', as he grew more and more out of touch with his real audience, creating an ideal one.

34. In the interests of Brecht, as in the 1960s, see below, pp. 142–3.

35. T. S. Eliot, *The Use of Poetry and the Use of Criticism*, pp. 146, 144.

36. G. Kozintsev in *Shakespeare 1971*, ed. Leech and Margeson, p. 193.

CHAPTER 7. 'MACBETH': THE SUBLIMATION OF SPECTACLE

1. Beaumont, *Knight of the Burning Pestle* (1607), shows Ralph the prentice reciting Hotspur's speech on honour.

2. Henry Paul, *The Royal Play of 'Macbeth'* (New York, 1950); Helen Gardner, 'Milton and the tragedy of Damnation', *Essays and Studies of the English Association*, New Series, Vol. I, 1948.

3. *English Institute Essays* (New York, 1950), reprinted in *Shakespeare the Tragedian*, ed. A. Harbage (New Jersey, 1964).

4. *Essays in Criticism*, Vol. VIII, No. 2 (April 1958), p. 147.

5. G. B. Harrison, *Shakespeare's Tragedies* (London, 1951); Mark Van Doran, *Shakespeare* (New York, 1936; London, 1941).

6. A. P. Rossiter, *Angel with Horns* (London, 1951), p. 217.

7. Willard Farnham, *Shakespeare's Tragic Frontier* (Berkley, 1950). E. M. W. Tillyard, *Shakespeare's History Plays* (London, 1944).

8. Sigmund Freud, *Some Character Types met with in Psycho Analysis* (1916), reprinted in John Wain, '*Macbeth*', *a Case Book* (London, 1968).

9. Inga-Stina Ewbank, 'Some uses and limitation of verbal symbolism', *Shakespeare Survey 24* (Cambridge, 1971), p. 14.

10. 'The Jacobean Shakespeare' in *Jacobean Theatre* (London, 1960) ed. Harris and Brown, p. 25.

11. Dennis Bartholomeusz, *Macbeth and the Players* (Cambridge, 1969).

12. The late eighteenth century saw popular versions of Shakespeare for chapbook audiences; and D. S. Bland (*Shakespeare Survey 19*, Cambridge, 1966) cites one in which the witches become gypsies and 'to Dunsinane great Burnham Wood/ Was marching like Jack-in-the-Green, sir/ Twas an army in bushes all crammed...'a matter of fact expression of that 'triumph of spring over winter' which modern critics treat much more respectfully.

13. A. L. Rowse, *Shakespeare the Man* (London, 1973); *Simon Forman* (London, 1974).

14. See J. P. Brockbank, 'History and Histrionics in *Cymbeline*' (*Shakespeare Survey 11*, Cambridge, 1958).

15. His silence concerning Elizabeth is taken as significant; the speech of Cranmer in *Henry VIII* is given to Fletcher and covert references to the death of Mary, Queen of Scots, are discovered in *King John*. (Peter Milward, *Shakespeare's Religious Background* (London, 1973, p. 67).

16. There is an example in the frontispiece to Sir Walter Raleigh's *History of the World*.

17. David M. Bergeron, *English Civic Pageantry 1558–1642* (London, 1971), p. 66.

18. Sporadic appearances of witches as 'spectacle' are found as early as *The Wisdom of Dr Dodipoll* (Paul's Boys, 1599).

19. *Shakespeare Survey 24* (Cambridge, 1971), p. 14.

20. The only playwright who follows Shakespeare in this blend of spectacle and imagery appears to be Webster, e.g. in the prison scenes of *The Duchess of Malfi*.

21. Mrs Siddons's most famous line.

22. Anne Righter, *Shakespeare and the Idea of the Play* (London, 1962), p. 132.

23. The phrase is Wilbur Sanders's.

CHAPTER 8: 'KING LEAR' AND THE KINGDOM OF FOOLS AND BEGGARS

1. The majority of writers vote for the priority of *King Lear*; my view approxi-

mates to that of Harold C. Goddard in *The Meaning of Shakespeare* (Chicago, 1951) who compares the sequence to that of Dostoievski's *Crime and Punishment* and *The Brothers Karamazov*.

2. e.g. Harry Levin, 'The Heights and the Depths' in *More Talking of Shakespeare*, ed. J. Garrett (London, 1959); Winifred Nowottny, 'Lear's Questions' in *Shakespeare Survey 10* (Cambridge, 1957).

3. Marvin Rosenberg, *The Masks of Lear* (Los Angeles, 1972).

4. Frank Kermode, preface to *King Lear* in *The Riverside Shakespeare* (Boston, 1974); Mary Lascelles, in *Shakespeare Survey 26* (Cambridge, 1973).

5. Donald McKinnon, on Golgotha in *The Borderlands of Theology* (Guildford, 1968) pp. 103, 93, and 'Subjective and Objective Conceptions of Atonement' in *Prospect for Theology*, essays presented to Herbert Farmer (London, 1967), p. 175.

6. See S. L. Goldberg, *An Essay on 'King Lear'* (Cambridge, 1974), pp. 88–9. 'What his case exhibits is the world's power really to hurt – the opaque, irreducible brutality of what people can do and suffer. It exhibits this as much in what he himself threatens to Edgar, in the blind panic of his hurt and fear...It might have seemed otherwise that there was nothing for Lear to get worked up about ...or that his madness is merely a pathological condition...what Gloucester fears in life, and in himself, really is to be feared....'

7. Caroline Spurgeon and Wilson Knight principally.

8. Goldberg, *An Essay on 'King Lear'*, pp. 23–8.

9. Christopher Hill, *The Century of Revolution 1603–1714* (London, 1961), p. 96; cf. John F. Danby, *Shakespeare's Doctrine of Nature* (London, 1949) *passim*.

10. Peter Laslett, *The World We have Lost* (London, 1965), p. 181; cf. below Chapter 9 (on *Coriolanus*), p. 175.

11. Later, he imagines something like Cornwall's 'revenges' on Gloucester – 'to have ten thousand with red-hot spits come hissing in upon them'.

12. See William Willeford, *The Fool and His Sceptre* (London, 1969).

13. The scene is treated at length by Harry Levin (see above note 2). Alvin Kiernan suggests the grotesque figure represents the last thing Gloucester *saw*.

14. The image of a Summer King could be used as a cruel mockery, as Margaret of Anjou mocks York in *2 Henry VI*.

15. Winifred Nowottny in the article cited above, note 2.

16. *Hickscorner* (1513); *Youth* (1520); see T. W. Craik, *The Tudor Interlude* (Leicester, 1958) Chapter v. Used by Jonson (see above, p. 97).

17. The distinction is Maynard Mack's from *King Lear in Our Time* (Berkeley, 1965).

18. Maynard Mack (see last note) pp. 63–5; Rosalie Colie, *Shakespeare's Living Art* (Princeton, 1974), p. 302.

19. In 1601 the pageant of the Summer Lord at South Kyme led to a Star Chamber case and ended in the ruin of the family who staged it – see C. L. Barber, *Shakespeare's Festive Comedy* (Princeton, 1959), Chapter 3; this derives from N. J. O'Conor, *Godes Peace and the Queenes* (Harvard, 1934).

20. What follows is indebted to a paper by my brother, H. L. Bradbrook.

21. The single word of non-English origin is 'scald' from 'calidus'.

22. See Anne Barton, 'Shakespeare and the Limits of Language', *Shakespeare Survey 24* (Cambridge, 1971).

23. See above Chapter 6 pp. 114–15; in this chapter note 9 for the views of Hill and Danby, and Chapter 6 note 24 for the article by Glynne Wickham.

24. J. R. Tanner, *English Constitutional Conflicts of the Seventeenth Century* (Cambridge, 1928), p. 29.

25. Marie Axton, *The Drama of Political Faith in the Age of Elizabeth* (Cambridge Ph.D. thesis, 1966, Chapter x). I am indebted to Mrs Axton for the following arguments.

26. The pageant would normally have been given on St Simon and St Jude's Day, when the Lord Mayor took office but was postponed on account of a violent storm.

27. I take *goujeres* in the old Cornish sense of the fiend – here something like Grendal. *Starv'd* is used in its archaic sense of 'dead'.

28. His last words 'Look on her, look, her lips...' may be interpreted in many ways, including some vision that he sees there.

29. As Ben Jonson learned when he replaced grandeur by *The Gypsies Metamorphosed, Christmas his Masque, For the Honour of Wales*, and offered as a play *Bartholomew Fair*. It needed a certain intimacy to gauge James's measure. See above, Chapter 4, p. 75.

30. 'Dad' would be the modern equivalent.

31. The *social* study of filial and political conflicts, of exile, of self-destruction through rage, was to issue in a play whose classic limits put it at the opposite pole from this – in *Coriolanus*.

32. From *Rilke's Last Poems*, translated by Leishman, *Selected Poems* (London, 1941), p. 49. The poem describes the Harrowing of Hell.

CHAPTER 9. IMAGES OF LOVE AND WAR:
'OTHELLO', 'CORIOLANUS', 'ANTHONY AND CLEOPATRA'

1. King James's poem begins with a prologue from the Devil. Richard Knolles' *Generall Historie of the Turkes* appeared in 1603; see G. K. Hunter, *Shakespeare Survey 21* (Cambridge, 1968); cf. also his 'English Folly and Italian Vice' in *Jacobean Theatre*, Stratford on Avon Series 1 (London, 1960), pp. 81–111.

2. T. J. B. Spencer in *Shakespeare Survey 10* (Cambridge, 1957).

3. The customs of Venice are discussed by Alvin Kiernan in the Preface to the Signet *Othello*, and by Allan Bloom in *American Political Science Review* LIV (1960), with rejoinder by Sigard Burckholt.

4. The unfortunate Anne was six feet tall, plain of visage, and whilst treated with some respect by James, never was in his confidence; he had deeply humiliated and offended her by putting her infants into other hands away from court. One may contrast Juliet at the masque

> O she doth teach torches to burn bright
> It seems she hangs upon the cheek of night
> As a rich jewel in an Ethiop's ear'.   (I.v.44–46)

5. See Eldred Jones, *Othello's Countrymen* (Oxford, 1965). The quotation is from *Lust's Dominion*. Webster's use of Moors (Zanche, Florence in disguise in *The White Devil*, Jolanta in *The Devil's Law Case*) derives from Shakespeare, I would think.

6. John Bayley, *The Characters of Love* (London, 1960), pp. 174–6, 194–201. Cf. also Michael Goldman, *The Actor's Freedom* (New York, 1975), p. 40.

7. Bradley saw 'a certain limitation, a partial suppression of that element in Shakespeare which unites him with the mystical poets and the great philosophers'. On the other hand, compare Othello's easy rebuttal of the charge of black magic in Act I with his assumption of some such supernatural power behind Iago, the 'demi-devil', in Act v.

8. Albert Gerard, in arguing that Othello's runaway match was a gratuitous insult to Brabantio (*Shakespeare Survey 10*, Cambridge, 1957, p. 101), overlooks the impossibility of his having voluntarily consented to it – as, for example, Donne's employer reacted when Donne secretly married his niece. Brabantio refused to take his daughter into his house again.

9. A. E. Housman, *A Shropshire Lad* (London, 1896), xxxv.

10. It is hardly necessary today to controvert the views of Eliot and Leavis; the work has been done by, among others, John Holloway in *The Story of the Night* (London, 1960) and John Bayley, *The Characters of Love*.

11. See Rosalie Colie, *Shakespeare's Living Art* (Princeton, 1974), pp. 149–67.

12. Adultery was an ecclesiastical, not a civil offence.

13. Fletcher's heroes, from Arbaces of *A King and No King* to the absurd Petillus of *Bonduca*, a decade later, develop the simplicities of the soldier in love. Jealousy became a mainspring of tragic action, although in such plays as Massinger's *Emperor of the East* or Ford's *Love's Sacrifice*, the effect was deplorable. For the influence of *Othello*, see David Frost, *The School of Shakespeare* (Cambridge, 1968), pp. 110–18 and 228–32.

14. Bayley, *The Characters of Love*, pp. 205–6.

15. J. W. Lever, *The Tragedy of State* (London, 1971).

16. K. M. Burton, 'Political Tragedies of Chapman and Jonson,' *Essays in Criticism* Vol. 2 (4), 1952, pp. 397–412.

17. See Nicholas Brooke's edition, *The Revels Plays* (London, 1964), pp. lx–lxxiv.

18. He eventually amended some lines, e.g. 'So soon, all best turns/With princes, do convert to injuries' (III.i.302–3) became 'So soon, all best turns/With doubtful princes, turns deep injuries In estimation...'

19. Kemble and Mrs Siddons excelled in this play; Volumnia was considered her finest part. It was Olivier's first triumph in 1937 (with Sybil Thorndike as Volumnia). See the New Arden (ed. J. P. Brockbank, 1976) pp. 74–89.

20. Compare Blake's Albion:

> His right food stretches to the sea on Dover Cliff, his head
> On Canterbury rests; his right hand covers lofty Wales,
> His left Scotland; his bosom girt with gold involves
> York, Edinburgh, Durham and Carlisle –
> His head bends over London...

21. This is Menenius' description, who adds, anachronistically, 'His "hum" is a battery'.

22. Compare Bates in *Henry V*: 'I believe, as cold a night as 'tis, he could wish himself in Thames up to the neck; and so I would he were, and I by him.' (IV.i.113–15).

23.   'patient fools
> Whose children he hath slain, their base throats tear
> With giving him glory' (v.vi.51–3)

24. Cf. Una Ellis-Fermor, *Shakespeare the Dramatist* (London, 1961) for intimations of this 'secret image.'

25. *De Republica Anglorum* (1565), ed. L. Alston, p. 46. (They could, however, serve on juries or as constables.)

26. *A Remonstrance against Presbytery* (1641) sig. I-4v.

27. T. F. Reddaway, *Shakespeare Survey 17* (Cambridge, 1964), p. 5, quotes the Journal of the Court of Common Council.

28. Cf. e.g. the Commons' assertion that their election and privileges were not derived from the Crown (Christopher Hill, *The Century of Revolution 1603–1714*, London, 1961, p. 10).

29. Willard Farnham, *Shakespeare's Tragic Frontier* (Berkeley, 1950), stresses the paradox of 'taints and honours'; E. M. Waith, *The Herculean Hero* (London, 1962) compares Shakespeare's Romans with Chapman's tragic heroes.

30. See my *Shakespeare the Craftsman* (London, 1969) Chapter VIII, for a discussion of this play.

31. J. W. Lever, *The Tragedy of State*, p. 11.

32. For a player, the ultimate worst thing is to be hissed off stage. In the intransigent young Coriolanus being 'whooped' out of Rome is there a memory of what had been inflicted on the actors in *Sejanus*, through the intransigence of Ben Jonson?

33. Bullough, *Narrative and Dramatic Sources of Shakespeare* (London, 1964), v, 261. See also pp. 270, 271, 276, 292.

34. Bullough, *Narrative and Dramatic Sources of Shakespeare*, v, 295.

35. Helen Morris in *Huntington Library Quarterly* (1968–9), pp. 271–8. Fulke Greville burnt his play of *Antony and Cleopatra* in case it should receive contemporary application – presumably to Elizabeth and Essex.

36. *The Masque of Blackness*, 151–4. Compare Zanche at the end of *The White Devil*, who boasts that death will not make her look pale, and Aaron in *Titus Andronicus* 'Coal black is better than another hue/In that it scorns to bear another hue' (IV.ii.99–100).

37. Kenneth Muir points out in *Shakespeare's Tragic Sequence* (London, 1972), p. 170, that Cleopatra's scenes with the messenger (II.v and III.vii) are really one scene, although several scenes in Rome intervene; the soothsayer who sends Antony to Egypt has been preceded by Enobarbus' description of the Cydnus meeting, almost in a 'place and scaffolds' style.

38. Cleopatra tells us 'Nature meant me/A wife, a silly harmless household Dove/Fond without Art and kind without Deceit' (IV.xi.99–101). F. R. Leavis made an extended comparison of Dryden and Shakespeare (*The Poetry of Experience*, London, 1975, pp. 144–54).

39. Quoted by Barbara Everett, in the essay prefixed to the Signet Classics Edition (London, 1964), p. xxiii.

40. Endnote to the play in his edition, 1765.

41. Cf. above, Chapter 2, pp. 19–21, for the popularity of death scenes. For *Antony and Cleopatra*, see the inaugural lecture by Anne Barton at Bedford College London in 1973, published under the title 'Nature's piece 'gainst Fancy'.

42. See below, Chapter 13, pp. 235ff. for a discussion of this play.

43. Proof is provided within a few years by the popular Red Bull company moving to the Cockpit. The relation between these 2 houses would repay investigation.

CHAPTER 10. ENTRY TO ROMANCE: 'PERICLES' AND 'CYMBELINE'

1. Sarah Lawrence Alumnae Magazine, vol. 31, no. I.

2. See my *Themes and Conventions of Elizabethan Tragedy* (Cambridge, 1952),

Chapter II, p. 20, for early examples of infernal music; compare the music for the masque of madmen in *The Duchess of Malfi* (which survives).

3. Without going into detail, I would accept Philip Edwards's view on the authenticity of the text as Shakespearean in origin. The first two acts seem to me rather better than the Bad Quarto of *Hamlet*. Edwards' edition of the New Penguin Shakespeare (London, 1976) summarizes his views.

4. Sir John Tatham, verses prefixed to R. Brome, *The Merry Beggars or The Jovial Crew*. The same mock condemnation is extended to Jonson and was evidently written at the time of his death, i.e. *c.* 1637.

5. On 5 June 1607, by marriage to Susannah Shakespeare, the physician John Hall became Shakespeare's heir.

6. From T. S. Eliot's poem, *Marina*.

7. I.ii.122–4, II.ii.37–47; cf. I.ii.30–1, 55–6, II.ii.36.

8. The Dorian Pentapolis in S.W. Asia Minor, perpetuated the memory of the five cities' common origin by a festival to Apollo. The five cities of Pentapolis were Lindos, Ialysis, Camiros (all Rhodian), Cos, Cnidos; originally Helicarnassus was part of the group (Herodotus I, 144). Shakespeare treats Pentapolis as the name of a region.

9. From John Arthos, '*Pericles, Prince of Tyre*, a study in the dramatic use of romance narrative', *Shakespeare Quarterly* IV, 3 (July 1963), pp. 267ff.

10. The link with *Comedy of Errors* has been already mentioned; in addition, through a common source the brothel scenes are linked with *Measure for Measure*–see G. Bullough, *Narrative and Dramatic Sources*, VII (London 1966), p. 371; Dionyza and Lady Macbeth and the whole anticipation of the final plays is familiar. The play is unusually full of reminiscences of the Bible, as editors have noted; these are not obtruded but make their effect indirectly, as befits a pagan story concerned with the gods as forces of the natural world.

11. ' "Thou that begetst him that did thee beget". Transformation in *Pericles* and *The Winter's Tale*', *Shakespeare Survey* 22, (Cambridge 1969).

12. The phrase is Leo Salingar's, *Shakespeare and the Tradition of Comedy* (Cambridge, 1974), p. 7.

13. The jailer's daughter in *Two Noble Kinsmen* is won by her humble suitor in the clothes of Palamon. See below, p. 240.

14. *Elizabethan Critical Essays*, ed. G. G. Smith, (Oxford, 1904), p. 217.

15. J. M. Nosworthy, Preface to New Arden Edition of *Cymbeline*, p. xvii.

16. Especially *Philaster*. I think it was the other way round; cf. Cambridge *New Shakespeare* (1960), p. xxiii.

17. See the edition cited in previous note, and the New Arden edition ed. J. M. Nosworthy.

18. See Hallett Smith, *Shakespeare's Romances* (San Marino, 1972) and Howard Felperin, *Shakespearean Romances* (Princeton, 1972).

19. As do Puntavolo in Jonson's *Every Man Out of His Humour*, Dapper in *The Alchemist*, and a number of Fletcherian characters. But compare the ritual quality of masques (Chapter 4, above).

20. The country gentleman, hero and victim of Middleton's *Michaelmas Term*. I have mentioned above, p. 197, Iachimo's resemblance in his assumptions and accent to the satirists of city comedy.

21. John Davies of Hereford in 1603 had addressed the 'Players' as men he loved for painting and poetry (noting in the margin W. S., R. B.).

> Fortune cannot be excused
> That hath for better uses you refus'd.
> Wit, courage, good shapes, good parts, and all good
> As long as all these goods are no worse use'd;
> And though the stage doth stain pure, gentle, blood,
> Yet generous ye are, in mind and mood
> (*Shakespeare Allusion Book*, ed. E. K. Chambers, 1932, I, 126)

22. Cf. Chapter 3, p. 43. Incidentally, Prince Henry detested hunting, probably because his father loved it, and would have been far from gratified by being shown in such as his main occupation.

23. In the poem with this title.

CHAPTER 11. OPEN FORM IN 'THE WINTER'S TALE'

1. In 'A Caveat for Critics' (*Scrutiny* x, 1942, p. 340) Leavis was responding to an anthropological view of *The Winter's Tale*; the essay reappears in *The Common Pursuit* (London, 1952). G. E. Bentley wrote on Shakespeare and Blackfriars in *Shakespeare Survey 1* (Cambridge, 1948).

2. See above, Chapter 4, pp. 70–2; and below, Chapter 13, pp. 236–7.

3. Ernst Schanzer, 'The Structural Pattern of *The Winter's Tale*', *Review of English Literature*, April 1964; and K. Muir, *Winter's Tale Casebook* (London, 1968), pp. 87–97.

4. In Beaumont's masque of the Inner Temple, the first antimasque is of statues that come to life. A statue on a grave comes to life in *The Trial of Chivalry* (1601). See my British Academy Lecture in 1965, *Shakespeare's Primitive Art*, for a further discussion of this convention.

5. See Rosalie Colie, *Shakespeare's Living Art* (Princeton, 1974), Chapter 6, for a comparison of *The Winter's Tale* with continental pastoral forms. She terms the play 'guileless' in characterization (p. 269) which seems to me a mis-reading.

6. Neville Coghill, 'Six Points of Stagecraft in *The Winter's Tale*', *Shakespeare Survey 11* (Cambridge, 1958), p. 35.

7. Edward Armstrong, *Shakespeare's Imagination* (New York, 1962), p. 206.

8. See above, Chapter 4, p. 50, and Chapter 10, p. 188.

9. Jean Jacquot noted that Shakespeare relied on 'word painting and the appeal to the mind's eye' and warns against over-estimating the effect of the masque (*Shakespeare, 1971*, ed. Leech and Margeson, Toronto, 1972, pp. 156–73).

10. L. G. Salingar, 'Time and Art in The Winter's Tale', *Renaissance Drama* IX, 66.

11. It is now in the United States.

12. Compare the anonymous *Comedy of Timon* which I have derived from the Inns of Court (see chapter on Timon in *Shakespeare the Craftsman*). By way of contrast, the lawyer-poet John Marston in his *Sophonisba* (1605/6) draws upon the success of Shakespeare's *Othello* (see Chapter 1, p. 8).

CHAPTER 12. 'THE TEMPEST'

1. I.ii.424–5.

2. v.i.243–4. For the 'maze' see III.iii.2, v.i.242; a word used by Milton in *Comus*.

3. George Puttenham, *The Arte of Poesie*, ed. G. D. Willcock and A. Walker (Cambridge, 1936), p. 19.

4. *John a Kent and John a Cumber, Wily Beguiled, Grim the Collier of Croydon, Friar Bacon and Friar Bungay*, and *The Old Wives' Tale; The Rare Triumphs of Love and Fortune* has a number of additional likenesses.

5. An antic comes out of a tree 'if possible it may be' in *John a Kent*. William Percy, in *The Faery Pastoral*, gives a full description of how this property worked; here it has faded to something remembered. In the masque of Ceres, on the other hand, some materials and dances from court performance may have been used again.

6. Neville Coghill, *Shakespeare's Professional Skills* (Cambridge, 1964), pp. 41–60. There are also some echoes in the Morris dance sequence of *Two Noble Kinsmen*.

7. *John a Kent and John a Cumber*, ll. 530–1, quoted in Coghill, p. 44. Cf. above, Chapter 2, p. 24.

8. William Strachey, in his *True Reportory*, extracts from which are reprinted in the New Arden edition of the play, Appendix A; quotation on p. 137. The islands were uninhabited. Compare the sense of providential felicity in the poem 'Bermudas' by Andrew Marvell, quoted below. Marvell's nephew Popple was Governor there; Marvell, as a tutor himself at John Oxenbridge's house, might have heard of the islands which Oxenbridge knew.

9. Sylvester Jourdain, *A Discovery of the Bermudas* (1610), quoted in the New Arden edition ed. Frank Kermode., p. 141.

10. Lines by Milton prefixed to the Second Folio.

11. Enid Welsford makes this point in *The Court Masque* (Cambridge, 1927), pp. 133ff.

12. See A. M. Nagler, *Shakespeare's Stage* (New Haven, 1958), p. 100.

13. During the sea storm (I.i) and the clowns' scene (ii.ii) there is thunder; the voice of Ariel's warning may have sounded to Sebastian like the 'hollow burst of bellowing' he speaks of (II.i.306); and again, in contrast with the soft music of the mock banquet (III.iii.82), sounds striked Alonso fearfully (III.iii.95–102).

14. Andrew Marvell, 'Bermudas', in *Poems*, ed. H. M. Margoliouth (Oxford, 1927), p. 17. The luscious fruit that offers itself is detailed at length. See below.

15. W. H. Auden, 'The Sea and the Mirror', in *For the Time Being* (London, 1945), p. 29.

16. The following passage is adapted from my British Academy Annual Shakespeare Lecture for 1965, 'Shakespeare's Primitive Art', *Proceedings of the British Academy*, II (London, 1966), pp. 232–3.

17. Providence is a powerful force in Marvell's poem on the Bermudas and was perhaps from the first invoked to explain the happy wreck. The order of the play is, of course, a pattern of providential control.

18. 'Bermudas', in Margoliouth's edition of *Poems*, p. 17.

19. Yeats used it in his *Deirdre* tragically. Chess was a recognized form of 'commoning' for young and noble courtiers.

20. Auden, 'The Sea and the Mirror', p. 10.

21. Ibid., pp. 9, 14, 15.

22. William Rankin's *Mirror of Monsters* (1587) most fully developed the analogy of the Devil's Chapel – with papal images – being in the Theatre.

23. Young actors were serving an apprenticeship by now, and must have been pleased to be out of their time to their masters. Ariel would presumably have been played by someone's hopeful apprentice.

CHAPTER 13. SHAKESPEARE AS COLLABORATOR

1. 'All art is a collaboration': Synge, preface to *Playboy of the Western World*.

2. T. M. Raysor, *Coleridge's Shakespearean Criticism* (London, 1930) pp. 1, 75.

3. Robert Bridges, *Collected Essays* (Oxford, 1927) pp. 1, 29.

4. See E. A. Honigmann *The Stability of Shakespeare's Text* (London, 1965).

5. In *Shakespeare Survey 1* (Cambridge, 1948).

6. Alfred Hart, *Shakespeare and the Homilies* (Melbourne, 1934); Edward Armstrong, *Shakespeare's Imagination* (London, 1946). The image clusters – a group of

subconsciously associated words – are much used by Kenneth Muir in what is the best study of the doubtful plays, *Shakespeare as Collaborator* (London, 1960).

7. There is, I would think, no case to be made for any of the other doubtful plays attributed to Shakespeare; a number of them are dealt with in Baldwin Maxwell's *Studies in the Shakespeare Apocrypha* (New York, 1956). C. F. Tucker Brooke's collection (London, 1908) remains the best edition of these plays.

8. The printer also published good quartos of *Love's Labour's Lost* (1598) and *Romeo and Juliet* (1599).

9. Capell was the first to do so.

10. See F. H. Hinsley *Sovereignty* (London, 1966) pp. 118–19.

11. Muir, *Shakespeare as Collaborator*, p. 44.

12. Quotations from *Edward III* and *The Two Noble Kinsmen* are from C. F. Tucker Brooke, ed., *The Shakespeare Apocrypha* (Cambridge, 1907).

13. William Empson *Some Versions of Pastoral* (London, 1935) Chapter 3.

14. In line 42, 'follow' is my emendation for 'fear.'

15. It was given before Anne of Denmark as entertainment by this family (see E. K. Chambers *William Shakespeare*, Oxford, 1930, II, 332).

16. The old plays of *The Rare Triumphs of Love and Fortune* and *Sir Clyamon and Sir Clamydes* are recalled in *Cymbeline*. As an actor Shakespeare must have learned many plays by heart.

17. See I. A. Shapiro, 'The Significance of a Date' *Shakespeare Survey 8* (Cambridge, 1955), pp. 104–5.

18. Peter Hall, in introduction to *The Wars of the Roses* (London, 1970), pp. viii, xxv.

19. Pierre Leyris, 'Le chante de cygne de Shakespeare', *Nouvelle revue française* 1 November 1970) No. 215.

20. Beaumont's masque is reprinted in *A Book of Masques in Honour of Allardyce Nicoll* (Cambridge, 1967).

21. See the Signet Classics Shakespeare Edition, ed. Clifford Leech, p. xxxvi.

22. See Elkin C. Wilson *Prince Henry in English Literature* (New York, 1946.)

23. Theodore Spencer in *Modern Philology* 26 (1928), 255–76; reprinted in Clifford Leech's edition of *The Two Noble Kinsmen* (New York, 1966).

24. See Marco Mincoff, *English Studies* (1952), 97–115, for a study of the imagery.

25. A mask of death's heads at a bridal occurred at the wedding of Alexander III of Scotland; see I. S. Ekeblad [Ewbank], 'The Impure Art of John Webster' *Review of English Studies* n.s. 9 (1958), reprinted in G. K. Hunter's *John Webster* (Harmondsworth, 1969). For Auden's views see his introduction to William Burton's Signet Classics edition of the *Sonnets* (London, 1964).

26. M. Leyris ascribes the mood to Shakespeare and quotes Yeats on his old age: *The Spur.*

27. See I.i.64–5, III.i.15–16, III.iv.16, v.iv.16–17, III.ii; and for Fate, I.ii.102, I.iii.41.

28. Stubbes, in *The Anatomy of Abuses* (1583), wrote a well-known rebuke to the traditional rites of May. The Morris Dance was a May Day celebration.

29. I. S. Ekeblad [Ewbank], 'The Impure Art of John Webster.' The comparison of the 'charivari' scenes from *The Duchess of Malfi* with the mad scenes of the Jailer's daughter is enlightening: both belonged to the King's Men and were staged in 1613.

30. *The John Fletcher Plays* (London, 1962), p. 32.

31. Norman Rabkin *Shakespeare and the Common Understanding* (New York, 1967), p. 230.

32. This jest was flung at Beaumont and Fletcher – see Aubrey's *Brief Lives* (A. Clark, ed., 1898), pp. 1, 96.

33. Muir *Shakespeare as Collaborator*, p. 110; Paul Bertram *Shakespeare and 'The Two Noble Kinsmen'* (New Brunswick, 1965). His case, which is mainly linguistic, has been strongly challenged by Cyrus Hoy in *Modern Philology* 67, 1 (1969).

CHAPTER 14. MASQUE AND PASTORAL

1. David Matthew, *The Age of Charles I* (London, 1951), p. 28.

2. Thomas Carew, whose *Coelum Britannicum* was to be given on Shrove Tuesday, 1634, to Aurelian Townshend, whose *Albion's Triumph* was given on Twelfth Night 1632, his *Tempe Restored* at Shrovetide. See *Poems*, ed. Rhodes Dunlop (Oxford, 1949), p. 77. The verse letter contains a description of the last-named masque.

3. Carew's *Coelum Britannicum* (Shrovetide, 1634); based on Bruno's *Spaccio delle Bestie Triomfante* (1584).

4. Edited by Clifford Leech in *A Book of Masques* presented to Allardyce Nicoll (Cambridge, 1967).

5. Not reprinted since Dyce's edition of the *Dramatic Works and Poems* in 1833.

6. See G. E. Bentley, *The Jacobean and Caroline Stage* (Oxford, 1956), IV, pp. 632–6 for a summary of the evidence. Simpson strongly favoured the first alternative but revision theories were popular in his time.

7. The comedy was staged by Queen Henrietta's Men at the Phoenix in Drury Lane. This was a recent and fashionable company controlled by Christopher Beeston who had been Burbage's apprentice in his youth. Jonson resented the failure of his last play at Blackfriars and accused the King's Men of 'negligence', so perhaps they refused this one; Queen Henrietta's Men often took risks.

8. For 'Medley', cf. above Chapter 2, p. 20, and Chapter 3, p. 46.

9. The action combines parade and merry-go-round; in Act I all the characters come on in turn, culminating in the procession of Lady Tub and her usher. Act II sees the bride being rapidly swapped from one group to another, ending with Squire Tub, Act III starts up a new action, which in Act IV reverses the merry-go-round of Act II; after a fresh bout of swapping, the bride ends up with Lady Tub's usher. All is suddenly resolved and the 'motion' concludes, two serving men getting their brides, whilst the humorous men get the booty (fifty pounds apiece).

10. The most notorious case was that of the Dymokes at South Kyme (see above, Chapter 8, note 19) but the structure recalls *John a Kent and John a Cumber* (*c.* 1590), *Two Angry Women of Abingdon* (1588), *Englishmen for My Money* (1597), *The Wise Woman of Hogsden* (1599) as well as *The Merry Wives of Windsor* (1600).

11. Valentine's Day, 1613, had marked the heights of Jacobean masquing.

12. In similar fashion, in *Perkin Warbeck* Ford drew on Shakespeare's chronicle history. This play was brilliantly revived at Stratford in 1975.

13. F. R. Leavis, *Revaluations* (London, 1936), pp. 47–9, 'On Milton's Verse'. 'It shows the momentary predominance in Milton of Shakespeare.' The observation is not new; it is found in an edition of 1756: 'Milton seems to have imitated Shakespeare's manner more than in any other of his works'. See Ethel Seaton, '*Comus* and Shakespeare' in *Essays and Studies of the English Association*, XXXI (1945) for detailed discussion of Milton's use of *The Tempest* and *Romeo and Juliet* especially.

14. Compare Vindice's sinister silk worms (Chapter 6, p. 18).

15. In a Cambridge Ph.D. thesis (unpublished) by Eleanor Relle.

16. See above, Chapter 4, note 52.

17. The lease which ran to 1629 originally, had been extended to 1635, and then to 1644.

INDEX

Works are entered under authors; collaborative works under the first author.
Except for quotations, references from the notes are not entered separately.

Index

286